CONTEMPORARY BRITISH THEATRE

Contemporary British Theatre

Edited by

THEODORE SHANK
Theatre Department
University of California
San Diego

Published in Great Britain by
MACMILLAN PRESS LTD
Houndmills, Basingstoke, Hampshire RG21 6XS
and London
Companies and representatives
throughout the world

A catalogue record for this book is available
from the British Library.

ISBN 0–333–56582–7 hardcover
ISBN 0–333–68406–0 paperback

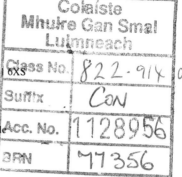

Published in the United States of America by
ST. MARTIN'S PRESS, INC.,
Scholarly and Reference Division,
175 Fifth Avenue,
New York, N.Y. 10010

ISBN 0–312–09631–3 (cloth)
ISBN 0–312–17224–9 (paperback)

Library of Congress Cataloging-in-Publication Data
Contemporary British theatre / edited by Theodore Shank.
    p.   cm.
Includes index.
ISBN 0–312–09631–3 (cloth)
1. Theater—Great Britain—History—20th century.   I. Shank,
Theodore.
PN2595.C63   1993
792'.0941'0904—dc20   93–2642
                                                   CIP

Contents

Preface to the 1996 Reprint

In the short time since the original publication of *Contemporary British Theatre* there have been a few noteworthy tendencies.

Among the important influences on British theatre have been the international festivals which bring productions from every continent and provide spice for what might otherwise be a provincial diet. The Edinburgh International Festival and the Fringe Festival which has grown up around it, are the oldest and largest of the festivals and they continue strong. While only a few theatre companies were presented by the main festival in 1995 – including French and German productions by Patrice Chéreau, Luc Bondy, Pina Bausch, and the Berliner Ensemble under the direction of Peter Zadek – there were more than 600 groups performing on the Fringe which is open to any company that can find a space and pay their expenses. And there are smaller, younger festivals. Since 1990 Barclays New Stages Festival, produced by the Royal Court Theatre in London, has sponsored more than fifty young experimental British companies. The Almeida Theatre annual presents a July festival of new opera, and the Turning World Festival, produced in part by the Place Theatre, brings small dance-theatre companies from various parts of the world.

Chief among the British theatre festivals is LIFT, the London International Festival of Theatre, which takes place in the summers of odd-numbered years. Beginning in 1981, the directors Rose Fenton and Lucy Neal have travelled widely to bring a variety of innovative productions to London. During the one-month Festival in 1995 they brought performances from France, Japan, Bali, Mexico, Germany, South Africa, India, Canada, Romania, Tunisia, China, Australia, Norway, and Algeria in addition to sponsoring British productions. 'Our love of theatre', they say in their programme introduction, 'is based on an insatiable desire to see experiment take place. LIFT loves to explore new forms, develop new landscapes, make new connections, chart new futures.' The directors of LIFT are not content merely to bring productions to London for the entertainment of audiences, they aim to have an impact on the art of theatre in Britain. Toward that end they present daily dialogues between artists performing at the Festival and local artists, there are after-show discussions between spectators and artists, and they offer an educational programme which allows communities in London to work with international artists on productions which are then performed before the public as part of the Festival. And LIFT even facilitates collaborations between foreign artists and British theatre companies. For the 1995 Festival, LIFT arranged for the leaders of the Afro-Brazilian company, Bando de Teatro Olodum, to create with London's Black Theatre Co-operative a production of *Zumbi*, named for the eighteenth-century slave hero of Brazil and intertwining his story with the experience of black people in Britain.

The presence of these international festivals contributes to an apparent contradiction. There are two opposite tendencies existing side by side – increasing nationalism and increasing international-ism, especially Europeanization. On the one hand, Scotland and Wales, no longer willing for the Arts Council of Great Britain to be their principal dispenser of subsidies, have their own arts councils and the former ACGB has become the Arts Council of England. On the other hand, Scotland with its Edinburgh Festival, in some respects was already more internationally attuned than England and, in fact, Glasgow had been selected European City of Culture for 1990. And now theatre in England, perhaps because of the combined influence of the international festivals, the growing importance of the European Community, and the opening of the Channel Tunnel connecting England and France, has begun to feel the influence of Europe on its aesthetics. Grants are available from the European Community for collaborative work and there is evidence, even in the British theatrical mainstream, of an expressionist postmodern aesthetics which had previously been more German and French than British. A prime example of this is the production by Steven Daldry of J.B. Priestley's *An Inspector Calls* **[cover photo]** which is emblematic of the nineties in that it takes a play from the past and deconstructs its meaning by way of making it relevant to contemporary audiences. In this case the production concept was especially well served by staging the interior scenes with the actors crammed into a kind of Edwardian doll's house surrounded by a landscape of bomb craters. At the end of the play, as the family disintegrates, the house self-destructs.

Daldry's production of *An Inspector Calls* is one of the bright spots in a tendency which bodes ill for the future of British theatre.

The large subsidized theatres have become increasingly inclined to produce revivals of old plays at the expense of new ones. The usual rationale is that the theatres can no longer afford to present works which do not have the built-in appeal of name recognition. We had come to expect this argument from the commercial theatres, but why from the well-subsidized Royal Shakespeare Company and the Royal National Theatre? Why are they not leading their audiences instead of merely catering to their established tastes which, necessarily, are based on what they have already seen? Why are these theatres not presenting more new work by contemporary artists who write about the world they share with their audiences? Who are to be the playwrights of the future if the theatres with large subsidies, those theatres which can most afford to present contemporary playwrights, incline toward presenting either plays by writers of the past or plays by a handful of living writers with name recognition such as Harold Pinter, Alan Ayckbourn, Tom Stoppard, and David Hare or established Americans such as David Mamet, Arthur Miller, and Richard Nelson. True, there is an attempt to have it both ways by commissioning younger playwrights to adapt the works of well-known authors of the past. The practice does provide a modicum of income for these writers, but does very little to encourage them to create works which are uniquely their own and which reflect the ambience of the contemporary world in which we live. Are all of the playwrights to become television and movie writers because only these media are willing to produce original work? Fortunately there are smaller theatres such as the Bush, the Royal Court, and the Hampstead in London, and the Traverse Theatre in Edinburgh which are dedicated to the production of new plays. But we may be seeing the end of a historical tradition – a tradition in which the principal subsidized British theatres were also the principal producers of new work. Hopefully it is not an end but only a hiatus.

THEODORE SHANK

Additional Comments from the Contributors for the 1996 Reprint

The original edition of *Contemporary British Theatre*, published in 1994, was the work of fourteen people, experts in their particular areas of theatre. It was appropriate, therefore, in providing a preface for this new edition, to ask these contributors to comment on the significant developments and trends in their areas since writing their original essays. In some instances the status quo prevailed and no further comments were required. And sadly, in the brief time that has passed, two of the contributors have died – the young American scholar Lynn Sobieski, who wrote on three of the ground-breaking innovative theatres in England, and Alasdair Cameron, the expert on experimental theatre in Scotland. Their loss is surely felt by their students and colleagues as well as by all of us who have benefited from their insights.

Following are brief comments by the contributors who believed updates were needed in the areas of their original essays.

TONY DUNN ON 'SATED, STARVED OR SATISFIED: THE LANGUAGES OF THEATRE IN BRITAIN TODAY'

The tendency in our culture for image to mimic flesh has accelerated in the last few years and the term 'virtual reality' is now in common usage. The resultant crisis in representation has profoundly affected the British political class. It knows for whom it speaks – the money institutions – but no longer to whom it speaks nor in which language. Right and Left combined to laugh out of court John Major's slogan 'Back to Basics' in 1994. There are no basics in a society of depthless image and free-floating individuals. The theatricals of the Tory leadership contest in 1995 revealed a surer instinct for what the people have come to expect from mediatic Toryism – a show. The contest followed the narrative convention of TV soaps, continuous domestic excitation without final relief, and the people were mollified.

The most stimulating practitioners of live theatre have long anticipated the menace of virtual reality. To counter it they have either framed electronic images in their live performances, or they have foregrounded the living body as an existential event. Tim Etchells of Forced Entertainment underlines, in an interview with Clare Bayley, this pro-active stance towards the media when he defines the company's aim as making 'theatre for those of us raised in a house with the TV permanently on' (*The Independent*, 24 February 1995). The crises of childhood and adolescence, he points out, are now played out in tandem with their simulacra on television. Irony, however, and physicality are not enough, as Theatre de Complicite have recognised. They now work their brilliant choreographic skills onto texts of linguistic weight and density. Their *Street of Crocodiles*, adapted from the stories of Bruno Schulz, a German-speaking Jew, was co-produced by the Royal National Theatre and presented at the Cottesloe in 1992 and the Young Vic in 1994. It was followed by their version of a John Berger story, *The Three Lives of Lucie Cabrol*, which was a success at the Manchester Drama Festival in January 1994 and had an acclaimed run at the Shaftesbury Theatre a year later. This first crossover of performance art into the commercial West End was followed, in December 1994, by another production at the Royal National Theatre, *Out of a House Walked a Man*. The text itself, by an obscure Russian surrealist Daniil Kharms, had to be unearthed by the company in St Petersburg. Complicite have the right priorities – to hunt out a blotched manuscript in Russia rather than splice videos in London.

While Complicite transmutes the texts of foreigners, the originality of Howard Barker's texts is still unrecognised by the major subsidised theatres. They order these matters better abroad. The Odéon Theatre in Paris hosted in February 1995 *Hated Nightfall* and *The Castle*, lethal exposés of the ruses of power, past and present, in the visceral language Barker alone has invented. His version of *Uncle Vanya* is scheduled for an English and European tour in February 1996, and 1997 should see the premiere, on a large continental non-theatre site, of his epic *Rome*. Barker's bodies, male and female, are always at war and always articulate. They speak an imaginative prose of startling image and virtuoso rhythm. The physicality of his company, The Wrestling School, is agonistic and real. The historical intuitiveness and the dramatic skills of Howard Barker are one of our few defences against meretricious simulation.

JATINDER VERMA ON 'CULTURAL TRANSFORMATIONS'

Since writing my original essay on translation as a form of transformation, I have also come to appreciate circumstances in which the act of transformation is also a form of appropriation – appropriating the artifacts and sensibilities of others for one's own use.

Since writing the original essay, Europe has become an all-pervasive reality in Britain. The opening of the Channel Tunnel has effected a geographic link and the political and economic union with Europe is now an ever-present shadow for Britons. It is in this context that questions of culture, more specifically of Britishness, have become most acute. The issue of identity has been raised by sports commentators questioning the loyalty of black British sportsmen and women when they are playing for England and by politicians enjoining schools to teach Britishness. This problematic identity is, in fact, peculiarly England's; the Scots, Welsh, and Irish see themselves, on the whole, as Scots, etc., first and British second, with European a distant third. The English, bereft of Empire, dominated by the United States on the one hand, and Germany and France within the European Community on the other, have been forced to ponder what they are as a distinct ethnicity. The 'we' that was so replete in the English language when English men and women talked of Britain, is now much more cautiously, even hesitantly, applied.

One current production is, for me, most significant of the times: *Titus Andronicus*. Initiated by the Royal National Theatre Studio in a co-production with the Market Theatre, Johannesburg, it is an inter-cultural production on a grand scale, involving black South African actors and white English ones. The actor Anthony Sher, whose roots are in South Africa, is the motive force for this production. With the 'liberation' of South Africa under Nelson Mandela, it is a chance for this fine actor to end his exile. During the 25 years or so of Sher's exile in England (mainly with the Royal Shakespeare Company), did he not notice blacks in Britain? To date, neither of the major English repertory companies – the RSC and the Royal National – nor indeed any of the major stars within these companies, have initiated a co-production with an Asian or black company in Britain.

Within such a context, it is plausible to argue that both myself and Yvonne Brewster – directors of independent Asian (Tara Arts) and Black (Talawa) theatre companies – were 'appropriated' by the major companies when in 1990–91 each of us was invited in to direct productions. What had seemed the beginning of a transformation of the Royal National in particular, pales into a pragmatic appropriation when one considers that company's repertoire since our productions. A caveat is looming: my company (Tara Arts) will be co-producing Edmond Rostand's *Cyrano* with the RNT using my adaptation with Ranjit Bolt. Will this prove to be another false dawn? Or is it suggestive of real changes in English theatre? The jury, as they say, is out on this matter.

Perhaps 'English' culture has such a long history of appropriation, legated by its Imperial past, that it can do little else. However, appropriation can be a two-way street. It could be argued, for example, that my own productions, which have largely concentrated on Western classics of late, are a form of reverse-appropriation: the 'Third World', if you like, fights back! My adaptations of *The Government Inspector* (which was originally directed by Anuradha Kapur from New Delhi), *Tartuffe*, *Troilus and Cressida* and, more recently, *Cyrano* (which Anuradha will also direct), have wrenched those texts from the familiar contexts in the West, relocating them vigorously within an Asian sensibility.

This First World/Third World dialectic, within which my work can best be placed, is replete with paradoxes. I live in the First World and, to an extent, am not immune to its sensibilities and textures in its relations with the Third World. This is exemplified by my work. In drawing so heavily upon the sensibility of Indian theatre, where does my work differ from that of a Peter Brook or an Ariane Mnouchkine who do the same? Is mine not also a case of appropriation? I don't know the answer to this in terms of aesthetic practice; but I do feel that where my work differs is that, to an extent greater than a Brook or a Mnouchkine, mine is a self-discovery, making some sort of a whole out of the fractures engendered by migration. I exist *in* the border; perhaps Mnouchkine, Brook, and their fellow European directors look out *from* a border.

This reflection on transformations in contemporary British theatre is far from conclusive; we are living at a time of major cultural shifts. Perhaps out of this will emerge a reconstructed sense of modern Englishness. To that re-invention, I and Tara Arts remain committed.

SHERIDAN MORLEY ON 'SPREAD A LITTLE HAPPINESS: WEST END MUSICALS'

The situation regarding British musicals on stage has not radically altered since *Contemporary British Theatre* went to press in 1994: the patient is no better or worse, he is much the same. True, we have had one major new Lloyd Webber, *Sunset Boulevard*, which seems to have created more drama with its various superstar performers and their offstage encounters than is actually available on the set. The show pays homage to its composer's lifelong interest in Hollywood movies, and has the wisdom to stay very close in its book and lyrics (Don Black and Christopher Hampton) to the model, Billy Wilder's classic movie of 1950.

Elsewhere around the West End, there has been a headlong flight to songbook shows celebrating a single singer (Nat King Cole, Al Jolson) or composer (Cole Porter, Louis Jordan), since these are usually cheap to stage, demand small casts, often of one, and can reasonably be expected to pick up an audience from those who buy favourite CDs or tune in to nostalgic radio shows.

Which still leaves the question of where the brave new shows are to come from, if not Lloyd Webber alone? They are out there somewhere, in workshops and regional theatres and summer festivals, but the cost of getting them into London, and the risks involved in failure, grow more prohibitive by the month. Meanwhile the Royal National Theatre's musical programme gives us *Carousel* and Sondheim and more Sondheim: not much room for adventure or experiment there either.

TIM ETCHELLS ON 'DIVERSE ASSEMBLY: SOME TRENDS IN RECENT PERFORMANCE'

Artists working in the crossover zone between theatre, fine arts performance, and new dance have continued the blurring and slipping as they move even further, sometimes completely, into each other's disciplines. Theatre-maker Graeme Miller's evocative installation piece, *The Sound Observatory* (a map/portrait of Birmingham via sounds collected in its streets), has led to new works such as *Listening Ground* (a guided audio walk through Salisbury) in which the only performers are those experiencing the walk and the people of Salisbury itself. In dance, meanwhile, Lloyd Newson has taken his DV8 Physical Theatre even further towards their incorporation of text with *MSM*, a largely text-based piece. The title *MSM* is a sociological term for Men who have Sex with Men and the piece used documentary interview material collected by the company to unpick the constructions of masculine sexuality in cottaging, the practice of men having sexual encounters with other men in public lavatories.

Pete Brooks' work has undergone yet another shift – away from textual minimalism and towards its most fully and spectacularly cinematic incarnation to date. In *Clair de Luz* (1993–4) all of the action is seen through a gauze cinema screen, the dimensions of which change to produce close-ups and CinemaScope effects.

Although exciting for audiences, and therefore very much in demand, these cross-disciplinary borrowings and incorporations have sometimes proved difficult for funders, and hence, for the artists themselves. Late in 1994 the Drama Department of the Arts Council of England suggested to several of its better-known experimental clients (my own company, Forced Entertainment, included) that other departments of the Arts Council might be 'more appropriate' sources of funding. At the same time dancer Nigel Charnock was under threat from the Arts Council Dance Department because his recent work had included too much talking and not enough dancing. These contemporary battles of definition are, of course, the embodiment of a debate about history, about strands of performance that are acknowledged and strands which are not, about strands of performance which are given the means by which to flourish and those which are not. I'd like not to be bleak, but in many ways the future for experiment in a British culture that is increasingly focused on a return to a past we never even had is not looking good.

If I were writing my chapter now I'd need to expand my all-too-brief mentions of some of the artists and correct at least one omission. In particular Keith Khan's work has developed in extraordinary ways, best exemplified perhaps by his 1993 piece *Moti Roti* – a combination of carnival, quotation, and reference to Indian cinema and postmodern deconstruction which spoke to festival and local audiences during the London International Festival of Theatre (LIFT) 1993. Desperate Optimists aren't mentioned in my chapter, but are deserving for their highly personal, highly politicised pieces, especially *Hope* (1994), which are very much at the centre of recent developments where theatre meets task-based performance.

Of the younger artists Blast Theory have stayed the distance, developing a promenade form that incorporates sound, movement, and multimedia to speak about contemporary issues. Reckless Sleepers and Index have also continued to grow and develop – the former pursuing projects in which the audience–performer relationship is spatially re-invented whilst Index are making less and less theatre as their installation works such as *Train Up a Child* and *Alphabet of Dogs* win considerable praise.

For our own part, in Forced Entertainment, I think our work continues to be subject to many of the movements and blurrings described above. Since 'Diverse Assembly' was written we have made a number of collaborative works for art galleries – *Red Rooms* (1993) and *Ground Plans for Paradise* (1994), both made with photographer Hugo Glendinning – and a number of site-specific projects – *Dreams' Winter* (1994), for the Great Hall of Manchester Central Library, and *Nights in this City* (1995) which involved a coach trip around Sheffield. There is a growing focus in our work, both in and out of theatres, on its contract with the spectator, on the ethical and political dimensions of spectatorhood and voyeurism and on the function of performance as a kind of public, and thus communal, bearing witness to the events of its time. I hope that, in its own way, 'Diverse Assembly' is also a useful bearing witness.

DAVID HUGHES ON 'THE WELSH NATIONAL THEATRE: THE AVANT-GARDE IN THE DIASPORA'

The Welsh National Theatre is comprised of relatively small-scale groups working mostly in the urban centres of the south where the population is concentrated, but also in the small communities throughout Wales, rather than in a single cultural centre. This reflects the demographic, linguistic, political, cultural, and economic splits of the country.

There is agreement among the theatre leaders in Wales that the situation has changed quite considerably in the last three or four years. Janec Alexander, Theatre Coordinator for Chapter Art Centre, believes Welsh theatre has matured through international touring by companies such as Man Act and Volcano. This notion of maturing is also signalled by an emergence into mainstream culture proper. Brith Gof have created television documentaries and made-for-TV pieces, and their income from TV rivals that from the Arts Council. Also, the international reputation of both Brith Gof and Y Cwmni has benefitted from performing at London's Royal Court Theatre as part of Barclays New Stages festivals.

The two ground-breaking companies which had stood out in scale and prestige – Moving Being and the Centre for Performance Research – have undergone important changes. Moving Being continue to produce occasional grant-aided projects such as *Darwin* and *Anna Freud*. However, when the Welsh Arts Council began withdrawing support, the company gave up their space in St Stephens Church. The church, which housed them and nurtured other groups, is now run as a commercial venture. Y Cwmni, one of the St Stephens groups, and Volcano have now been around long enough in a permanent production mode for splinter and subgroups to be spawned. The Practice is effectively defunct, but the newer, younger groups are taking the stage and the subsidies.

The Centre for Performance Research have also given up their space – the gym in Chapter's schoolyard – and now locate their projects around Wales and England as appropriate. They are behind a new academic journal for performance and live art to be called *Performance Research*. Richard Gough, Artistic Director of the CPR, has taken up a post as Senior Research Fellow at the Drama Department of Aberystwyth University which will become a partner in much of Centre's work, and it seems likely that CPR will ultimately be absorbed by Aberystwyth. This kind of move, writes Simon Thorne (Co-director of Man Act), 'is completely in line with the general trend in Britain for all kinds of innovative thinking in performance languages to be placed within academic institutions.'

The notion of a mainstream National Theatre of Wales is once again a live and contentious issue with Michael Bogdanov (former director of the English Shakespeare Company who has Welsh connections through his mother) returning to Wales to launch a bid to establish such an operation in conjunction with Phil Clark, director of productions at Cardiff's mainstream Sherman Theatre. Launched in the summer of 1995, the plan is to consolidate the circuit of theatre buildings and main-stage companies in Wales as well as to produce a number of heritage projects such as performances about 'steel' in Port Talbot and 'drovers' in Carmarthen.

Bogdanov's announcement of his plan assumed that all the small-scale groups working in Wales would agree with him and stand behind him. However, this was not the case. The general feeling among these companies is that the bid will fizzle out like other attempts to create a mainstream national theatre. However, Bogdanov, with his European plaudits and work for the RSC, is a bigger fish than others who have attempted to set up a National Theatre. The Lottery Fund and the Millennium Fund are on the look-out for big, prestigious projects and this might just fit the bill.

The geographical centre of theatre in Wales has clearly fractured. Whilst in the 1970s and indeed up to the early 1990s, Chapter Art Centre was *the* centre, a hub, a main focus of work, support and energy, the loci of energy are now much more spread out. The Cardiff Bay area has plans for an opera house, a Dance and Choreographic Centre for Wales at the enormous old Coal Exchange building, and Maggie Russell's venue, The Point, is already functioning there. The monopoly for care, nurturing and commissioning work has been taken away from Chapter which is essentially threatened by the new initiatives, and in a contest for Lottery and Millennium funds, might well lose out to the National Theatre or Dance and Choreographic Centre bids.

Note

Thanks to the following who provided information for this update: Janec Alexander (Theatre Coordinator, Chapter Arts Centre), Simon Thorne (performer and Co-director, Man Act), Maggie Russell (Project Associate, Magdalena Project), Geoff Moore (Artistic Director, Moving Being), and Mike Pearson (Co-director, Brith Gof).

JANE EDWARDES ON 'DIRECTORS: THE NEW GENERATION'

Naturalism is still out of fashion with the young directors who continue to make their names by directing the classics. The only difference is that the classics are getting more recent. It took the epic sweep and emotional range of Tony Kushner's *Angels in*

America to persuade Declan Donnellan to direct a new play. The arrival of Stephen Daldry on the scene with his extraordinary production of J.B. Priestley's *An Inspector Calls*, transforming it from what had become a rep pot-boiler into a piece of expressionistic theatre, spoke to a new generation that is visually literate and brought up on movies rather than books. His subsequent production of Sophie Treadwell's *Machinal* at the Royal National Theatre used machinery that had lain rusting beneath the stage since the building opened. This flamboyant approach can be extraordinarily exciting; at the Royal Court, where Daldry is Artistic Director, there is a good chance that he will put theatre at the centre of this country's culture once more as he brings a classical bravura to new work. The danger is that when applied to a new play, as with Daldry's production of Meredith Oakes' *The Editing Process*, the world of the play will be swamped by the directorial flourishes.

Daldry, Sean Matthias, who 'outed' Noel Coward with his production of *Design for Living*, and Richard Jones dominate a group of directors who, with varying degrees of success, bewitch an audience with their theatricality and the power of their imagination. At the other end of the spectrum, there are those directors who want audiences to become involved by being forced to use their own imaginations. While increasingly design-conscious, these directors continue to concentrate above all on what happens between the actors. Katie Mitchell's production of Strindberg's *Easter*, Donnellan's all-male *As You Like It*, Deborah Warner's *Richard II* with Fiona Shaw as Richard, and Theatre de Complicite's adaptation of John Berger's *The Three Lives of Lucie Cabrol*, in which the actors played everything from blueberry bushes to slaughtered pigs, all drew the audience in to play its part in the production. Theatre has always revolved between the bare planks and the spectacular; it's just that these days the door revolves even faster.

MATT WOLF ON 'RECENT TENDENCIES IN DESIGN'

Summer 1995, and British design seems more buoyant than ever. If the musical set-maker was king during the 1980s, his straight play colleagues have now well and fully caught up. Who would have imagined four years ago that a British theatrical warhorse, *An*

Inspector Calls [**cover photo**], would give rise to a set from Ian MacNeil that would be one of the most talked-about designs London, and Broadway, has ever known? In conjunction with director Stephen Daldry, MacNeil turned Priestley's Yorkshire call to social consciousness into a fiery example of theatrical expressionism, in which the Birlings' tiny jewel of a house exists to be shattered, along with the smug, self-absorbed values of its inhabitants. That it was good spectacle as well merely made for a pleasingly subversive kind of irony, since the production ended up attracting exactly that audience which the play itself attacks.

An Inspector Calls began in a Royal National Theatre auditorium, the Lyttelton, that continues to suggest itself as among the most amazing design spaces anywhere. Re-imagining Rodgers and Hammerstein's *Carousel* for keeps, Bob Crowley gave audiences a clean, shimmering New England vista which Andrew Wyeth and Norman Rockwell could both have called home. Jean Cocteau's *Les Parents Terribles* (renamed *Indiscretions* on Broadway) made a London and New York star out of the gifted Stephen Brimson Lewis, whose two extraordinary designs – including the spiral staircase of an actor's nightmares and an audience's dreams – balanced the camp and the serious in the same heady manner as the play itself. The ever-astonishing Anthony Ward surpassed his work on *Napoli Milionaria* with *La Grande Magia*, also by Eduardo de Filippo. From Magritte-like hotel setting by the sea to a conjurer's shabby home and beyond, Ward continues his experiments with light, shade, and perspective that make the stage seem literally to breathe. Vicki Mortimer, Rob Howell, Neil Warmington, Tom Piper; the list of rising talent goes on in a country whose design savvy continues to grow.

List of Photographs

Notes on the Contributors

Claire Armitstead is Arts Editor for *The Guardian*. She has worked as theatre critic on the *South Wales Argus*, Theatre Editor for the *Hampstead and Highgate Express*, and theatre reviewer and feature writer for the *Financial Times*. She read English Literature at St Hilda's College, Oxford.

Alasdair Cameron was a lecturer in Theatre at the University of Glasgow. He reviewed for *The Times*, was Assistant Editor of *Theatre Research International*, published many articles on Scottish theatre, and edited *Scot Free*, an anthology of Scottish plays (Nick Hern Books). His early career was in professional theatre. He died in 1994.

Ruby Cohn is professor of comparative drama at the University of California (Davis). She has published three books on Samuel Beckett, and another seven books on various aspects of contemporary theatre.

Tony Dunn is Senior Lecturer in Literary and Cultural Studies at Portsmouth University. He has contributed many features and articles on contemporary theatre to *Plays & Players* and *New Socialist*, and he is a regular reviewer for *Tribune* newspaper. He is at present writing a book on domesticity and culture in Britain from the 1950s.

Jane Edwardes has worked in the Film and Theatre sections of *Time Out*, and in 1986 she became Theatre Editor. She has written for *The Times*, *Plays International*, *Plays & Players*, *Times Educational Supplement*, *20/20* and occasionally broadcasts. She has also worked in Fringe Theatre.

Martin Esslin was born in Budapest, educated at the University of Vienna and the Reinhardt Seminar of Dramatic Art. He joined the BBC in 1940 and served as Head of Radio Drama 1963–77. In 1977 he became Dramaturg at the Magic Theatre in San Francisco and Professor of Drama at Stanford University. Among his many publications are books on *The Theatre of the Absurd*, Pinter, Samuel Beckett and *Mediations; Essays on Brecht, Beckett and the Media*.

Tim Etchells has been writer and director with Sheffield-based

Forced Entertainment Theatre Co-Operative since its formation in 1984. Alongside his work with the company he has written widely on new theatre, performance and fine art installation as well as teaching in a variety of contexts. His novel, *Helen* ©, is in progress.

David Hughes is a critic of dance, performance and fine art. He has served as the artistic director of the improvisation group Reflex Action Theatre in Cardiff. He edits *Live Art Listings,* is launching an international magazine of performance, directs The Working Party's programming wing in London and performs with the group No Mean Feat. Formerly a lecturer in the School of Performing Arts, Leicester University, he now teaches at Nottingham University.

Sheridan Morley is the drama critic of the *International Herald Tribune* and *The Spectator*. Musicals he has devised include *Noel & Gertie* and a tribute to Vivian Ellis, *Spread a Little Happiness*. In 1990 he won the Arts Journalist of the Year Award, and now hosts the BBC Radio 2 Arts Programmes. He is the author of more than 20 books on the theatre.

Theodore Shank is Professor of Theatre at the University of California, San Diego. His articles and books on contemporary theatre have been published in at least fifteen countries, he is an award-winning playwright and director, and he has served on several theatre committees of the Arts Council of Great Britain. He is founding editor of the international journal *TheatreForum*.

Lynn Sobieski taught at the University of Michigan, the University of Texas (Austin), and New York University where she received her Ph.D. She worked as a dramaturg at theatres in New York and in Germany on a Fulbright-Hays Grant, and she published articles on contemporary German and British theatre. She was editing a collection of essays on *Postmodernism and Contemporary Performance* and was writing a book on 'performance theatre' in Britain when she died in 1994.

Ian Stuart is a Lecturer in Drama at the University of Southern California. He earned a Ph.D. in Dramatic Art at the University of California, Santa Barbara. His studies of Edward Bond's production work have appeared in *New Theatre Quarterly* (May 1991) and *Australasian Drama Studies* (October 1991).

Jatinder Verma was born in East Africa and migrated to Britain where he earned degrees at the Universities of York and Sussex. In 1976 he founded Tara Arts and has served as its Artistic Director ever since. In 1990 he became the first 'immigrant/Black' to direct at the Royal National Theatre.

Matt Wolf is London arts correspondent for The Associated Press and theatre critic for *Variety*. His freelance articles have appeared regularly in *The Times* of London, *The New York Times, Harpers & Queen* and *American Theatre* magazine.

Part I

1

The Multiplicity of British Theatre

Theodore Shank

In this book 'contemporary theatre' refers to the work of those artists in Britain who are creating unique forms of theatre to express what it is like to be alive today. Primary attention is given to those artists who, rather than beginning with conventions of the past, are exploring means uniquely expressive of the tensions and pressure of our time even though some works may be in response to older plays or literature or history. Sometimes text and character are primary; at other times visual images, movement, sound/music, even the form itself may dominate. There are unlimited possibilities as artists search for the means to express the variety of experience which comes from living in a multi-ethnic, multi-cultural and multi-national country. The result is a complex and dynamic British theatre.

In Britain, as elsewhere, there is an 'official' culture consisting of the beliefs and behaviour of people who are perceived as having political and economic power and there are other cultures existing along side the dominant one. The people of this official culture in Britain are English; they are middle-class, white, hold traditional English values, and they reside in the Home Counties near London. The unofficial cultures are made up of peoples who are not perceived as being a part of the English establishment; they may be distinguished geographically (they may live in the north of England or in Scotland or Wales) or ethnically – especially the people of Asian or African descent. Members of these ethnic minorities are sometimes considered immigrants even if they were born in England. This 'official' view of British culture does not reflect its true complexity. Not only does Britain have several geographic and ethnic cultures, these are not the only sorts of divisions that are reflected in theatre work. England, of course, is not Britain – there are also Scotland and Wales and there are nationalistic movements within these countries which see their cultures as unique and not well served by the theatre of the official English culture. And there are other sorts of divisions – philosophical, social, political and aesthetic – and each has its ardent adherents.

At the 1991 Edinburgh Festival a panel of theatre practitioners and critics from England, Scotland, Wales and Ireland discussed the concept of national theatres and attempted to answer a number of related questions: Do these individual nations have separate cultural identities? If so what are they? Should they be preserved at a time of greater cultural exchange and increasing Europeanisation? Do nations need national theatres to express their identity? ('Theatres').

The discussion began with moderator Michael Billington, the respected drama critic of *The Guardian*, suggesting that the typical image of English theatre is that it is ironic and text-based; Scottish theatre is hard-headed and realistic; Irish theatre is word-drunk and tragi-comic; and Welsh theatre, not having a written dramatic tradition, tends toward performance art and takes place outside of conventional theatre buildings. It was suggested by others that it is the English sense of superiority and smugness that allows for irony and self deprecation – a luxury which the other British nationalities and ethnic groups do not have. An ironic multiplicity of perspectives may also reflect a belief that there is no common bond between people. Some English politicians see only fragmentation of their culture rather than acknowledging a multitude of unique cultures. For them there is no such thing as society, there are only individuals and families. On the other hand, there are those who believe, as does Fintan O'Toole, the literary advisor of Dublin's Abbey Theatre, that there are societies that can form the bases of national theatres.

There are responsibilities, there are values, there are things we have in common that make us feel a part of each other. Those things are open ended and constantly changing, but they do exist. If you want that, a national theatre is a good thing to have because it has the responsibility of saying there are things we have to say that you may not come to on your own; there are things we have to show that you may not have noticed before. It is dangerous and challenging; but if you don't do it, it ultimately will lead to a bland Europeanisation. ('Theatres')

According to Mike Pearson, a founder of the Welsh company Brith Gof, the tendency in Wales toward a theatre that is not based in language and which is often presented in unconventional spaces is pragmatic. There is no tradition of dramatic literature in Wales, he says, no tradition of social realism or discursive narrative technique, no great circuit of playhouses in which to perform. A programme note for Brith Gof's production of *Patagonia* mentions another reason for performing in non-theatre spaces. They prefer to perform in 'buildings in which a community works, plays and worships: chapels and cathedrals, barns, cattle markets and disused factories.' And they have ambitions for a theatre that is uniquely Welsh.

Brith Gof is convinced that a new, vibrant and distinctive theatre tradition is possible in Wales which is relevant to the hopes, fears and aspirations of a small nation. Such a tradition is firmly rooted in the Welsh language, culture and history. . . . It will necessitate new structures and forms of performance with the dynamic juxtaposition of sung and spoken voice, physical image and action, music and poetry. And all this may bear little relation to the 'well-made play'. (Brith Gof)

The Scottish representative on the Edinburgh panel, Neil Wallace, agreed with Billington's characterization of Scottish theatre as angry, typified by John McGrath's politically-focused 7:84 Theatre Company. This company and others are also populist, attempting to communicate with people who have no theatre-going tradition. Other tendencies are evident in Glasgow's Citizens' Theatre which is especially receptive to European influences rather than looking to London for models. And the Traverse Theatre in Edinburgh is dedicated to the presentation of new work – especially those by Scottish writers. But many feel something is missing. The 1992 *Charter for the Arts in Scotland*, a document prepared by a consortium of arts organizations after wide consultation with artists and others, demands a national theatre:

The renaissance in Scotland's indigenous culture is echoed in a strong cry for a Scottish National Theatre. Scotland supports a lively theatre network, but . . . . there is widespread belief in the need to develop and promote the Scottish dramatic repertoire, encourage Scottish writing for the stage and help actors develop and maintain the skills necessary for effective performance of drama.

The artistic director of the West Yorkshire Playhouse, Jude Kelly, who was the English representative on the panel, believes that most people think of English theatre as plays with upper-middle-class characters who live in country houses in one of England's Home Counties. Except for musicals, this is the typical fare of the commercial theatres of the West End which reflect what Billington referred to as the official English culture. Such productions also make up a small portion of the two so-called 'national theatres' in London – The Royal National Theatre and the Royal Shakespeare Company – which receive the largest subsidies from the government through the Arts Council of Great Britain. In part the justification for these large subsidies is that the National and the RSC are intended to serve as the national theatres for all of Britain; but it has been suggested that it would be more appropriate to call them 'English National Theatres' in that they do not often reflect the national aspirations or cultures of Scotland or Wales and only infrequently produce plays by writers from those countries. However, they are more adventurous than the commercial theatres and somewhat more reflective of the cultural variety of the country. While their repertoires consist, to a large extent, of English classics or new plays by established playwrights of England, they also present works by lesser known writers such as Jim Cartwright who lives in Lancashire and reflects the culture of northern England, and occasionally by writers from British minorities such as Mustapha Matura or Derek Walcott. And the Royal National Theatre has engaged directors with minority perspectives – particularly Jatinder Verma and Yvonne Brewster – to direct productions which, in addition to playing at the National's Cottesloe Theatre, have toured to various parts of Britain and abroad.

In addition to their work at the National Theatre, Matura, Verma and Brewster are each directors of their own theatre companies producing plays with actors of Asian or African descent. In the beginning, forming their own companies was probably a necessity if they were to work in the theatre. Matura's first London-produced play was at the Institute of Contemporary Arts in 1970. In 1978 he and Charlie Hanson founded the Black Theatre Co-operative to produce another of his plays. Although at least 17 of his plays had been produced at fringe theatres in London, and several of them had earned prestigious awards, it was not until 1991 that one of his plays was presented in London by one of the national companies. In fact, *The Coup* was the first Caribbean play produced by the National Theatre. A play by his Trinidadian countryman, Errol John, had been produced in London as early as 1958, but that play (*Moon on a Rainbow Shawl*) did not provide much of a breakthrough for other writers. 'Caribbean culture and literature have been marginalised', Matura says. However, writers such as 'Marquez and Rushdie have made British audiences more aware of the value of looking at a life that does not relate to the English. The English have become broader because of travel to other countries and have increased tolerance and acceptance that there is life elsewhere' (Matura).

Yvonne Brewster, director of the Talawa Theatre Company, directs for her own company and for the National Theatre. She has directed all-black productions of *The Importance of Being Earnest* and a Nigerian-set *Oedipus*, and she has set a predominantly-black *Blood Wedding* in Cuba. Similarly, Jatinder Verma directs his own company, Tara Arts, and also directs at the National Theatre. He has directed productions of *The Government Inspector* [Photo 4] and *Tartuffe* with Asian casts. But such casting is uncommon. Except for productions by ethnic-specific companies such as Talawa or Tara, most productions are by white directors with almost exclusively white casts. A few black actors, such as Josette Simon who has played major roles at the RSC, are exceptions. And plays written by white British playwrights rarely reflect the multi-cultural make-up of Britain's population. Even though most British playwrights hold liberal or even radical views, says Michael Billington,

> you could comb the plays of Osborne, Wesker, Ayckbourn, Stoppard, Nichols (with the major exception of *National Health*), Frayn, Gray, Hampton and numerous others without finding many indications that we inhabit a pluralistic, multi-racial society. (Billington)

By this practice, Verma believes, 'British theatre is promoting a kind of myth that does not correspond to people's experience as they walk down the street.'

It may be that this tendency to make non-white Britons invisible feeds what Verma describes as a tendency of non-English Britons 'to be more English than the English'. He calls it 'colonisation of the mind' – a legacy of colonialism which results in people losing their own distinctive character. He satirized this tendency in his *Government Inspector* which he set in post-colonial India [**see Verma essay**]. However, it is not only descendants of people from former British colonies who aspire to be English; some Scottish and Welsh people feel colonised as well. And the tendency infects some white English people who are outside the official English culture. Certainly many theatre people have lost their regional ways of speaking. A version of this theme is at the centre of *The Rise and Fall of Little Voice* (National Theatre, 1992) by Jim Cartwright who was born in Lancashire and continues to live there. The title character of the play, set in 'a Northern Town', is a shy, withdrawn young woman who denies her own personality and voice; she can only sing when imitating one of several famous singers. The happy ending comes when she accepts herself and her own voice, rich with northern dialect though out of tune.

Jatinder Verma would keep the distinctive varieties of speech. He is fascinated by

> the aesthetic consequences of putting a Yorkshireman next to a Scotsman next to an African next to an Asian on the stage. The signs they represent by different ways of speaking English and different colours of skin suggest a possibility of cultural encounters, of different world views operating on the same text. That, in terms of its implications on the theatrical language, is immensely exciting. (Billington)

Such a production would certainly be at odds with the stereotypical view of English theatre.

There are other areas of contemporary theatre performance which are counter to the traditional. While the forms of such works are yet to be named and are often simply called 'experimental' or 'live art', they can perhaps be divided into those which emphasise visual imagery and those in which the principal means of expression is physical movement. Until recently it was sometimes remarked that many English directors did not see, that they were concerned with vocal expression, the subtle shades of meaning in the language and a mastering of verse, but they had less interest in the visual aspects of a production. And it was a cliché that English actors act only from the neck up, that their focus on language and voice was to the exclusion of the body as an expressive instrument. This is, of course, not true of actors such as Laurence Olivier, Ian McKellen, Maggie Smith, Tilda Swinton, Antony Sher and Ian McDiarmid. But there is an English tradition for plays which depend on wit, intelligence and a command of verse which make no large demands on the body. So it is surprising that some young performers are creating works that are especially physically demanding.

The members of DV8 Physical Theatre **[Photo 2]** create productions collectively with director-choreographer Lloyd Newson. These works put into focus arduous physical movement which often is brutal but can be sensuous or gentle. The movement serves to express a thematic emotive idea around which a work is structured. The idea might be loneliness and desperation as in *Dead Dreams of Monochrome Men* or could be striving, hopeful, even flirtatious as in *If Only . . .* (1990). A programme note says *If Only . . .* 'is a direct response to the despair and loneliness evoked by . . . *Dead Dreams of Monochrome Men* in which the performers were slaves to their desires and the environment they inhabited, victims of the sadness and oppression which surrounded them.'

If Only . . . tests the physical endurance of the performers as they struggle against gravity in various ways. But there is hope; there is the possibility of non-gravity, of flight. Men are at times suspended from a cable and pulley in the flies at each side of the stage. One man tries to fly out from the wall. He and a woman also try to fly without the cable. It is as if they did not understand gravity, as if they should be able to fly, so they fight unsuccessfully against this unknown force. They defy gravity, but gravity always wins. They never give up, even though they are physically exhausted.

A programme note for *If Only . . .* describes the objectives which guide the work of DV8:

> The company's work is about taking risks, breaking down the barriers between dance, theatre and personal politics, and above all, about communicating new ideas directly, clearly and unpretentiously.
>
> Dancers struggle with an unknown force to gain control of their bodies; one falls, another seeks to fly. Each player struggles to find a voice so as to be heard, but their words remain soundless.
>
> 'If Only . . . ' looks at our attempts to determine the paths our

lives take, examining the relentless search for fulfilment, and the belief that there is something better within our reach, if only we know where and how to find it.

DV8 Physical Theatre is the best known and most travelled of the physical theatre companies in Britain, but there are others including the younger group V-TOL Dance Company (the name stands for Vertical Take-Off and Landing) directed and choreographed by Mark Murphy. And such work is not unique to Britain, there is a kinship with such companies as La La La Human Steps in Canada, and the works of choreographers Pina Bausch in Germany, Anne Teresa de Keersmaeker and Wim Vandekeybus in Belgium, some of the work of Joe Goode in the USA and others.

Groups whose work depends importantly on visual images have a longer British history. The surreal images of the People Show [Photo 8], the oldest of such groups, first appeared in the late sixties and the group continues to perform. Others of importance, but of shorter duration, are Geraldine Pilgrim's Hesitate and Demonstrate and Lumiere & Son under the leadership of director Hilary Westlake and writer David Gale [see Sobieski essay]. Another enduring company, and the furthest ranging in the scope of its work, is Welfare State International which continues under the direction of John Fox who founded the company with Sue Gill in 1968.

The Welfare State company – also known as Engineers of the Imagination, Civic Magicians and Guardians of the Unpredictable – are a core group of about ten visual artists, musicians, performers, engineers and pyrotechnicians that can be enlarged for specific projects. The company is based in Ulverston, a small town in South Cumbria, but has created special site-specific projects throughout Britain and in other European countries as well as in Canada, Australia and Japan. Their visual images, achieved with costumes, props, lanterns, masks, giant puppets, ice sculptures and fireworks, combine traditions of mummers, carnival and musical hall and suggest a world of Britain in the Dark Ages as it might have been depicted by Bosch or Breughel. Their work ranges from miniature pieces, which have been presented with audience and performers inside a bus, to gigantic outdoor productions involving more than a hundred people. *The Raising of the Titanic*, commissioned by the London International Festival of Theatre (LIFT) in 1983, was presented on an estuary of the Thames. The performance made use of both the dock and the water from which a skeletal Titanic was raised providing an occasion for its ghosts to perform songs and comic routines as they acted out the events leading up to the sinking. To John Fox, the sinking of the Titanic is an apt metaphor for the demise of Europe. The company's production for LIFT 1991 was *Lord Dynamite* [Photo 3], a full-scale opera commemorating the life of the inventor Alfred Nobel. The magnitude of the performance required two football pitches with the audience watching from an earthen mound between them. John Fox is not only an imaginative and skilled director and visual artist, but a poet with a fine dramatic sense which serves him well in writing librettos and scripts. Productions are celebratory in spirit and performers interact with the spectators. Often performances end with participants and audience dancing together.

None of these unique companies, whether imagistically or physically focused, has a performance space of its own. All of them tour throughout Britain and most of them to the Continent as well. In Britain performances are often sponsored by art centres which occasionally offer commissions. Some of these are discussed in the following essays, especially Cardiff's Chapter Arts Centre and two venues in Glasgow – Tramway and the Third Eye which has metamorphosed into the Glasgow Centre for Contemporary Arts. In London the principal venues are Riverside Studios, directed by Jonathan Lamede, which presents a variety of theatre work; The Place, under the direction of John Ashford, which sponsors work by dance theatre companies; and the Institute of Contemporary Arts, directed by Mik Flood, formerly of the Chapter Arts Centre, which gives most of it attention to young exploratory groups. These venues present not only the work of British companies, but at least as often they sponsor the work of companies from various parts of Europe and even from Asia, Africa and the Americas.

In part these Centres reflect a shifting kinship which is also occurring within British companies. In the late sixties and seventies the greatest influences on young British theatre groups were companies from the USA – specifically La Mama, the Living Theatre and the Open Theatre – though the work of Jerzy Grotowski also had an impact. Without suggesting which came first, as the economic alliances of Britain gradually shifted from the USA to Europe, especially with the growing importance of the European Economic Community, aesthetic relationships have also shifted. One reason is that European governments are much more generous than Britain (and certainly more generous than the USA) in providing funds to assist their theatre companies to tour to Britain and for British groups to visit Europe. So British artists have had an opportunity to see work which inevitably leaves its mark, subliminally at least, and seems to have an impact on their work. Such influences have caused some to worry that the ultimate result could be a bland Europeanisation of British theatre. This concern is one of Fintan O'Toole's arguments for national theatres that would help preserve cultural uniqueness ('Theatres'). It is perhaps ironic that as nationalism increases among some of the peoples of Europe, including Scotland and Wales, there is a growing internationalism in the arts.

Internationalism seems to have had less of an impact on text-based theatre – perhaps because the restraint of different languages has inhibited international touring of such works. And those British theatres which give primary attention to producing new plays look most diligently for British plays and the accompanying potential support from the Arts Council in the form of commission money and residencies for the playwrights.

The Royal Court has long been the best known theatre ardently dedicated to presenting the premiere productions of new British plays. Since John Osborne's *Look Back in Anger* opened there in 1956, the theatre has introduced many of the playwrights who have been responsible for late twentieth-century British (especially English) drama. In addition to Osborne, there were John Arden, Edward Bond, Ann Jellicoe, Joe Orton, N.F. Simpson and David Storey. Playwrights of the last decade whose works have premiered at the Court include Howard Barker, Howard Brenton, Caryl Churchill, Andrea Dunbar, Terry Johnson, Paul Kember, Hanif Kureishi, Louise Page, Winsome Pinnock, Timberlake Wertenbaker and others. Critics and some artistic directors perennially decry the dearth of talented young playwrights and often blame it on the difficulty of making a living writing for the live theatre compared with television and film. While the current Artistic Director of the Royal Court, Max Stafford-Clark, believes that writing for the stage is the most demanding writing medium and agrees that most playwrights do not have easy financial lives, he thinks there is no dearth of young talented playwrights. Rather he believes there is a dearth of young directors who are eager to direct new work.

It's small wonder that few directors choose to risk time and energy in the volatile field of new writing when critical acclaim and career advancement awaits above average productions of minor classics. Promising young directors will remain reluctant to exchange one-sided dialogues with the dead for the tensions of collaborating with the living while their efforts remain invisible and unperceived by the myopia of critics. (Stafford-Clark) [See Edwardes essay]

In the late eighties and early nineties other factors inclined theatres toward more conservative programming and less expensive productions. This meant taking fewer risks with unknown playwrights, but the impact was more general. Under the Conservative government of Margaret Thatcher there was a kind of trickle-down conservative attitude which dampened the enthusiasm of artistic directors for risk taking; and government support for theatre did not keep up with the rapidly rising costs of production and the economic recession. Artistic directors became increasingly worried about theatre finances. Terry Hands, Artistic Director of the RSC during this period, points out that their subsidy went from 44 percent of total income in 1985 to 27 percent in 1990. In 1981 the RSC had taken 'a policy decision to go into spectacle' which meant rather sumptuous sets, but four or five years later the accumulating economic problems of the 'Thatcher years' made elaborate sets impossible. And, according to Hand, the 'Thatcher years' also brought an end to the regional theatres, 'our breeding ground', and 'nearly destroyed the RSC as well' (quoted in Coveney).

It is probably a combination of necessity and the aesthetic pendulum that has led to greater simplicity in the nineties. Newer directors such as Sam Mendes and Declan Donnellan together with designers such as Bob Crowley have replaced monumental pictorialism, which was often a literal depiction of a place, with a suggestive symbolism which frees the spectator's imagination [see essays by Edwardes and Wolf]. Unlike the detailed world for which director Trevor Nunn had a proclivity in the early eighties, Sam Mendes says he tends 'to look for simple organic properties that can have a hundred meanings' (quoted in Wardle).

The number of premiere productions in the late eighties and early nineties may not actually have decreased, but many of these at the National, the RSC, the Royal Court and in the West End drew upon the familiar – the work of earlier writers or history or movies which would spark recognition in the minds of potential spectators. There were adaptations of literary works such as Laclos' *Les Liaisons Dangereuses* (adapted by Christopher Hampton), Bulgakov's *Black*

Snow (by Keith Dewhurst), Homer's *Odyssey* (Derek Walcott) and Robert Louis Stevenson's *Dr Jekyll and Mr Hyde* (David Edgar). Playwrights were commissioned to make new versions or new translations of well-known plays such as Lope de Vega's *Fuente Ovejuna* (by Adrian Mitchell), Wilde's *Salomé* (Steven Berkoff), Chekhov's *The Seagull* (Michael Frayn) and *Uncle Vanya* (Pam Gems), Ibsen's *The Pretenders* (Chris Hannan), Tirso de Molina's *The Last Days of Don Juan* (Nick Dear), Molière's *Le Bourgeois Gentilhomme* (Nick Dear), etc. There were new plays based on historical figures or events such as Alan Bennett's *The Madness of George III* and Richard Nelson's *Columbus*. There were adaptations and conflations of ancient Greek plays including *The Thebans* by Wertenbaker [see Cohn essay]. The usual direction of stage to screen was reversed with adaptations of movies including *Some Like it Hot, Casablanca, The Manchurian Candidate, The Blue Angel*. Such borrowings, of course, are not unusual. The Greeks did it, so did the Romans, Shakespeare, Molière, and the forgotten nineteenth-century playwrights who adapted the novels of Dickens and others as soon as they were published. It provides work for playwrights, but it can also inhibit their ability to develop unique forms to express personal emotive experience of what is happening in their world.

Nevertheless, a handful of theatres in England and Scotland continue their dedication to new plays, all be it with two eyes on the box office. In addition to the Royal Court, under the direction of Max Stafford-Clark and Stephen Daldry, the most prolific are the Traverse Theatre in Edinburgh where artistic director Ian Brown is especially interested in encouraging Scottish writers such as John Clifford and the Bush Theatre, above a London pub, directed by Dominic Dromgoole, which has completed its twentieth year of producing new plays by such writers as Stephen Poliakoff, Robert Holman, Sharman MacDonald, Terry Johnson, and Doug Lucie. Other theatres still actively producing new plays, though most often by established playwrights, are the Hampstead Theatre, under the direction of Jenny Topper, a former director of the Bush; the Royal National Theatre directed by Richard Eyre; and the Royal Shakespeare Company under the direction of Adrian Noble. Despite the dedication of these theatres, the enthusiasm for the production of new plays clearly diminished in the eighties.

There are other tendencies in theatre practice of the early nineties which relate to the changing times. Beginning in the late sixties and continuing through most of the seventies there was a burgeoning of small idealistic theatre groups with marxist political agendas. Often these groups were structured as collectives and developed their own plays which they toured throughout Britain. The most prominent of these – the Scottish and English companies of 7:84 (named for the statistic that in Britain 7 percent of the people own 84 percent of the wealth), Red Ladder, Cartoon Archetypal Slogan Theatre (CAST), Belt and Braces Roadshow, North West Spanner, Broadside Mobile Workers Theatre – received support from the Arts Council of Great Britain; but during the Thatcher government, in the eighties, the funds for many of these companies were cut off or devolved to Regional Arts Associations.

These theatre groups were not alone in their political idealism. Text based playwriting since the end of the sixties has been driven by a belief in socialism in general and sometimes Marxism in particular. Playwrights such as John Arden, Edward Bond, Arnold Wesker, John McGrath, Tom McGrath, Trevor Griffiths, David Hare, Howard Brenton, Caryl Churchill and David Edgar wrote plays focused on social issues which were critical of the British establishment, of capitalism. And they seemed to know the answers; they believed with Oscar Wilde who wrote, 'A map of the world that doesn't include Utopia isn't worth even glancing at.' (Wilde) David Hare wrote a play called *The Map of the World*. There was an implicit suggestion in these plays that Utopia was another name for socialism and on the map it was in the neighbourhood of Eastern Europe. A series of events in that part of the world dampened enthusiasm. The fall of communist governments and the embracing of a free-market economy by much-admired people such as Vaclav Havel, was more than most idealism could withstand. And when the Labour party in 1992 lost to the Tories for the fourth time running, these writers could no longer locate Utopia on the map. For most the last glow was gone. They were left without the moral and intellectual framework which had shaped their writing. They were at sea without a map or a compass. Howard Brenton described the situation that he and others had to face:

> The 'British epic' theatre with its 'issue plays' that my generation of playwrights invented and wrote through the seventies and eighties . . . has died on us. This is normal artistic life; what was once white-hot invention becomes dead convention, mere theatricality. We need new ways of dramatising what people are thinking and feeling out there.

Ironically, we could become rebels against the official orthodoxy we ourselves helped to make. (Brenton)

Brenton feels that his new play, *Berlin Bertie* (1992), 'takes a sledge-hammer to the "right on" clichés that have debilitated recent radical theatre in Britain' because it is 'psychological, character-driven' and, although the play is 'very realistic', each of the five characters has a 'disruptive' aside to the audience in verse (Brenton). So his new approach was the old one of psychological realism driven by the experience of the characters, and he makes a gesture toward formal exploration in his use of monologues. The play does not chart a route to a new Utopia but, rather, suggests there might not be one after all.

A younger playwright, Gregory Motton, responding to Brenton's comments, has no investment in the social-issue focus of the older generation. To him the popular view of theatre as a form of social criticism 'provides simple and very traditional fare'. It deals with the safe external world 'where wrongs are committed and reported, where other people are guilty of injustices.' He decries the 'moral-istic tone' with its 'hollow Victorian ring'. And the playwrights are politically impotent. Audiences go to the National Theatre to see a play by Hare or Brenton 'but they don't grasp what they are watching . . . you only have to watch the swine striding past the beggars on their way out with their noses in the air to see that.'

Writers whose consciousness is formed by what they read in the papers are writing plays somewhat less stimulating than journalism, less penetrating than the biographies and factual books they depend upon.

The limitations of political ideology are neither suitable nor desirable in an art form. Art, if it is anything, is to do with truth, a vain, failed attempt at truth – the opposite of politics which is not vain but purposeful, and which expects not to fail but to succeed, and is famously full of lies . . . . It deals, as does the theatre it spawns, with the knowable and known, whereas art deals with the unknowable and the unknown.

Issue theatre describes the self-evident as effectively as poss-ible. If it does no more, it feels it succeeds. . . . [But] to invent truth, the artist must descend into the limitless unknown of the human soul; resist the obvious and go to the hidden heart of things where meaning itself is sparse. He cannot know what he will find, he must withhold judgment, be illogical and perverse, obscene and offensive. He can have no aim and can never achieve it. (Motton)

Motton's comments might well be the manifesto for several young theatre groups who are exploring a renewed aestheticism drawing upon their subjective response to the brutal ambience of their world. They may be collectively structured like many of the political theatre groups of the seventies, but their aim is not the analysis or criticism of society or political structures. In some instances these new groups actually predate individual playwrights like Motton. Because these groups develop their own texts and perform their own work they need not find producers willing to risk presenting work outside the conventional models of theatre as social criticism or as entertainment. Perhaps it is this self-suffiency that has allowed Welfare State International and the People Show to survive. More recently formed groups include DV8 Physical Theatre, Forced Entertainment [Photo 10], Dogs in Honey [Photo 6], Station House Opera, Mayhew & Edmunds, Insomniac Productions, Blast Theory, V-TOL and perhaps a dozen more [see essays by Cameron, Dunn and Hughes]. New ones emerge and existing ones disintegrate every few months. Much of this work uses means and techniques that a purist might think belonged to dance or music or visual arts or electronics, but fortunately there are at least two sources of financial support. Barclays New Stages, funded by Barclays Bank, was formed 'to provide financial aid for independent theatre – a dimension of the arts which is traditionally under-funded' by government and business sponsors. (Barclays) And the Arts Council created a category of funding called New Collaborations with a budget in its second year (1992–93) of £350,000, an increase of 75 percent over its first year.

It is inevitable in art that an expressive form devised by an artist or a group to reflect their relationship to a time is then repeated by other artists if, indeed, the form is genuinely effective in expressing the time and communicating some sense of it to an audience. By repetition the new form or technique becomes a convention that outlasts the time and, although it no longer is expressive, may continue in use because of its momentum. In some arts adjustments to the shifting times are quickly made – newer concepts arise and forms and techniques are invented or resurrected to express them. But the cumbersome nature of theatrical production and the costs involved tend to make it one of the most conservative of the arts. It is lethargic and clumsy in its response to the changing emotive climate of a culture. It is fortunate for the theatre as an art that there is a continuous stream of young artists who do not carry the baggage of the past, artists who can look anew at our world and tell us what we didn't know that we knew.

REFERENCES

Arts Council. Press Release, 29 November 1991.

Barclays New Stages. Programme for the Festival of Independent Theatre, 18 May–6 June 1992.

Billington, Michael. 'The Colour of Saying', *The Guardian* (London), 1 November 1990.

Brenton, Howard. 'Poetic Passport to a New Era', *The Guardian* (London), 7 April 1992.

Brith Gof. Programme for *Patagonia*, 1992.

Charter for the Arts in Scotland (draft). The Steering Group which prepared the document represented the Scottish Arts Council, the Scottish Museums Council, the Scottish Film Council, and the Convention of Scottish Local Authorities, May 1992.

Coveney, Michael. Interview with Peter Hall, Adrian Noble and Terry Hands, *The Observer*, 28 June 1992.

DV8 Physical Theatre. Programme for *If Only . . .*, Queen Elizabeth Hall, 11 August 1990.

Matura, Mustapha. Interview by the author, London, 6 September 1991.

Stafford-Clark, Max. 'Looking Back in Anger', *The Guardian* (London), 28 May 1991.

Motton, Gregory. 'At the Stage of Hollow Moralising', *The Guardian* (London), 16 April 1992.

'Theatres and Nations', a panel discussion moderated by Michael Billington at the Edinburgh Festival, sponsored by *The Guardian* (London), 18 August 1991. Other members of the panel: Jude Kelly (Artistic Director, West Yorkshire Playhouse, Leeds), Fintan O'Toole (critic and literary advisor to the Abbey Theatre, Dublin), Mike Pearson (founder and member of Brith Gof, Cardiff) and Neil Wallace (Program Director, Tramway, Glasgow).

Wardle, Irving. 'Beyond His Years', an interview with Sam Mendes, *The Independent on Sunday*, 12 April 1992.

Wilde, Oscar. 'The Soul of Man Under Socialism', quoted in Tony Dunn's 'Writers of the Seventies', *Plays and Players*, May 1984, p. 12.

2

Sated, Starved or Satisfied: The Languages of Theatre in Britain Today

Tony Dunn

I

That politics and theatre have much in common is a truism. The fall of Margaret Thatcher followed exactly the sequence of a typical Greek tragedy as analysed by Aristotle and preserved in the student notes on his lectures which we call the *Poetics*. But her downfall was more than a banal conceit. It was the high point of a process that had been accelerating throughout the decade. In 1980s Britain a number of different developments combined to make possible, for the first time, the permanent theatricalisation of everyday life. Media-technology became more compact, more economical and more accessible. Home-videos, Walkmen, Car-phones and VDU's plugged the people into their own mobile dramas. Conservative anti-union legislation was traditional and in the Government's first five years was aimed at traditional targets, the heavy industries of steel, coal and the railways. Dramas of confrontation, particularly with the miners, were familiar from the 1970s, extraordinary sagas with a long class-history. But a side-effect was to demonstrate the mobility of new lightweight TV cameras, needing much smaller crews. When the print-unions were broken in the Wapping dispute of 1986, the way was open for much more rapid editing and production of verbi-visual stories by journalists. The result, according to Mark Lawson of *The Independent*, was an increase in media-outlets so that 'for the first time British politicians employed image-makers to help them fill the newly available space' (*The*

19

Independent, 1 December 1990). The new term 'photo-opportunity'
meant a constant alertness by politicians to the possibilities of being
photographed. In 1980s Britain to be was to be visible.

Imagistic lightness was displacing discursive heaviness. Lewis
Mumford, quoting Toynbee, observes, in *The City in History* (134–5),
how creative cultures tend, by lessening their bulk and simplifying
their design, to 'etherialise' their technology. He proposes the city,
where the interplay between the concrete and the symbolic is
most complex, as the crucial space for such a process. The 1987
deregulation of the City of London, that dramatic orgasm called
the Big Bang, was not just a technical matter of changed relations
between client, broker and stock-market. It installed London as
the junction of global, financial information, etherialised into electronic impulses appearing as figures on banks of screens. Money
has always been an esoteric matter in Britain, inextricable from
arguments about class and education. But monitors are familiar
conventions of soap opera. The interweave of deals and love-affairs
has made *Capital City* (1989 on) a most successful series, but the title
is more layered than *Dallas* or *LA Law*. It suggests that the city is
defined as a place where capital is; that such a city is 'capital', that
is an excellent place to be; and that the city is the capital, London,
historically a non-industrial centre. The Thatcher Government's bias
towards finance capital and against industrial capital, and towards
the centralised control of all local finance, underpinned, at the policy
level, these symbolic shifts.

Shakespeare is a political conservative, but in play after play he
warns against autocracy. Henry V is the ideal king because he can
talk man-to-man with the common soldier as well as leading from
the front in wartime and squashing aristocratic cabals. Menenius
has as much contempt for the common people and their tribunes as
Coriolanus. But Coriolanus is a political menace because he cuts off
all communication with them whereas Menenius can talk to them
in their own language. Mrs. Thatcher and her PR team devised a
language for the people appropriate to televisual politics. Linguistically it was aphoristic and dogmatic – 'There are new industries
in other people's pleasures', 'There's no such thing as society' –
and visually it was iconic, the all-inclusive and irrefragable image
of perfect coiffure, steel-blue eyes and sharp-edged handbag. The
people were actively invited into this theatre of the housewife
superstar, not as bit players, but as authenticators of her enterprise
dream. The people would realise their status as a collection of free

individuals, not through work, or class or community, but through money. Shares in public utilities and tax-reductions were more than political ploys. They were part of a larger project, to remodel the British people like the American people, for whom there is no contradiction between money-making and good citizenship. Mrs. Thatcher lost her common touch when her pride, by now regal, caused the Poll Tax to be transformed into a counter-icon of mass democracy. But she made a more profound miscalculation. Since the eighteenth century the source of all rights and laws in the American Constitution has been The People. Britain has no written constitution and the source of rights and laws is an ambiguous compromise, the Queen in Parliament. Citizenship is a legal fiction and 'the people' has no constitutional existence whatever. It is, in Britain, everyone and therefore no-one. It had been shaped by class, region or community. Mrs. Thatcher tried to profile this amorphous entity as the profit-making individual. She failed, but her opportunistic populism has ensured that 'the people', if only like the Ghost in *Hamlet*, has to be listened to and remembered. The secrecy of the Thatcher Government created mounting demands in the 1980s for a written constitution. The centralising obsession of the Thatcher Government exacerbated demands for separate assemblies by the Celtic regions of the Kingdom. If, in the next ten years, 'the people' is recontoured as a Republican or a Federalist democrat, Mrs. Thatcher's home policies, by a dramatic irony that is almost Greek, will be largely responsible.

Feminists were highly critical of Mrs. Thatcher since her support for the nuclear family and 'Victorian values' seemed to check their programme for female emancipation from domesticity. 'The personal is political' (Tuttle, 245–6) claimed not only that what goes on in the home (sex, eating, child-care) is as political as the world of work, money and wars, but also that the two worlds are umbilically connected. The walls of a home are porous boundaries and the everyday life within them – and what could be more everyday than the domestic round? – is as worthy of deciphering and revaluation as the world at large. The home, on this account, is not a haven from the world. It is the world in microcosm, with 'inside' and 'outside' as merely contingent terms. The relationship between what Mrs. Thatcher said and the policies effected by her Government was often as arbitrary as the Saussurean sign. There is convincing evidence that in 1980s-Britain family life became visible as never before. The law penetrated to the core of the family with

judgements on domestic rape and child-abuse, and publicised legislation on one-parent families. Social scientists documented the rise
in illegitimacy – from 10% of live births in 1979 to 28% in 1989. The
heart of the economy was re-located in private home-ownership and
domestic credit. Parents were mobilised as overseers of the educations system. Books such as Charles Forty's *Objects of Desire: Design
and Society 1750–1980* and Christina Hardyment's *From Mangle to
Microwave, the Mechanization of the Household* epitomise growing
academic research into the social signification of everyday processes
in the home. The Design Museum was opened in 1989 and has
mounted exhibitions on such topics as the Citroen DS and Creativity
in Everyday Life. Communications technology has by now set up an
intense two-way traffic between the home and the world through
24-hour satellite TV, fax machines, specialist telephone lines and an
expanded network of radio stations. Politicians resigned to spend
more time with their families. Advertising publicised, by the end
of the decade, the most intimate body processes – menstruation
and AIDS. As the birth-rate fell and easy credit was encouraged,
what children there were became the privileged conduits into the
home of the worlds of style and fashion. Terrestrial TV, taking off
from such long-established family sagas as *Coronation Street* and
The Archers, multiplied the genre throughout the 1980s. *Dallas* and
Dynasty were only exotic in their settings. Their dramatisations of
family squabbles were as irresolvable, and as addictive, as those
in *Brookside* and *Eastenders*. The Australian soaps, *Neighbours* and
Home and Away, have taken the genre to its logical conclusion.
They are ultra-realist sagas of everyday life, where the most banal
and the most catastrophic of events are, helped by the Australian
accents, flattened into even narratives without end. The women,
old and young, are the most powerful figures, inside and outside
the home. Not only is the personal political; the political can only
be personal.

Such hyper-domestication of political life was anticipated by the
shrewdest analyst of media, Marshall McLuhan, more than thirty
years ago. The global growth of electronic technology would induce,
he forecast, a shift from an alienated, objective stance towards
events to an in-depth empathy with them. 'We are suddenly eager
to have things and people declare their beings totally' (McLuhan,
13) elucidates both soap-opera figures and born-again religionists.
Not everyone feels competent to pronounce on politics or economics. Everyone has views on domestic matters. McLuhan suggested

the model for the new, electronic community would be not the city, but the global village with all its petty jealousies and ancestral rancours. Appropriately he uses a theatre metaphor to characterise this relationship. Satellites encircling the globe create, as it were, a proscenium arch around it so that everyone is now actor and audience in their own village dramas.

II

But what of theatre proper? What is its role and function in this electronic culture? In several important respects it has distinguished itself from, and provided a critique of the mediatic society described above. In recent years it has seemed as if the beauty and grace of men's and women's bodies, as framed by the camera in sporting events and fashion magazines, have virtually detached themselves from the musculature and bone-structure of these bodies. Sweat even, in rock-videos, seems artful and translucent. Live theatre foregrounds the body as physique with viscera. Its beauty or ugliness is a function not only of convention but also of a relationship with other bodies in a space with depth. Live theatre grounds the body in its physical density whereas the electronic theatre etherialises the body into an image. It does this much more rapidly than live theatre ever can. Cutting substitutes for dialogue, and the interval between an event and its playback has become minimal. Live theatre, by contrast, takes its, and your, time to present a unique event. It guards the space between performer and audience which, in a period of 'consumer choice', is elitist in contrast to the demotic politics of rewind and replay. Those forms of live theatre that have made greatest use of image and new technology, that is musicals such as *Les Misérables* (1985) **[Photo 7]** and *Starlight Express* (1984), have been the most popular. The more a play has had language itself as its subject the more coterie it has seemed. But ever since the late 1960s it has been impossible to trace clear frontiers between demotic and elitist art. 'Crossover' has been both a marketing technique and an aesthetic strategy. Covent Garden Opera, relayed to the general public with subtitles in the Plaza, or Pavarotti's 'Nessun Dorma' signalling World Cup Football are examples of the former. They correlate, however, with a more varied audience for opera in recent years for performances by the English National Opera and Opera North. Opera is now not considered a snob art in Britain.

A more complex example of crossover is the development of Performance Art in this country in the last five years or so. This hybrid theatre of drama, music, dance and objects proposes that discontinuity radically challenges the 'grand narratives' of the bourgeois State. Yet the brevity of its pieces, between sixty and ninety minutes long, pushes it towards a structure of imagistic moments. With roots in the libertarian 1960s, this theatre always foregrounds the human body, often naked, and the sequences, by now a convention, of bruising physical encounter emphasise its material existence. But political struggle in Britain is now conducted on two simultaneous levels, the clash of bodies in riots and strikes, and the clash of ideas in language. Grand narratives are not over. A new one, whose subject is 'democracy', has been unfolding from Eastern Europe to China in the last two years. An old one, whose subject is 'economic man', has been recounted to us for the last decade. In comparison the strangled articulacy of performance art tells only half the story.

One of the most talented companies in this field is the Theatre de Complicite. The name acknowledges an ironic collusion with mainstream, electronic culture. A small season of two shows at the Almeida Theatre in December 1988 illustrated the strengths and limitations of performance art. The first, *More Bigger Snacks Now* (a revival from 1985), was a beautifully choreographed series of fantasies by four young men. A dilapidated sitting-room with wonky TV, lampshade, a couple of chairs and a high-backed double sofa was the setting for the opening mini-dramas of the 'Phantom £20 Note' and 'The Last Cigarette'. The Captain (Tim Barlow) finds a cigarette and, dragging on his bruiser's mouth, saunters towards the audience as his mates cry 'Marlboro! Marlboro!' Plates wheel through the air and glasses loop from hand to hand as three of the men set up the fourth as a guest at an expensive restaurant created out of battered formica table, broken-down chair and a biscuit on a plate. Back to the flat with the Idiot (Simon McBurney) grinning a mouth full of ugly fillings in a narrow, rattish face topped by oil-slicked hair. He gasps 'Let's have a party! Let's have a party! Let's make it nice! Let's make it beautiful!' But there are no women, nor do they need any for this very accurate description of male creativity about wealth, glory and exploration. So, improvising baggage-check and customs, they set off to Brazil, or Canada, or Australia. They mount the airplane steps of chair and table and chorus 'we go, we go, we go' into the fading spotlight.

The show was enormously enjoyable not only because of the

ensemble skills but also because of cultural recognition. It was not a parody, but a fast and affectionate replay of 1950s British absurdist theatre of which the best example is N.F. Simpson's *One way Pendulum* (1959). The scruffy settings and delusions of grandeur recalled 23, Railway Cuttings East Cheam, the fictional address of Anthony Aloysius Hancock, frustrated hero of *Hancock's Half Hour*. Spike Milligan's *The Bed Sitting Room* was the model for the expansion and contraction of stage space, and it needed only a tilt of the story-line towards, say, detective or thriller action for us to find ourselves watching performance art Pinter. Complicite's production of Dürenmatt's *The Visit* opened with the scene on the railway station of Güllen acted in the same tradition of British rubbish. A gangling British Rail guard, a stocky Mediterranean police-chief, a dwarf and a pop-eyed citizen wearing odd socks stumbled, jerked and inanely gestured up and down the platform as imaginary trains whizzed by. But the grotesque, always lurking beneath the surface of this humour, was exposed when a train stopped and a small woman descended. She was supported by attendants in cream-linen suits and shades. Her green ski-pants covered an artificial right leg, her black gloves a prosthetic left hand. She levered herself across the stage on crutches topped with fur. Clara Zachanasian had returned home as a rich heiress to have her revenge on the townspeople who expelled her years ago for her illegitimate child, and on Alfred Schill, the storekeeper who was the father. Kathryn Hunter played Clara with a voice hoarse from a thousand cigarettes, a crippled vamp, ruthless and black-humoured. Christine Keeler was crossed with Marlene Dietrich to manufacture a female of palaces and night-clubs, whose sophistication was worlds away from provincial Güllen, but whose rich vindictiveness caused economic chaos in the town and a magnificent final scene where Alfred is hunted to death in the town-hall basement. The repetitive circlings and sudden physical clashes skilfully integrated performance art technique into a major text of European theatre. The text, however, pre-dated the company, and the quality of Dürenmatt's writing showed up the derivative nature of the script for *More Bigger Snacks Now*.

This gap between script and technique has been even more marked in the recent work of Steve Berkoff. The first play of a double-bill at The Warehouse over Christmas 1985 was *Harry's Christmas*, written by Berkoff. It was a solo piece for a man (played by Berkoff) sitting in an armchair in his bedsitter, bemoaning his small number of Xmas cards and taking us back through the

histories they represent. It was banal, tedious and humourless. Tony
Hancock would have made something of it, but Berkoff doesn't
have the skills at sitcom. The second piece, Berkoff's stage-version
of Poe's 'The Tell-Tale Heart', was a brilliant theatricalisation of the
grotesque. Alone on stage Berkoff, in the frock-coat, breeches and
necktie of a dilapidated count, writhed, hissed and extruded out of
Poe's tale its horrific core. His knee trembled up, his hand clawed
the air in front, his right eye seemed to enlarge into a key-hole.
The deadlocked pull between movement and immobility enacted
the claustrophobia of the tale as he never moved from his spot
centre-stage.

The horror of confinement was also dramatised in his adaptation
of Kafka's *Metamorphosis* at the Mermaid in July of the following
year. The stage was dominated by a cage of tubular bars which
fanned out from a hutch at the back. Tim Roth, as Gregor, with
minimal make-up, became the insect as his limbs were transformed
into splayed, waving insect-legs that hooked onto the bars of the
cage or folded themselves under his body. Gregor's family tends to
be forgotten because of the horror of the son, but Berkoff has read his
text very carefully and his production gave particular prominence
to the father. He throws the apple that causes Gregor's death, but
he is also the only person who touches him when he lifts him back
into his cage. An Oedipal reading of a story by a middle-European
Jew in the early twentieth century makes good historical sense and
sharpens the physical clashes on stage.

Two months later (September 1986) Berkoff presented his story
of the Falklands War in *Sink the Belgrano!* at the Half Moon Theatre.
Moving uneasily between agit-prop and artifice, with a War Cabinet
of politicians called Maggot, Pimp and Nit speaking blank-verse of
cod Elizabethan intercut with fragments from *Henry V* and *Macbeth*,
the piece added nothing to the drama we already knew. One passage
almost saved it. The young crew is lying down inside the submarine
traced flat on the stage. Their commander describes the pleasure of
combat as they move underwater. The beauty of the marine depths
is paralleled with the aesthetics of slaughter. This is the site of
fascism and psychologically very shrewd, but Berkoff's blank verse
is too dog-trot a medium to explore the complexity, and the play
switches, with relief, to the cartoon-comedy of the War Cabinet.
Mrs. Thatcher, as we have seen, had her own agenda for classical
theatre and Berkoff's collage could only be a feeble imitation of it.

Berkoff's most intelligent reading to date of a classical text has been his production of *Salomé* for the National Theatre in 1989. Wilde, under cover of the Biblical story, dramatised typical 1890s fears of male castration by erotically confident women as they swept into the taboo area of politics. But Wilde's language is laughably outdated for a modern audience. It is the stilted vocabulary of the 'sinful' nineties with its references to pale moons, white roses, cedars of Lebanon and exotic perfumes. Berkoff discerned beneath it the sharper-edged outlines of the next period of female emancipation. His *Salomé* was therefore set in the 1920s. He made the references to whiteness and paleness the visual motif of the production. Wilde's Soldiers, Courtiers and Jews were transformed into a gaggle of Bright Young Things in evening-dress and white face-paint. They giggled, squabbled, Charlestoned and, at the end, killed Salomé on Herod's orders. Herod himself, played by Berkoff, strained his white mask into grimaces as he groaned at Salomé to 'Daaaaaaance' or grotesquely elongated the vowels of the treasures – 'chrysolites and beryls' – he offered her. Twisted through Berkoff's scarlet lips and amplified by the arm-sweeps that almost toppled him off his tubular chair, his speech sounded like a private language-game, the frantic yelps of empty-headed socialites in Waugh's early novels, or a manic joke to ward off the boredom of yet another provincial evening at the Palace. Kate Schlesinger's Salomé was a giddy girl in white, the most passionate sex was a kiss on the mouth, and the music was Chopin-edged jazz from a black pianist on stage. This was the world of Scott Fitzgerald as well as Evelyn Waugh, both caustic fictioneers of a heartless, frenzied society of money. Against it stood Iokanaan the Baptist. He barely moves as the court swayed round him on its high-heeled, stilted walk. The natural brown and white of his body contrasted with the artificial pallor of everyone-else. Unlike Wilde Berkoff had him on stage throughout. He passed up Wilde's *coup de théâtre* when he rises from his cistern to denounce the court, as he downplayed the Dance of the Seven Veils almost to the level of family charades. Through costumes and speech-inflections theatricality was spread throughout this production, so as to let the audience focus on a very 1980s politics, the politics of sexual gaze.

'You must not look at her', says Herod's page to the young Syrian Captain. 'I have told you not to look at her', rasps Herodias to her husband Herod. Only Iokanaan refuses to gaze at Salomé. Who offers and who accepts *le régard* came to dominate the play. Salomé only gets to look her fill on Iokanaan when she holds his dead head in her hands. Berkoff uncovered in Wilde's play a more accurate power-diagram of the gaze than the vulgar feminists of today. His proposition was that it is the man who looks at the woman who is trapped and overcome. It is the woman who is looked at who possesses power. And the attractive man who refuses to look at the beautiful woman has ultimate power over her. Salomé pants like a predator for Iokanaan, not because he will not kiss her, but because he will not look at her. She holds his sex in her hands when she holds his head, but its eyes are dead and its lips are cold. As with his production of *Metamorphosis*, Berkoff's stylisation has led to creative reinterpretation.

There is a boundary however between re-reading and appropriation. Berkoff crossed it with his production of Kafka's *The Trial* in 1990 for the National Theatre. The visual motif was a success. Everyone except Joseph K held themselves in the frame of a tall, grey-painted rectangle. These converted easily into rooms, housed, offices, corridors, roofs and the labyrinthine passages where the poor clerk loses himself and his reason. Antony Sher, hair brilliantined flat and in waistcoat, high stiff collar and spongebag trousers, plays Joseph K with a downbeat tenderness. But Berkoff's theatre is always striving to burst out into physical violence. Joseph's encounter with his lawyer is quite matter-of-fact in the novel. In Berkoff's version he is bloated in his suit like a balloon and almost bursts after a laughing sequence (at Joseph's naivete) of nearly ten minutes where he rolls all over the stage, his couch and his assistants. This was more Dickens than Kafka and they are very different writers. Joseph's sex-life is important in the novel, but the women are not given especial prominence in it. They showed a lot more leg, breast and red-lip here than the text warranted. There was nothing sexist about this elaboration. It was the importing into a cool text of a body heat from an earlier period of libertarianism that was wrong.

The Trial seemed dated, as did a revival of *Decadence* in 1991 at the White Bear Theatre Club in South London. First shown in 1981 the theme, the interdependence of sex and violence between aristocrats and workers, goes back at least to *fin-de-siècle* narratives by Stevenson and Wilde. The blank verse is the usual parody of an earlier convention. The White Bear is a tiny theatre so the sweat literally pored through his white face-paint as Roger Monk strained every vein to try and go beyond even his skin to project the rage of working class Les and the fetishism of upper class Steve. Portia

Booroff, a haughty red-knickered Helen, rode Steve exhaustingly to hounds, then switched into a young, foul-mouthed slag called Sybil. The actors gave their all but the text, which demands violence in playing it, does not provide a correlative to this in linguistic or psychological richness.

The introductory music for the production was Ian Dury's 'Billericay Dicky'. Its witty melding of contemporary cultural references with social stereotypes like the East End wide-boy represents the linguistic crossover that Berkoff devised in the early eighties. In *West* (1983) Mike, a gang-leader from East London, slips easily between classical reference and local geography to produce the cultural grab-bag of a street-wise illiterate like Shakespeare's Pistol:

A face like that won't launch a thousand ships or pull the scrubbers to their beds in Edmonton/Gants Hill/or Waltham Cross/so let him have his scars/his medals that he flaunts to all/to put the shits up any villain that doth take a fancy to him/for a bout of bundle round the back. (14)

The late 1970s and the early 1980s was the period when the cultural mix of the 1960s, avant-gardist and art-college, finally filtered through to popular culture. The surrealist video-promos for Queen's 'Bohemian Rhapsody' (1975) and the Boomtown Rats' 'I Don't Like Monday' (1979) are evidence of this. Yobbos speaking verse had the same shock-value as a female, Tory Prime Minister. Each side, for different reasons, then developed an obsession with image and collage. But avant-garde art, by definition, is oppositional and marginal. Pop culture is essential to the communications hegemony of the modern capitalist State. Each has lived off the other but now popular culture, as the much larger beast, seems about to swallow the avant-garde and performance art in particular. David Gale, founder-member of the distinguished company Lumiere & Son, in a paper given at a conference on performance art at the Riverside Studios in 1986, described how, ten years on, many practitioners felt 'sated and starved at the same time'. He was not just imaging performance art as an unwelcome guest at the capitalist feast. He was also pinpointing its inability to go beyond image and physique into narrative and debate. And it may be that this kind of theatre is primarily valuable to artists in regimes of repressive linearity and as a way of circumventing

verbal censorship. Certainly companies from former fascist and
communist countries have mounted extraordinary spectacles at,
for example, the biannual London International Festival of Theatre
(LIFT) seasons.

The contrast with a British performance, Mayhew and Edmunds
and Co.'s *The Devine Ecstasy of Destruction* at the 1991 LIFT, was
instructive. Thick smoke gradually cleared to reveal to the audience
squatting in the ICA's theatre a De Sade, with Sumo wrestler's
stomach and glittering cod-piece, spot-lit on a platform high to the
rear of the playing-space, who urged on with cackles and curses a
young man and woman in black leotards to more and more athletic
efforts at copulation, whipping, bondage and ejaculation. Chains
and halters were wound down from the roof by the young woman
to enact De Sade's increasingly frenzied quotes from *Justine* and *The
120 Days of Sodom*. He tore off his wig, jumped down into the arena
and showed them how it's done in a complicated buggery sequence.
This raised the first extended laugh from an audience embarrassed
by the poor casting and inadequate plotting. The British are always
uncomfortable with libertinage, but there was enough French here
for them to take it seriously. The embarrassment came from the mis-
match between energy and text. A group of youngsters was sweat-
ing away with a lot of equipment (PVC suits, swords and wigs) at
subjects (sex, death, perversion) they couldn't know anything about
because of the secular, laissez-faire culture that has bred them.

III

Any new theatre has eventually to come to terms with the texts
and institutions of classical theatre, ancient and modern. Precisely
because of its traditions and stylisation the theatre of Shakespeare,
Sophocles and Brecht marks off art from everyday life. Its standard
of quality also exposes the gimcrack tragedy of a Mrs Thatcher.
The body is foregrounded for disciplined mimesis rather than to
exemplify abstract political theory. Re-evaluation is the constant
task of directors and designers, but the most illuminating productions of Shakespeare recently have been, as with Adrian Noble's *The
Plantagenets* (RSC Stratford 1988; Barbican 1989) and Peter Hall's *The
Tempest* (National, 1988), where the costuming has been Renaissance
and the language has been thoroughly mined for its ambiguities and
resonances.

Debates about the Politicisation of Shakespeare are endless, but the recent work of contemporary political writers such as Trevor Griffiths, Caryl Churchill, Howard Brenton and David Edgar marks a watershed in their development. Although the majority had their associations with the fringe and mixed-media theatre in the late 1960s, their prime interest has always been in language for rational debate of public issues. Marx and Brecht led them away from obsessions with the image in hermetic spaces to epic narratives with large companies.

Trevor Griffiths' *The Party* (National Theatre 1973; RSC 1985; TV production 1988) is set in a room but contains a central speech of twenty minutes by the old Trotskyite John Tagg which expands political concerns far beyond four walls, to encompass the Third World, the history of the Soviet Union, the May '68 events in Paris and the roles of 'minority' groups such as woman and blacks in a future revolution. Striving to erect an edifice of historical logic, Tagg sublimates his passion in the brick-by-brick jargon of the revolutionary left. This extraordinary speech is the apogée of naturalist political theatre in our time and, with the collapse of communism, a threnody for a bankrupt discourse. While Tagg speaks, the TV relays images of the fighting in Paris. His host, Joe Shawcross, is a successful TV producer of Northern working-class origin. Tagg despises the media, but the structure of Griffiths' play, whereby Tagg, rigid and upright in his chair, is, as it were, 'soft-focused' by the stumbling, drunken playwright Sloman, the smoothie London School of Economics lecturer Ford and the gentle liberal Shawcross, demonstrates how wavering the lines of demarcation have become in the new electronic environment.

The 1980s, these playwrights sensed, would be the era of the middle-man. Marlene, the Thatcherite heroine of Caryl Churchill's *Top Girls* (Royal Court, 1982; revived 1991), runs an employment agency and resists the call to domestic responsibility by her dull country sister Joyce. *Serious Money* (Royal Court, 1987), with songs in the interval by Ian Dury, paraded the world of commodity-dealers, traders and bankers with such zestful accuracy that the theatre was packed by audiences from The City. David Edgar's Martin Glass in *Maydays* (RSC, 1983), Ian McEwan's James Penfield in the film *The Ploughman's Lunch* (1983), and Howard Brenton and David Hare's Andrew May in *Pravda* (National Theatre, 1985), are all journalists of liberal inclinations who opportunistically ally themselves with power. Only Howard Barker's Downchild, in the play of that name (RSC, The Pit, 1985) has no ideals to betray because, as a homosexual and a gossip-columnist, he has always lived along the hazy line of inside-outsider.

The morality of the media is a limited field since it is difficult to say anything original about the treachery of middle-men, and even more difficult to invent an original language in which to say it. Performance artists were shrewder, in the 1980s, when they made the effects of media the content of their theatre. The disintegration of communism, however, would seem to offer excellent opportunities to *marxisant* writers for dialectical debate within epic structures. But here also the playwrights' language has failed to match the drama of the events. Howard Brenton and Tariq Ali composed a tragi-farce, *Moscow Gold* (RSC, 1990), out of recent episodes in the Soviet Union. The tragedy was the post-glasnost career of a KGB man, his wife who is a cleaner at the Kremlin, their son and his girlfriend. But this familiar domestic tale, with its worm's eye view of politics, could not explain the machinations of Brezhnev, Andropov and Gorbachev. These were treated farcically, with Brezhnev's coffin presiding over Politburo meetings and Raisa using Gorbachev's rump to trace out the future map of Eastern Europe as he sweats off weight in a gym. Lenin descended in a chair from the flies reading the *Financial Times* and declaring that since socialism and communism are equally unstable 'the world is yet to be made'. With a march of all the Soviet nationalities round the stage and a series of full-scale Politburo confrontations, it was the visual language of the set, a magnificent revolve of huge red table, bedroom and prison backed by a creaking Stalin statue against the scaffolding, that provided imaginative excitement.

The dialogue of David Edgar's *The Shape of the Table* (National Theatre, 1990) was even duller. Students and intellectuals debated their biographies and reform programmes with communist party hacks across and round the tables of the title which are in the ante-chamber to the main meeting room of the communist government. In interview Edgar said that 'the important language of politics isn't grand, public rhetoric but lengthy negotiations over arcane detail. The final straw is often the misplaced comma' (*Tribune*, 9). A theatre of grammar is possible. Ionesco's *The Lesson* is an example. But although Edgar challenges the old politics of language he doesn't invent a new language of politics. Lutz, the Party Secretary, and Pavel Prus, the oppositional writer, stiffly confront each other and learn, by the end, a kind of respect for each other. There are allusions throughout to a fairy-story with a happy ending of church-bells and this becomes a metaphor for false narrative. Unfortunately Edgar's own narrative isn't dramatic enough to overcome the fairy-story nor is the fairy-story fantastic enough to capture the actions of the characters. Prus muses at the end that communism was a kind of awful holiday-trip with a mad schoolteacher who 'takes a group of pupils up a mountain and when the weather turns be can't cope and the whole thing ends in tears' (Edgar, 83). Edgar should have started here, with how accident, repressed and unacknowledged, produced the crazy doublespeak of Marxist-Leninism. John Tagg uses it with confidence, but in Griffiths' play he is already dying of cancer. Edgar thought he was writing history, but he has only mimed a corpse.

The hand of Trotsky's traindriver drifting in a bottle of formaldehyde is Howard Barker's symbol for the peculiar sclerosis of body and language under communism in *Fair Slaughter* (Royal Court, 1977). But the bottle is also functional to the plot in that Old Gocher, in Wandsworth prison-hospital for murder, wants to get the hand back to Russia and reunite it with the rest of his comrade's body that he buried fifty years ago. Old Gocher persuades his prison-warder Leary to help him escape and Leary persuades Gocher they have arrived in Murmansk when they have only got to the South Downs. There they meet Stavely, Gocher's former commanding-officer in Russia who also stage-managed Gocher's later career as a popular entertainer and has now escaped from a party of lunatics on an outing. Stavely loves art and finishes the play drooling about Picasso. Gocher loves communism and finishes with a hallucination of the train-driver shunting round him in an engine-mime. Leary has been drawn into Gocher's world and he exits from the play carrying the bottle.

Fair Slaughter is fifteen years old but, as the excellent 1991 production by the Cold Harbour Company at Greenwich Theatre Studio showed, this sardonic (not cynical) commentary on deluded idealism is even more pertinent today. Barker would never set out to research a play 'about' Gorbachev or Eastern Europe. He wrote his 'crisis of communism' play years before Brenton or Edgar, not because he is clairvoyant, but because his extraordinary linguistic ability led him to create imaginative rather than mediatised worlds of politics. Like Oscar Wilde he has always understood that the true artist is never of his times, but always ahead of them or behind them. His 'nuclear' play *The Castle* (The Pit, 1985) is set in the Middle

Ages and his 'feminist' play *Scenes From An Execution* (Radio 3, 1984; stage-version, The Almeida, 1990) in Renaissance Venice. His 'education' play, *The Bite of the Night* (The Pit, 1988), prospects down through a Troy with more levels than even Schliemann discovered to try and find truth. Dr Savage, last classics teacher in a ruined University, is accompanied in this 'Ruinad' by his wife Creusa who torments him as the leader of Mums' Troy and Laughing Troy, and by Helen, symbol of unattainable female beauty, who speaks objectively about her effect on men as she is gradually dismembered as the play proceeds. She finishes up as a trunk in a sack. Society hunts beauty but cannot tolerate the disorder it provokes. Savage's son wants to boil Helen into soap so every woman can cleanse herself into a Helen at a profit to him. Helen's daughter Gay is a brisk, tanned and depthless young woman whose goal is instant happiness and who resents the pain that both Helen and Savage recognise as the precondition for knowledge. Bodies clash but, even with Helen, never stop speaking. *The Bite of the Night* is a four-hour narrative which interlocks the fall of Troy with the murder of desire. Scholarship is ruined, beauty is mangled and the social vision of the new order is one of passionless marketing.

Barker is as savage as his hero in his attacks on liberal notions of equality and right-wing notions of natural order. He synthesises performance artists' emphasis on the body as an ensemble of irrational drives with political playwrights' concerns for analysis and debate. But above all his plays represent the outstanding achievement in British theatre in the last decade because he uses the fullest resources of language in the service of plots that exemplify moral dilemmas and hold theatrical attention by their cunning intricacy. With the same rapidity that his characters change sides in the wars that are the perennial settings for his fictions, his protagonists speak in every register from classical syntax to demotic obscenity. The Duchess of Devonshire, mistress to Charles II in *Victory* (Royal Court, 1983; Greenwich, 1991) but free for a moment from the fetid libertinage of the court, gazes out over the Thames estuary:

. . . . Oh, this is pure, this is absolute life, I never felt so whole and so completely independent, this is the third letter in a week begging me back and in verse too. All very flattering but really it is pure dick, a woman should never forget a poem is actually dick, should she? I don't believe before Mr. Van Oots anyone went near a beach, you can't smell the seaweed in a painting, can you? (Barker, 1983, 39)

The play of 'dick' against 'Mr. Van Oots' transgresses conventional boundaries between the material body and fine art but, as a crowd of beggars shuffles after her under the pier, the speech is sardonic, comic and relevant to the plot. In an earlier scene, in the vaults of the newly-created Bank of England, Barker has anticipated the conspiratorial corruption of the banking fraternity which is now so publicly exposed when he creates a group of builders and traders who are hugging the nations gold against monarchists and republicans alike. The title of Brenton and Ali's play, *Moscow Gold*, comes alive in this play. The register shifts between past and present in a brilliant cameo of greed and economics:

> MOBBERLEY (*dragging some gold bars on a small trolley*)   **Got a bit of England, sir!**
> PARRY   Oh, put it back, Frank –
> MOBBERLEY (*picking up a bar*)   In my grubby paw got boys and girls –
> HAMBRO   Just give us the keys –
> MOBBERLEY   **Got woods and fields and shops and rivers –**
> HAMBRO   Put them on the table, there's a good –
> MOBBERLEY   **An' fish an' fences, gardens, cradles, virgins, cots!**
> HAMBRO   Frank, I am the Governor of this place!
> MONCRIEFF   Leave him.
> MOBBERLEY   Leave me, Billy. I am hanging on to **my bit.** (*He sits at the empty chair.*) Did I miss anything?
> UNDY   You missed the oath.
> MOBBERLEY   (*putting the gold bar on his lap*). Fuck the oath. (*He turns to his neighbour.*) I am keeping my gold indoors.
> (Barker, 1983, 31)

Shortly after, to the consternation of the bankers ('Fuck, it's the mad shagman' says Undy), Charles enters with the cry of 'Oh, there's a do! There's a do in my bank!' He has brought Nell Gwynn with him who wants to take an ingot to rub her tits on, but Hambro patiently explains that each brick represents the accumulated wealth of others and that paper money is a far more efficient method of wealth-transfer. The aphrodisiac of money has never been better dramatised, and the isolation of Charles from the real centres of power in Restoration England is subtly underlined.

The emotions have always been a difficult area for political writers to negotiate. The sex in Brecht's plays was in inverse proportion to the sex in his life, and many a feminist now makes a career writing soap-operas or blockbuster family sagas. The principal female characters in Brenton and Edgar's recent work have been beacons of moral virtue through the male fog. Barker has devised a procedure, for male and female characters alike, whereby they do not express their feelings but display them. Their emotional topography is revealed to them by the some lightning-flashes of language that reveal it to us. Their abrupt veerings and sudden darts surprise them as much as us. In *The Castle* Stucley has returned home from the Crusades to find his demesne has been feminised by co-operative farming and his wife, Ann, is living with a lesbian witch called Skinner. Stucley tries to explain to Ann how her image sustained him throughout the years of slaughter, but he concludes:

> . . . everything is contrary, must be, musn't it, I who jumped in every pond of murder kept this one thing pure in my head, pictured you half-naked on an English night, your skin which was translucent from one angle and deep-furrowed from another, your odour even which I caught once in the middle of a scrap, do you believe that, even smells are stored, I'm sorry I chucked your loom out of the window, amazing strength comes out of temper, it's half a ton that thing if it's – trust me, what does that mean? (Barker, 1985, 9)

Barker does not want to elicit sympathy for Stucley in this passage. He wants to restrain the contours of his rage by the larger history of his life and avoid, through precise image, the clichés of nostalgia and self-pity. Ann is caught in an emotional tug-of-war between Stucley and Skinner, whom she also begs, in the language of soap-opera, to trust her and read her love by signs rather than declarations. Skinner is almost fooled:

> I do. I do trust signs. (*Pause*) We do not make a thing of flesh, do we, the love of women is more – they could eat flesh from off your body, we – no, actually I could eat yours, I could! Tell me why you love me! (Barker, 1985, 18)

Theoretically this could be read as a compressed demolition of Victorian myths of women's spirituality and structuralist theories of *l'écriture féminine*. Dramatically, punctuation just about paces Skinner's confusion, and the imagery contributes to the major clash in the play, between the body with its powers of natural production and consumption, and the military castle, the creation of abstract engineering. Katrin in *The Europeans* (The Wrestling School, 1992), pushed even further up against the limits of language when she describes her rape by the Turks, discovers that the subject of her story is turning out to be language itself:

> My mouth which I had held to be the very shape and seat of intimacy they smothered with wet and fluid – I don't think you could call them kisses – **yes, yes, kisses, they were kisses** I try to hide behind the language, oh, the language I do twist like bars of brass to shelter in, no, they were **kisses** because a kiss can be made of hatred – kisses, yes, oh, yes . . . (Barker, 1990, 5)

As much as the Shakespearean 'shape and seat of intimacy', it is this ability to abstract themselves out of their turmoil without breaking pace that distinguishes Barker's characters from those of his contemporaries.

The complexity and fertility of Barker's work offends the delicacy of ideologues the length of the political spectrum. He has long been on the offensive against received ideas in the British theatre and it is probably for this reason that, unlike Brenton and company, his truly epic plays have never had performances on the large stages of the National or the RSC at Barbican. The very successful season of three plays (*Downchild, Crimes in Hot Countries, The Castle*) in 1985 was crammed into the RSC's studio theatre, The Pit. This is a disgraceful state of affairs but Barker is held in such regard by actors that a group of them formed a company, The Wrestling School, in 1987 to perform his work and thus emphasize the importance, for radical theatre today, of such unfashionable components as complex plotting and a language that embeds demotic nouns in classical syntax. The most recent productions have been of *The Seven Lears* and *Golgo* (Sheffield Crucible and Leicester Haymarket Theatre, 1989), *Victory* (Greenwich, 1991), *A Hard Heart* (Almeida, 1992), *Terrible Mouth*, with music by Nigel Osborne (Almeida, 1992), and *Ego in Arcadia* and *The Europeans* (The Wrestling School, 1992).

Howard Barker should be stage-centre but it is clear why he has been locked up in the studio. The premise of this essay has been that the collisions and collusions between the electronic image and the material body in 1980s Britain produced, on the whole, theatrical work limited by conventions it only half recognised. The lucid originality of Barker's work stands out against the scams and self-deceptions of the last decade. His illiberalism seemed to mirror that of the Thatcherite Right and therefore his plays offered little consolation to artistic directors of a vaguely left-of-centre position. Thatcher has gone, but Barker is continuing his courageous attack on the crass sentimentality that permeates the latest nostrum of the Left, sexual politics.

REFERENCES

Barker, Howard. *Victory.* London: John Calder, 1983.
Barker, Howard. *The Castle and Scenes from an Execution.* London: John Calder, 1985.
Barker, Howard. *The Europeans and Judith.* London: John Calder, 1990.
Berkoff, Steve. *West and other Plays.* London: Faber & Faber, 1985.
Edgar, David. Interview with David Edgar by Tony Dunn. *Tribune,* 9 November 1990.
Edgar, David. *The Shape of the Table.* London: Nick Hern Books, 1990.
Forty, Adrian. *Objects of Desire: Design and Society 1750 to 1980.* London: Thames and Hudson, 1986.
Hardyment, Christina. *From Mangle to Microwave: The Mechanisation of the Household.* London: Polity Press, 1988.
McLuhan, Marshall. *Understanding Media.* London: Sphere Books, 1964.
Mumford, Lewis. *The City in History.* Harmondsworth: Penguin, 1961.
Tuttle, Lisa (ed.). *The Encyclopedia of Feminism.* London: Arrow Books, 1987.

Part II

3

Digging the Greeks: New Versions of Old Classics

Ruby Cohn

With hindsight, we can appreciate the harmony between T. S. Eliot's Greek-based modern plays and his self-declared stance – *'classicist in literature*, royalist in politics, and Anglo-Catholic in religion' (my emphasis). But British playwrights who abhor Eliot's attitude have also turned to ancient Greece. Perhaps these playwrights were inspired by the forays of two renowned English directors – John Barton's ten-play *Greeks* in 1980 and Peter Hall's *Oresteia* in 1981 (in a version by Tony Harrison). Unlike these directors, however, the playwrights (with the exception of Harrison) restrict their archaeology to a single play. Timberlake Wertenbaker and Howard Barker dramatize Greek myths; Joe Orton, on the one hand, Caryl Churchill and David Lan, on the other, adapt the same Greek tragedy, *The Bacchae* of Euripides; Steven Berkoff, Edward Bond, and Tony Harrison read different dramas of classical Greece in their own distinctive voices. Dating from 1967 to 1988, these Greek structures are garbed in each playwright's individual idiom, so there is no point to examining them chronologically. Instead, I propose to move from the sombre to the light, as in the tragic tetralogy of the Dionysian Festival at Athens in the Fifth Century BC.

Non-dramatic material was dramatized in two Royal Shakespeare Company productions of 1988 – Timberlake Wertenbaker's lyrical *The Love of the Nightingale* at The Other Place in Stratford and Howard Barker's epic *Bite of the Night* in London's Barbican Pit. Although based on a violent myth of classical Greece, *The Love of the Nightingale* is spare and quiet on the stage. Several Greek poets – Apollodorus, Hyginus, Pausanias, Strabo, Thucydides – narrate the bloody tale of Tereus, Procne, and Philomele, but Sophocles'

tragedy titled *Tereus* is no longer extant. In his *Metamorphoses* Roman
Ovid conflated his Greek sources for his own purpose. Although
Wertenbaker reads Classical Greek, it is upon Ovid's version that
she relies for her 21-scene drama that plays without intermission in
an hour and a half.

Vaguely classical in costume, Wertenbaker's Male and Female
Choruses comment individually on the clear, linear plot involving
the main characters. Thracian Tereus, the wartime ally of King
Pandion of Athens, is awarded his daughter Procne in marriage.
After five years and the birth of a son, Procne requests her husband
to bring her sister Philomele to Thrace: 'I must have someone to talk
to.' On the voyage Tereus rapes Philomele, cuts out her tongue that
threatens to proclaim his crime, and, imprisoning his victim, reports
her death to Procne in Thrace. But mute Philomele manages to
inform Procne of the violation, and the two sisters reunite to wreak
a dreadful vengeance. They kill Itys, the son of Tereus, and serve
him to his father at a grisly meal. When Tereus threatens vengeance,
they are transformed into birds.

Wertenbaker omits the cannibalism, and she invents two new
characters – Philomele's old servant Niobe, whose home has been
destroyed by the Athenians, and Tereus' Captain, who dies in
an attempt to save Philomele from the Thracian king. Two new
threads weave Wertenbaker's 21 scenes into a whole – interrogation
and theatre. Interrogation – asking questions – sustains Philomele
through her human and avian forms. We first hear Philomele asking
girlish questions of sexual curiosity; we last see her as a nightingale,
instructing her nephew Itys to ask questions. In the body of the play
Philomele's questions cast doubt on the royal patriarchal authority
of her father and her brother-in-law. In contrast, Procne poses no
questions until she is confronted with the rape of her sister.

That rape is revealed through Wertenbaker's own love – of
theatre – as theatricalised by the plays within her plays. And
Athenian love of drama is exploited by Wertenbaker, who confers
the city's taste upon the young Philomele. She understands aesthetic
distance, but the adulterous passion of the Thracian Tereus is ignited
by the staged performance of the adulterous passion of Phaedra
for Hippolytus, a play within the play. Before the offstage rape,
Wertenbaker's Tereus pleads with Philomele: 'I am Phaedra.'

Theatre can be dangerously suggestive, but also revelatory.
Wertenbaker changes mute Philomele's tapestry of the original
myth to a puppet play at a Bacchic revel: '*The rape is re-enacted in*

a gross and comic way . . . Philomele then stages a very brutal illustration of the cutting of the female doll's tongue.' (In the London performance this dumbshow within the larger play was neither gross nor comic, but sobering.)

Since Sophocles's tragic *Tereus* exists only in a few fragments, we cannot reconstruct the attitude of his Chorus, but it is unlikely that Wertenbaker reflects him by her double chorus – Male and Female, five members in each, who speak individually except for one line: 'These sorrows have fallen upon us unforeseen.' Although Wertenbaker's two choruses are not in explicit competition, they react differently to the unforeseen; the Females try to warn Procne of male hegemony in Thrace, but even though the Males are suspicious of Tereus, they squelch their own questions, and they disappear before the end of the play (Rabey, 526). Yet it is the Male Chorus who inform the modern audience that we are witnessing 'a myth for our times.'

Ovid, like his Greek predecessors, is sympathetic to the wronged sisters, as is Wertenbaker, but she alone traces their separate maturations. Her Procne, who early preaches 'Measure in all things', learns to castigate her own passivity, and yet she doubts the evidence of the puppet play within the play until she looks into the tongueless mouth of Philomele. The younger sister transforms from a pubescent beauty to a Bacchic murderess; it is she who stabs the child Itys to death, but, wiser as a nightingale, it is also she who teaches the resurrected child to ask questions. The child's father, a Puritanical Tereus, grows increasingly lustful and cruel during the course of the play; after the rape and mutilation of Philomele, he finds a voiceless victim attractive. To the wronged sisters he thunders his last human words: 'I will kill you both.' It is a vain threat, for he is finally silent and impotent in the gaudy plumage of the hoopoe.

The final play to be performed at Stratford's Other Place, Wertenbaker's *Love of the Nightingale* transferred in 1989 to The Pit in London, where a bleached white set reenforced the distancing effects of two choruses, as well as two plays within the main action – an abridged *Hippolytus* and a dumbshow of rape and maiming. Throughout the three main characters moved with deliberation, sometimes resembling a frieze, and the two sisters seemed aware of their own myth. Katy Behean as Philomele grew within a scant hour from a silly princess into a wise old bird, still questioning. And implicitly urging us too to question, in the words of the child Itys:

'What is right?' – a pervasive theme in Timberlake Wertenbaker's drama.

In contrast to Wertenbaker's exploration of a linear Greek myth, two playwrights cull fragments of *The Iliad*. Edward Bond's *The Woman* (1978) does so by way of Greek tragedy. Although Bond had long admired Euripides, Greek tragedy was new terrain for this autodidact, after his bouts with Shakespeare. Bond had thematised his previous plays on the evils of British capitalism, but with *The Woman* he struck at the base of Western culture in the Trojan War: 'Greek society created us. We live in the world of the Greeks' (Hay and Roberts, 1978, 12).

With his usual fecundity, Bond began to work on *The Fool* and *The Woman* at the same time, the latter nourished mainly by Euripides' *Trojan Women*. Between 1974 and 1977, Bond spent two holidays on Malta: 'I wanted to soak myself in the Mediterranean background . . . just to face the sun on the rocks, as it were, as simple as that. I re-read all the extant Greek tragedies while I was there, and the comedies too' (Hay and Roberts, 1980, 239). Although *The Woman* was not commissioned by the National Theatre, Bond admits: 'I had in the back of my mind a description of the [National's] Olivier theatre that I'd read in a newspaper' (241). On the vast Olivier stage Bond made his English directorial debut, relying on a completed script, as is habitual with directors. That script features familiar classical names – Ajax, Nestor, Thersites, Hecuba, Ismene, Cassandra, and the child Astyanax, but, except for the last of these, the characters who bear Greek names behave differently from the originals, for Bond is less concerned with individuals than with the mythic climate of a 'civilization' based on exploitation and imperialism.

Structurally, *The Woman* splits in two – fourteen scenes in Part I, zigzagging between Troy and the Greek camp, between public rhetoric and private confidences, between men at war and two peace-loving women, Ismene and Hecuba; nine scenes in Part II follow the changing seasons on a nameless island. Part I draws upon Homer's *Iliad* and upon Greek tragedies that derive from it – Euripides' *Trojan Women* and *Hecuba*. (Both James Bulman and David Hirst argue, too, for the relevance of Sophocles's Theban plays.) For Helen Bond substitutes a stone Goddess of Good Fortune – 'a plain, grey, schematized female shape', which we barely see. Part II is largely Bond's invention, although he retrieves three characters with classical names – the Trojan woman Hecuba, her adoptive daughter Ismene, and the Greek elder statesman Nestor. Loosely linking these 'Scenes of War and Freedom' (Part I being War, Part II a precarious Freedom) is the Greek Heros, 'Achilles, Agamemnon, and Odysseus all rolled into one: warrior, king, politician' (Bulman, 507). And superstitious believer of myths, so that Heros wages war and ploughs the sea in quest of a statue of the Goddess of Good Fortune.

Joyous Greek cries of 'Dead.' open Bond's drama, for Priam of Troy has died of old age. A Greek delegation of Thersites and Ismene try to persuade Hecuba to surrender. When Trojan Hecuba and Greek Ismene meet in intimacy, they do not speak in Giralducian trivialities but in dismay at the ongoing war. Hecuba convinces Ismene that the Greeks will destroy Troy with or without the statue, and Ismene therefore refuses to return to her perfidious camp. From the walls of Troy, across the crimson-floored battle-field of the Olivier stage, Ismene harangues Greek soldiers to return to their home, and, like Sophocles's Antigone, she is sentenced to death by immurement. When a victorious Heros orders the child Astyanax flung to death from the walls of Troy, Hecuba blinds herself with the gesture of Oedipus, but without his guilt. After the looting and burning of Troy, Part I ends on a few Greek soldiers seeking the jewels of the immured Ismene.

Part II takes place twelve years later in a fishing community on a free and nameless island far from Athens – visually a gray tilted disk on the Olivier stage – where blind Hecuba and mind-damaged Ismene live humbly. Greek Nestor intrudes upon them, ostensibly to invite Hecuba to Athens, but actually to persuade her to divulge the hiding-place of the Good Fortune statue, which was lost at sea. A month later a runaway crippled slave, the Dark Man, seeks refuge at the hut of Hecuba and Ismene. Another month and the Dark Man has made love to the Ismene whom he is the first to find beautiful. Still another month, and Greek Heros personally superintends the dredging of the sea for the statue. A few months later, Nestor returns from Athens to order Heros home, and, like the Euripidean Hecuba, Bond's heroine tricks her way to vengeance upon her enemy. With the words 'Remember Troy!' Hecuba persuades Nestor not to avenge Heros, but to return to Athens before the first storm of winter. Blind Hecuba dies in that storm, but Ismene and the Dark Man, maimed and mutually supportive, face the new day and the new season.

From his earliest notes for *The Woman* Bond gave voice to women:

'I have tried to have all the moral decisions made by women' (Itzin, 13). In Part I, therefore, and in sharp contrast to Euripides, Bond's Queen of Troy pleads for peace, and the Antigone-like Ismene risks her life when she opposes a powerful ruler. Both women undertake moral action, but Ismene is naive, and Hecuba wily. By Part II a mind-damaged Ismene is no longer capable of moral decisions, but Hecuba renounces her private peace for public action – the assassination of Heros. Bond's tempered optimism lies in a union of a nameless Dark Man with a childlike Ismene – a union blessed by a Hecuba drawn from the matter of Troy, but coloured in contemporary moral shades.

Howard Barker's morality is more ambiguous in *The Bite of the Night* (1988), and more obliquely derived from Homer, without the mediation of classical tragedy. Barker's program note reads: 'In this epic play Doctor Savage, the last classics teacher at a defunct university, discarding his family in a wilful spasm of freedom and accompanied by Hogbin, a wayward student, revisits the eleven Troys of antiquity and encounters the source of Eros, Helen of Troy, as well as her creator, Homer.' But Barker's five-hour drama rambles more waywardly than this sentence promises. Although based on Homer's portrait of the most seductive of women, *The Bite of the Night* is largely a Barker invention.

Barker's several (not eleven) Troys are neither historical nor mythic, but imaginary and even fantastic, e.g. Paper Troy (as celebrated in books), Mums' Troy (propagating infants), Laughing Troy (trivializing pain), Fragrant Troy (with compulsory scents). All Troys prove to be infernos in which Helen is victimized. Homer confesses: 'If I had not made Helen, Helen would not have been disfigured.' Barker's Helen knows that Homer is her creator, and she intuits that Professor Savage will destroy her.

Barker's drama is subtitled 'An education', and presumably the student is our coeval, Dr Savage, who journeys back to Homeric Troy, which is burned not by Greeks but by soldiers with English names. Their leader Shade enlists Savage to write a constitution for the new Troy, freed of Helen's sin. Blamed on all sides, Helen suffers the amputation of her limbs, in what is cruelly called 'The Pruning of Helen.' Her voluble torso is then wheeled around by a blind Homer. Since she is still considered dangerous, the English-named soldiers arrange her execution by the ex-student Hogbin. Instead of killing her, however, Hogbin commits suicide. An imperturbable witness to these events, Savage cries out at a cake of soap, for in it he smells the odour of Hogbin's body (an obscene reminder of the Holocaust).

A totalitarian Fragrant Troy celebrates the public coupling of Savage and his wife Creusa (the name of the dead wife of Aeneas in *The Aeneid*). The son of Creusa and Savage is an adult soap salesman who addresses limbless Helen with smooth clichés, and she senses that her end is near. When one of the soldiers strangles Helen, her mute husband breaks into speech, and the whole populace of Troy tries to touch her corpse for luck. In a limbless but indomitable Old Woman, Savage recognizes another Helen, and he systematically buries her alive, after which he throttles Helen's daughter Gay.

At the play's end Savage wanders through the rubble of Troy. Archaeologists who have figured briefly in *The Bite of the Night* point out the sights of the Trojan dig. Schliemann pontificates about the University: 'The corridors of inordinate length where tortured thinkers thrashed each other in pursuit of a deity they called Truth' – Barker's target is clearly a modern and not a Trojan university, but the sentence also applies to Barker's play, which ends, after Savage and a resurrected Hogbin thrash about, on a high note of irony. Noticing Savage, the archaeologist Schliemann asks him: 'Are you on the tour?' And elusive Truth is absent.

Prodigiously and prodigally ambitious, *The Bite of the Night* lectures its audience even in the program: ' . . . the audience does not struggle for permanent coherence, which is associated with the narrative of naturalism, but experiences the play moment by moment, contradiction by contradiction.' Some memorable moments: Hogbin in a coat of ubiquitous book-filled pockets, Savage grovelling at Homer's feet, the caging of Shade in a wicker basket that is hoisted high, Helen's torso in a baby-carriage pushed by blind Homer, Hogbin lending gestures to armless Helen, Savage sniffing at a bar of soap.

Arrogant and sometimes self-indulgent, Barker means to outrage us into feeling as he imposes modern dilemmas upon classical Greece in order to puncture genteel cultural shibboleths about the value of the classics. His poets, soldiers, and academics may conspire to demolish Helen, but her spirit is invincible. Lush and diffuse, *The Bite of the Night* aspires to be another *Iliad*, where Ilium or Troy suffers not from warring armies but from warring ideas promulgated by episodic characters.

Although classical tragedy was performed at the City of Athens Dionysian Festival, the god came from Thrace, and sober Athens may have sympathized with Pentheus of Thebes in his suspicion of the Bacchic revels. But a playwright who lived and died in violence, appreciated the position of the wild outsider. Joe Orton's biographer John Lahr informs us that *The Erpingham Camp* was conceived in 1964 as a film treatment for Lindsay Anderson, a director whom Orton met at the Royal Court. He then 'developed it as a [parodic?] Brechtian epic' (20), but in 1965 it underwent still another genre change for an ITV series on 'The Seven Deadly Sins'; broadcast in 1966, it apparently satirized the sin of Pride. Lahr categorically notes Orton's debt to *The Bacchae*, but although the biographer documents his subject's innumerable sexual exploits, he .does not trace the autodidact Orton's exposure to Greek tragedy in general, and to *The Bacchae* of Euripides in particular.

Lahr does quote from Orton's letter to Anderson:

> This is a story of an eruption, an explosion, an outburst . . . of inspiration. A representative group of sturdy, honest English folk, respectably pleasuring themselves at an August Holiday Camp, find themselves subjected to the influence of an intense, demonic leader . . . . they abandon themselves under the tutelage of Don to impulse . . . Propriety, in the person of the dubious Manager of the Camp, rashly attempts to intrude and to veto. But the forces of impulse are too strong; and catastrophe can be the only result. (Lahr, 338)

In the stage version of 1967 Don (for Dionysus) becomes Chief Redcoat Riley (a surname used by Eliot and Pinter), and the Pentheus-figure is a dictatorial director of a holiday camp. Lacking analogues for Cadmus, Tiresias, and Agave, *The Erpingham Camp* introduces Bacchic revels of holiday campers. Like Euripides' *Bacchae*, Orton's play is climaxed by the death of the Pentheus figure. As in Euripides, that death takes place off stage, but there is no corresponding horror at a mangled corpse, for Orton is bent on the comic.

When Orton first wrote Anderson, he was interviewed on radio: 'I always say to myself that the theatre is the Temple of Dionysus, and not Apollo. You do the Dionysus thing on your typewriter, and then you allow a little Apollo in, just a little to shape and guide it along certain lines you may want to go along' (Lahr, 15). What Orton preserves between his 1964 film treatment and the 1967 stage play *The Erpingham Camp* is 'the Dionysus thing.'

Riley-Dionysus enkindles a riot by slapping a pregnant woman, but the holiday campers themselves are far more violent than he. They insult and pummel Erpingham, and yet he dies, as Martin Esslin notes, 'not under any assault by orgiastic, unchained revellers, but merely because the floorboards of his office give way so that he drops down among the dancers on the ballroom floor' (Bigsby, 103). Lying in state beneath four dozen red balloons, Erpingham is dead, but so is the riot, which has not frayed the fibres of society. 'A little Apollo' finally calms 'the Dionysus thing', despite Orton's taste for the latter in his life and other work. It is a moot point whether Orton's Dionysian proclivity constitutes radical subversion, as claimed in book-length studies by the critics Bigsby and Lahr. Orton's one debt to classical Greece, *The Erpingham Camp* is less a celebration of impulse than a calculated coupling of aphorism and anarchy, sprinkled with satire. Only when Orton abandoned the *figure* of Dionysus would his Dionysian farce soar to *What the Butler Saw*.

In sharp contrast, two Dionysus-figures help theatricalise the involved modernization of *The Bacchae, A Mouthful of Birds* (1986) by Caryl Churchill and David Lan, who participated in the Joint Stock Company workshop on women and violence: 'We began with *The Bacchae* and the idea of possession. . . . *A Mouthful of Birds* tells the stories of seven possessed people. . . . Our new play, which began with *The Bacchae*, is itself possessed by it' (Lan, 6). Churchill amplifies: 'What really happened with *The Bacchae*, I suppose, was that it was one example of the kind of things that we were exploring, rather than it being that we were trying to find ways of doing *The Bacchae*' (Cousin, 9).

On an 'undefended day' each of the seven modern characters is possessed by a spirit or a passion: 1. Lena, frustrated in her relationship with Roy, is possessed by a spirit that urges her to murder their baby. 2. Marcia, a black switchboard operator, is also a medium possessed by a Baron Sunday, but she is displaced by white Sybil who seizes her occult power. 3. Dan, a vicar possessed by Dionysos, acquires the ability to kill his victims in pleasurable deaths. 4. Paul, a married businessman dealing in wholesale meat, falls in love with a pig but loses her to an abattoir. 5. Yvonne, an acupuncturist, is also an alcoholic. 6. Derek and 7. Doreen are possessed by Pentheus and Agave, respectively, and it is they who relate most closely to Euripides.

Costume and prop are central to Act 2 of *A Mouthful of Birds*, which opens on a long autobiographical monologue of the nineteenth-century French hermaphrodite Herculine Barbin, spoken by an actress dressed as a man. Unemployed Derek, possessed by Herculine, is then dressed in her clothes, while repeating that same monologue. The acupuncturist Yvonne has an alcoholic fantasy of women in golden shoes, but she overcomes that possession to grow absorbed in painting her room. Derek as Pentheus is dressed as a woman by the two Dionysoses in tandem. Doreen, a secretary who is possessed by the violent events she hears on the radio, reacts violently to her neighbours, who respond with reciprocal violence. Exacerbated beyond endurance, and possessed by Agave, Doreen tears Pentheus to pieces. After these events 'Pentheus is brought by Dionysos into a dance of the whole company in which moments of Extreme Happiness and of violence from earlier parts of the play are repeated.'

In Part 3 the 'undefended day' is over, as is reliance on Euripides. Each character briefly reveals her or his new post-violence life as a result of possession. The exception is Doreen:

> I can find no rest. My head is filled with horrible images. I can't say I actually see them, it's more that I feel them. It seems that my mouth is full of birds which I crunch between my teeth. Their feathers, their blood and broken bones are choking me. I carry on my work as a secretary.

Since these are the final words of the Churchill/Lan derivation from *The Bacchae*, the striking image that gives the play its title may also apply to the characters who have enjoyed violence but who are horrified at its potential for destruction. Euripides' tragedy warns against flouting the divine and the irrational, which may be synonymous. Churchill and Lan hint at a calm after possession. Only Doreen knows no catharsis.

Of these several returns to Greek sources, Churchill and Lan stray almost as far as Barker, but a self-styled iconoclast, Steven Berkoff, is curiously closer in his *Greek* (1980), an obscenity-studded pastiche of Sophocles's *Oedipus*. Berkoff's decade on the Fringe had habituated critics to an energetic play by Berkoff, directed energetically by Berkoff, with Berkoff in the energetic main role, but in the first performances of *Greek* he limited himself to adapting and directing. (In the 1988 revival he played the Laius-figure, Dad.)

Berkoff's Eddie, his Oedipus-analogue, thrives on fighting and fornicating. Not unlike Oedipus and his vast theatre progeny, Eddie leaves his assumed parents to avoid the dire prophecy. Quarrelling with and killing a restaurant manager, Eddie absconds with his widow. In Eddie's answer to the riddle of the Sphinx, the third leg is not a stick but an erect phallus of man at the height of his virility. After cutting off the head of a bored Sphinx (a proto-feminist), Eddie and his new wife prosper in the catering business – both in sensuous sexuality and conspicuous wealth. When the happy couple invite Eddie's parents to bless their prosperity, the son learns the truth. Eddie is briefly contrite at his incestuous love, but Berkoff rejects the Greek conclusion: ' . . . it is healthier to love your mother than expiate your alleged sin by self mutilation' (Program note to the 1988 production).

Greek portrays a heroic Eddie who scorns conformity even before he scorns the incest taboo. Eddie closes Berkoff's play in defiant affirmation of his love for Jocasta: 'for your belly twice known/ for your hands twice caressed/ for your breath twice smelt, for your thighs, for your cunt twice known, once head first once cock first, loving cunt holy mother wife/ loving source of your being/ exit from paradise/ entrance to heaven.' For all the lexical poverty, and the wavering rhythms, repetition lends a certain force to the lines, especially in Berkoff's staging, which blends music, lighting, choral effects, and enactment of properties. However Berkoff's dialogue diminishes the best-known Greek myth, he inventively deploys four actors in whiteface to stylize an aggressive homage to his native East End of London.

In these several returns to Greek myth the playwrights are true to their respective modern themes – Wertenbaker's interrogation of gender, Bond's condemnation of imperialism, Barker's quest for a public-private code of conduct, Orton's taste for mockery, Churchill and Lan's investigation of the irrational, Berkoff's loyal regionalism – but Tony Harrison alone ponders a Greek myth in its own country and ours, specifically in the form of a satyr play. At the Dionysian Festival of fifth-century (BC) Athens three tragedies were capped by a farcical satyr-play, but our only extant example of that genre is Euripides' *Cyclops*. Tony Harrison, a poet, translator, and classical scholar who is proud of his working-class Yorkshire origins, dramatizes the search for Greek residua, as well as one of those very residua – some 400 lines of Sophocles's *Ichneutae*. In 1907 two Oxford University archaeologists, Bernard Grenfell and Arthur Hunt, discovered that fragmentary satyr play on a papyrus at Oxyrhynchus, some hundred miles south of Cairo. As the actor Jack Shepherd writes, Harrison's *Trackers* embraces three historical periods: 'a painstaking reconstruction of a Greek satyr play, an account of how that play came to be unearthed and an altogether different account of how a discerning class has come to *own* high culture, keeping it well out of the reach of the undiscerning masses' (Astley, 427).

Conceived for the ancient stadium of Delphi in 1988, Harrison's *Trackers of Oxyrhynchus* moved – with some revision – into the Olivier Theatre of the National in 1990. Sophocles' *Trackers* dramatizes the fourth Homeric Hymn, in which Apollo tracks his lost cattle to the infant Hermes who has invented the lyre from a tortoise shell and cowgut. As P. J. Parsons writes in the National Theatre Program: 'The satyrs tracked down the cattle; Grenfell and Hunt tracked down the papyrus; Tony Harrison's new play follows both tracks, as ancient satyr and modern scholars meet. . . . . ' And yet, they do not literally meet, for the two actors, Jack Shepherd and Barrie Rutter, play both modern scholars and Greek mythic figures.

Harrison's play begins with the modern trackers logging and deciphering papyri. An exhausted Grenfell imagines that he is Apollo seeking his lost cattle, and Hunt-Silenus offers to help. In orange body-stocking, asses' ears, prancers' tail, noisy clogs, and long limp phallus, Barrie Rutter/Silenus teaches Greek syllables to us the audience, and we thereby materialize the satyrs on stage – wearing the same costume as Silenus, but with rubber phalluses hilariously erect. In a parody of the Furies of the National Theatre *Oresteia* (English by Tony Harrison) who sniffed out Clytemnestra's blood, the satyrs sniff Apollo's cattle down to the strings of the lyre, from which they flee in fright. In a parody of Victorian translations of Greek, the nymph-caryatid Kyllene unveils the infant Hercules (the distinctly adult Brian Glover in diapers) with his new musical toy. Confiscating the lyre, Apollo pays the satyrs off with gold ingots that transform into boomboxes, significantly wrapped in the newspapers of the day of performance. Silenus rhapsodizes about 'low' art, and inveighs against the Olympian elitists. The ostracized satyrs become contemporary football hooligans who are uncontrollable by old Silenus. In an epilogue, however, eight satyrs gather the Greek letters of the name Sophocles, and with our help, the other four satyrs arrange the letters correctly to honour the ancient dramatist.

Almost to a man (and a rare woman), reviewers were outraged by Harrison's elevation of popular art as opposed to elitistism, and they pointed to the irony of espousing such art within the subsidized walls of the National Theatre. By the time I saw *The Trackers of Oxyrhynchus* (and of Tony Harrison) late in the National run, reviewers were gone, and audiences joined in the festive satyric spirit, relishing Harrison's inventive rhymes, nodding to Stephen Edwards' infectious music and the satyrs' precisely clumsy clogs; marvelling at Jocelyn Herbert's double-time set and costumes; and laughing aloud when we were tickled in our funny-bones. Harrison's serious romp instructs us about the Dionysian Festival of ancient Greece:

> Six hours of tragedy and half an hour of fun.
> But they were an entity conceived as one.
> As was the entity of Tony Harrison.

The classical scholar Marianne McDonald, praising Harrison's adaptations from the Greek, affirms: 'Both past and present inform each other and provide ways to interpret each other; these lenses distort but also enhance. The ancient texts are filters for modern ideas' (Astley, 479). And for modern idiomatic English, in the subversive spirit of the modern dramatist.

REFERENCES

Plays

Barker, Howard. *The Bite of the Night*. London: John Calder, 1988.
Berkoff, Steven. *Decadence* and *Greek*. London: John Calder, 1982.
Bond, Edward. *The Woman*. London: Eyre Methuen, 1979.
Churchill, Caryl and Lan, David. *A Mouthful of Birds*. London: Methuen, 1986.
Harrison, Tony. *The Trackers of Oxyrhynchus*. London: Faber & Faber, 1990.
Orton, Joe. *The Erpingham Camp* in *The Complete Plays*. London: Methuen, 1976.

Criticism

Astley, Neil (ed.). *Tony Harrison*. Newcastle upon Tyne: Bloodaxe Books, 1991.

Bigsby, C. W. E. *Contemporary English Drama*. London: Edward Arnold, 1981.

Brown, John Russell (ed.). *Modern British Dramatists*. Englewood Cliffs: Prentice-Hall, 1984.

Bulman, James. 'The *Woman* and Greek Myth: Bond's Theatre of History'. *Modern Drama*, December 1986.

Cousin, Geraldine. 'The Common Imagination and the Individual Voice', *New Theatre Quarterly*, February 1988.

Hay, Malcolm and Philip Roberts. *Bond: A Study of his Plays*. London: Eyre Methuen, 1980.

Hay, Malcolm and Philip Roberts. 'Edward Bond: Stages in a Life'. *Observer Magazine*, 6 August 1978.

Hirst, David L. *Edward Bond*. London: Macmillan, 1985.

Itzin, Cathy. 'Breakthrough for Bond', *Time Out*, 11–17 August 1978.

Lahr, John. *Prick Up Your Ears*. London: Penguin, 1980.

Rabey, David Ian. 'Defining Difference: Timberlake Wertenbaker's Drama of Language, Dispossession, and Discovery', *Modern Drama*, December 1990.

4

Cultural Transformations
Jatinder Verma

Any reading of contemporary British theatre cannot be disso-
ciated from the social transformations wrought by large-scale
'non-European' migrations since the 1950s. A product of the
need for cheap labour by British industries engaged in post-War
re-construction, migrations from the former British colonies of
the Caribbean, Eastern Africa and the Indian sub-continent have
fundamentally changed the image of many British cities and towns.
Inevitably, the introduction of such diverse populations – diverse by
virtue of colour of skin, of language, of dress, of food, of religion,
of value systems – has unleashed tensions in contemporary British
society. Each passing decade since the 1950s has witnessed varying
negotiations, as the 'natives' have sought to adjust to the presence
of 'foreigners' in their midst, and the latter have sought to possess
their adopted country as a new home-land.

British theatre has reflected these societal negotiations. In the
fifties and sixties, theatre by and large ignored the presence of
the immigrants. Confined in the main to service industries and
menial work (public transport, hospitals and light manufacturing
industries), the immigrant populations had not surfaced in the
imagination of the public at large. This despite the Notting Hill riots
of 1958, which first introduced the problematics of race in Britain.
The so-called 'Angry Decade' of British theatre is marked by its
absence of the immigrant phenomenon. This peculiar absence was
one of the contributory factors in the emergence, in the seventies,
of 'Black Theatre'. The rise of a second-generation of 'foreigners'
– children born of immigrant parents – along with an economic
recession that affected immigrant workers more acutely than others,
provided a powerful motive to *achieve presence*. In other words,
self-determination. The term 'Black' encompassed a diversity of

ethnicities: Indians, Pakistanis, Bangladeshis, Caribbeans, Africans. While individual theatre companies were characterised by their differing ethnicities, they shared certain characteristics in common: characteristics that lent efficacy to their common self-definition as 'Black'. These were (a) independence from white control; (b) opposition to the 'mainstream' – perceived as white and racist; (c) the presentation of 'Black' work – plays either dealing with contemporary realities or with the history of Britain's relationship with its colonies; and (d) the assertion of the right to public funds on a par with white companies.

Among the theatre companies that emerged in the seventies were Temba – an African theatre company led by actor-director Alton Kumalo (who had spent a season with the Royal Shakespeare Company playing largely minor roles); and Tara Arts – a theatre company run by and reflecting the South Asian experience both in Britain and historically. As the decade wore on into the eighties, these were added to by the emergence of the Black Theatre Co-operative, British-Asian Theatre Company, Hounslow Arts Co-operative, Asian Theatre Co-operative, Double-Edge Theatre, Carib Theatre, and, more recently, Talawa and Tamasha.

Such companies were perceived, and to a large extent continue to be seen, as 'marginal' to the 'mainstream' of British theatre. Nevertheless, by their existence and practice they exerted both explicit and implicit pressures upon existing theatres. Often the pressure was of a pragmatic kind: audiences were flocking to Black companies at the very moment when more established theatres were wrestling with the problems of dwindling audiences. As the eighties wore on, however, it became increasingly clear that Black theatre work was not only a question of pragmatics. While 'mainstream' British theatre was bemoaning the loss of its 'anger' (after the heady years of the sixties), Black theatre in the main reflected a passion, a vitality that was absent elsewhere. Race relations, naturally, was a theme mined by practically all the Black companies. Equally, some companies (notably Tara Arts) were developing styles of 'total theatre' that posed a challenge to the largely realistic conventions of the majority of British theatre.

Thus, by the late-eighties Black theatre had moved from a social statement to an aesthetic challenge to the 'mainstream' of British theatre. Naturally enough, it was in this same period that the question of 'integrated casting' became a central issue of debate in British theatre.

This, admittedly sketchy, account offers a context in which to locate my own theatre practice in Britain: both with my company, Tara Arts, and with my work at the Royal National Theatre.

I should state at the outset that I am a product of that immigrant phenomenon which has so transformed Britain. I came to Britain in early 1968 from Kenya in eastern Africa. *Transformation*, therefore, is for me an existential fact, rather than an objective reading of post-War British realities. I have been changed by Britain as much as, I hope, I am contributing to changing Britain's idea of itself.

'Transformation' has encompassed for me two attendant ideas: *translation* and *quotation*. As an Indian immigrant to Britain, I have often characterised myself as a 'translated man'. Based on the etymology of the word 'to translate' as meaning 'to bear across', I, too, have literally been 'borne across' from Africa to Britain (and, through my parents, from India to Africa). There is another sense in which the term best characterises me: the sense in which I choose to 'bear across' my ideas, my sensibility of theatre to another, dominant, sensibility in contemporary Britain. And, the sense in which what I do is 'translated' by others – often critics from the dominant culture. 'Quotation' seems to best describe my sense of 'culture'. Born a Punjabi-speaking Indian in eastern Africa, I was educated first under the British colonial system, then under independent Kenya's and finally, coming to Britain, in the British national education system. My 'culture' therefore could be said to be a rag-bag mixture of Indian, African and British: what Salman Rushdie terms, in *The Satanic Verses*, as 'selected discontinuities'. It is imaginary landscape full of bits – quotations – of several cultural traditions.

These two ideas have formed a central thread in my theatre work from the mid-seventies. I began with Rabindranath Tagore's Bengali play, *Sacrifice* (Tara Arts' inaugural production). Written in 1917 as a pacifist's response to the First World War, it was adapted to act as a metaphor for contemporary racial and cultural inequities; in the process, Tagore's own Edwardian English idiom was translated into a more contemporary style. Twelve years later I produced Gogol's *The Government Inspector* (again, for Tara Arts) [Photo 4]. In this production the twin ideas of translation and quotation had by now matured sufficiently to radically transform the perception of this classic of European theatre.

I chose to re-locate Gogol's play to a mythical small town in post-Independence India. Dispensing with the naturalistic structure

of Gogol's original, I employed techniques derived from Indian
theatre to re-invent the story. The primary techniques employed
were (a) the use of the Story-teller as both narrator and character; (b) the use of music (rhythm) and movement as elements in
characterisation; (c) the creation of a spoken text that embraced
song, verse, soliloquy and dialogue; and (d) an epic structure that
displaced time-and-space continuities.

While these techniques radically transformed the form in which
Gogol's text had hitherto been perceived in Britain, the creation of
a distinctive language, along with the displacement of the story
to post-Independence India, transformed the content of the play.
Gogol's satire thus became not only an attack on material corruption
but also, self-referentially, an attack on one of the abiding legacies of
colonialism – the 'colonisation of the mind'. The Indian characters
in my version were driven by the desire to be 'more English than
the English'; striving (to quote Salman Rushdie again in *The Satanic
Verses*) 'to be worthy of the challenge represented by the phrase *Civis
Britannicus sum*' (his italics). The grotesque nature of Gogol's satire
thus took on a peculiar poignancy – especially when performed
before Asian audiences – when, at the end, the story-teller turns
to the audience and says 'Laugh not, for then must you laugh at
yourselves'.

The distinctive language created for this play reflected the nature
of the theme: a deliberately theatrical language comprising archaic
Anglo-Indianisms and quotations from Chekhov, Eliot, Kipling,
Tennyson, Kalidasa, Shakespeare, Salman Rushdie and Indian
popular lyrics !

In essence, the production of *The Government Inspector* was a
re-invention: a deliberate attempt to confront the specificities of a
particular theatre text with the different specificities – in time, place
and cultural sensibility – of its performers. In other words, it was
an attempt not to mask the Blackness of the particular performers
behind the illusion of nineteenth century Russian characters. To
have done so would be tantamount, for me, to denying the particu-
larity of ourselves – and colour, ethnic origin, in Britain today, is but
one mark of our own distinction. As such, I have always opposed the
arguments put forward by some proponents of integrated casting of
'colour-blind casting'. I cannot ignore my colour in modern Britain,
no more than my audiences can. And, in any case, to do so would
be to deny what makes me human.

The process of 're-inventing' a classic was given a more cogent expression in my production, for the Royal National Theatre, of Molière's *Tartuffe*. The event in itself was significant: I would be the first of the immigrant generation to be invited to direct at the National Theatre. Inevitably perhaps, I chose as my actors members of my own company, Tara, which served to make the production even more significant: the first all-Asian play at the National!

I quote from my production note-book my thinking prior to the commencement of rehearsals:

> I am setting out to translate a seventeenth century French farce into an all-Asian company of performers of the National Theatre touring around Britain. [That entails expressing] the sense of Moliere's original in English. An English spoken by Asian actors . . . who therefore have their own history of the acquisition of English speech. In other words, who are themselves 'translated' men and women – in that they (or their not-too distant forbears) have been 'borne across' from one language and culture to another. In order, then, to lay bare the full dimension of 'translation', I must take account of the specificity of my performers (their history): *by conveying Moliere's original play-text into another form*; a form that allows the performers to make creative connections between their ancestral traditions and their English present. Otherwise, the process of translation would be partial; and, being partial, would re-bound unfairly on the Asian performers: they would be judged in the context of white actors' history of producing such translated texts. Judged, in other words, on speech itself (ways of speaking English).

The connotations of the word 'translate' were extensively exploited in the production. The main features were (a) the play as 'borne across' to seventeenth century India; (b) transposed 'in form' to Indian popular theatre conventions; (c) presented 'as a gift from the West' by a French traveller, François Bernier, to the Emperor Aurangzeb in a 'translation' by the Emperor's Court Poet; (d) the deliberate use of Indian languages, which at times were directly 'translated' by one of the two story-tellers; (e) the direct quotation from Indian and European texts, either as parody (in the case of Shakespeare) or as substitute for Moliere's original text.

Having established the conventions, the production sparkled into life on the occasions when the conventions were deliberately broken. The most potent example of this was when Orgon's children

exchange verses from the Indian epic romance of *Heer and Ranjha* (an
equivalent of Shakespeare's *Romeo and Juliet*). As the verse-exchange
in Urdu finished, one of the story-tellers strode forward to address
the audience: 'Another translation !', she declared. By this stage of
the performance, the convention having been well-established, a
murmur of recognition would ripple through the audience. Pausing
a moment, 'Why bother !', she'd say and run back to her position on
stage, the house having erupted in laughter.

This moment encased for me several sub-textual readings. In
some senses it was a defiant validation of a language which has
a history of absence on the British stages. In another sense it was
simply the recognition by all of the un-translatability of languages;
and, paradoxically, the recognition of a common human experience
by this fact of difference.

If I have talked at length about these two productions it is because
I know intimately the thinking which has informed them. They
suggest, however, merely one type of transformation currently
under-way in British theatre. These would be interesting to note,
if only to better locate my own work.

Talawa Theatre – an Afro-Caribbean theatre company directed
by Yvonne Brewster – staged Oscar Wilde's *The Importance of
Being Earnest* in 1990 with an all-Black cast. Without making any
formal changes to Wilde's play, nor seemingly seeking to challenge
the dominant text-based conventions of British theatre, Talawa
nevertheless effected a challenge: the mere presence of Black actors
proved potent. Especially the frisson created in performance with
lines such as 'gazing into his blue eyes'! This was followed by an
all-Black version of Shakespeare's *Anthony and Cleopatra*. Again,
without any formal or conventional transformations, the production
reclaimed for Cleopatra, at least, her ethnicity.

Cheek by Jowl, another touring theatre company (directed by
Declan Donnellan), but significantly not a Black company, has in
its work also suggested the nature of the transformations underway
today. It has for several years presented work with a racially-mixed
cast, without suggesting that this is a policy. Its recent all-male production of Shakespeare's *As You Like It*, featured a Black Rosalind.
The work of this company is to be distinguished from that of others
I have mentioned hitherto not only because it is not a Black-run
theatre company but, significantly, because it is engaged in a similar
transformative exercise, albeit through under-statemert. 'Let the
performance speak', it seems to suggest. An entirely valid approach,

though no less so than those of Black companies. The example of
Cheek by Jowl is now replicated in many other theatres: from the
largest theatre houses (the Royal National Theatre and the Royal
Shakespeare Company) to the smallest touring companies. In other
words, more and more plays, both 'new work' as well as the classics,
are engaging with multi-racial casting.

To summarise this essay, I would suggest that the nature of
transformations in contemporary British theatre are of two types:
pragmatic and aesthetic. Pragmatically, this has resulted, by the
1990s, in increasing racially-integrated casting as well as the presentation of what has been perceived hitherto as 'White' work by
all-Black casts (though this latter is still much less in vogue than the
former). This pragmatic approach has built on the gains of seventies
and eighties Black Theatre movement – in terms essentially of
increasingly diverse audiences – as producers and directors have
sought to draw on the creative vitality of the Black communities
that now form part of the British landscape.

Aesthetically, it has introduced – and to an extent validated – a
wider diversity of theatrical language. This is not the preserve of
international theatre festivals or individual offerings from overseas,
but a vital part of 'home-grown' British theatre. My own production of *Tartuffe*, which toured eight countries around Europe and
the Pacific under the auspices of the British Council, in addition
to extensive national touring and playing at the Royal National
Theatre in London, offers but one example of the different images
of contemporary British theatre. A more recent example is offered by
the Black musical, *Five Guys Named Moe* (based on the life of Louis
Jordan) by Clarke Peters. This has achieved phenomenal success in
London's West End. How far this aesthetic approach is effecting a
full-scale transformation of the dominant convention of text-based
theatre is yet too early to evaluate. But the fact that it is now a part
of what was perceived in earlier decades as the 'mainstream' as well
as part of the 'fringe', is in itself significant.

5
Edward Bond and the Royal National Theatre
Ian Stuart

Edward Bond envisaged that during his lifetime he would write a series of plays opening with *The Pope's Wedding* and closing with *The Sea*. However, Bond has admitted subsequently that, having completed this dramatic cycle, he discovered there were many other plays he wanted to write (Bond letter to Coult in Hay, 179).

Since the original 1973 Royal Court production of *The Sea*, Bond has written fifteen plays as well as two translations/adaptations; three librettos for musical theatre; a trilogy of television plays, *Olly's Prison*, which he plans to adapt for the stage; a full length film script of Melville's *Moby Dick*; and a number of short stories, poems and essays. Given such a prolific output, it may seem surprising that the only production of Bond's work for a decade at Britain's Royal National Theatre was not a more recent unproduced play, such as *Human Cannon* or *In the Company of Men*, but his earlier play *The Sea* staged in the 1991–2 season.

At the time of *The Woman* at the National Theatre (1978), Bond wrote in *Plays and Players*:

[The National] has resources of space, time, skill and technology that we can use to strengthen our work and relate it more closely to our age. We use advanced technology to travel to our jobs and to bake our bread, and there must also be times when we use it to create those images of ourselves which are essential to culture and human nature. (Bond, 'Us, Our Drama', 8)

But in an interview in December 1991, Bond attacks the National as a theatre which has 'no purpose other than to survive' (Interview,

22 December 1991). Why does Bond's opinion of the National seem to have changed so dramatically? What was Bond's approach to his work at the National from 1978? And why, despite his acclaimed productions of *The Woman* and *Summer* on London's South Bank, does the National not appoint him as director of his own plays?

In attempting to answer these questions, this essay traces Bond's production history at the National Theatre through *The Woman* (August 1978), and *Summer* (January 1982). An assessment will be made as to how Bond worked on the plays in the theatre including extracts from interviews with Bond and those involved in the production process. *The Sea*, directed by Sam Mendes in December 1991 with some assistance from Bond, will also be examined as giving further practical definition to Bond's relationship with the National Theatre.

Contrary to claims by Peter Lewis who states that '*The Woman* was the first play to be specifically written for the Olivier stage,' the National did not commission *The Woman* (Lewis). However, Bond has said that a description of the Olivier auditorium from a newspaper was in the 'back of his mind' as he wrote the play (Bond in Hay, 239). Peter Hall, then director of the National Theatre, believes that presenting *The Woman* on the Olivier stage was a 'landmark' in that it 'showed that people like Edward Bond could go the distance in a big space' (Hall interview). Bond's decision to use the stage of the Olivier Theatre when approached by the National, caused Peter Hall some administrative difficulties. However, Bond was determined to use this space to stage *The Woman* and so waited until the following year opening the production on 10 August 1978. In a letter, Bond wrote, 'If you stage *The Woman* in a small space then you affect the play because its epic size is clear. It would be a bit like going to the seaside for a holiday but then never going near the sea and instead staying inside the hotel' (Letter to Baraket, 3 February 1990). Bond discovered during rehearsals that this theatre was a perfect forum for the play. Soon after the opening Bond described the Olivier as a public place, 'where history is formed, classes clash and whole societies move. . . . The Olivier stage is ideally suited to this sort of theatre. It's like a public square or the meeting of several roads or a playing field or a factory floor or a place of assembly and debate.' In the Olivier he saw a theatre 'that can help us to create the new sort of acting we need to demonstrate our world to audiences' (Bond, 'Us, Our Drama', 8–9). He maintains that with *The Woman* he reached a position where he was making new demands on actors in writing (Bond, *Socialist Challenge*, in Hay). But some critics have argued that this different approach to acting failed in terms of practical theatre. John Peter wrote in the *Sunday Times* that 'the play contains almost no acting. It has no people, only types: Fallen Queen, Warlord, Woman. They have functions but no flesh. They can't be impersonated, only represented. You might weep for Hecuba; but would you weep for an archetype?'

The Woman is subtitled 'Scenes of War and Freedom.' As Ruby Cohn has observed, this helps divide the play into two sections: Part One revolving around the Trojan War, Part Two occurring twelve years later on the island where the central characters, Hecuba and Ismene, gain freedom from the Greeks and triumph over the Greek's leader, Heros (Cohn, 200–1).

Bond and his designer, Hayden Griffin, literally stripped the stage of the Olivier theatre, exposing the fire screen not normally seen by the public. This screen served as an important component in the play's action, rising half way at the end of Part One to represent the ruined wall of Troy. Fire and smoke billowed from the side furthest away from the audience to indicate what one critic described as, the 'holocaust inside' (Young). Part Two occurred on a large tilted disc representing the island with Hecuba's hut stage right and a few silver boulders stage left. The silver wall was present throughout lit to suggest an 'endless horizon of sea and sky surrounding the island' (Bond letter to Coult in Hay). There were no other scenic elements with the exception of a large red cloth for Part One that covered the stage representing the bloodshed of the Trojan wars. The use of this cloth prompted Bond to write 'On The Red Floor Covering', a short poem capturing the social distinction between the actors and those who 'walk before us on a red carpet' (*Bond Plays*, 275). Peter Hall recalls the 'colossal use of the vast space in an asymmetrical way which in a totally symmetrical theatre was very exciting. It gave an enormous dynamic to the staging and gave very strong meaning to every movement' (Hall interview).

Lighting was also vital to the creation of stage imagery. Malcolm Hay and Philip Roberts mention that Bond requested a 'spiral of light in scene six, flickering briefly on the steel wall at the back as Hecuba walked down towards the beach and into the storm on the night before the race' (Hay, 263).

As with Bond's subsequent productions, the lighting at times bathed the stage in a bright white light and at other times illuminated specific areas for the short scenes. Also consistent with Bond's later productions, the intensity of the lighting was increased during the scene changes, demystifying the theatrical experience for an audience and emphasizing that they were in the theatre watching a play. This harsh light and the absence of substantial pieces of scenery emphasized the size of the Olivier stage, a space that Bond fully utilized.

At least one actor had difficulties in understanding his approach in creating an acting style for the play. Nicky Henson, playing Heros, had the impression that Bond required an unemotive technique. According to Henson, Bond made it very clear that 'Victorian-emotional-sentimental acting,' was unacceptable. Although he wanted a different method, Henson felt that Bond could not explain what it was:

> What we would do is interpretive acting and he did not want us to interpret his words, just speak them. How does an actor do this, like an automaton and an audience just sit there and listen and, ironically, make their own interpretation of the work? (Henson)

Henson also had difficulty with his character:

> Heros was a conglomeration of everything Edward feels is worst in the world. This should have been a feast for an actor but instead you walked on and everyone knew who he was. There was nowhere to go from there. A Molière or Shakespeare might have made a smiling villain who you appreciated later was evil. . . Surely what is interesting is the good bits of bad people and the bad bits of good people. (Henson)

A possible explanation for an actor's confusion is that Bond clearly challenges performers, asking them to think in a way not required by a drama school training. For example, one of the difficulties for Bond as director was that the acting at the National Theatre in 1978 came from a tradition antithetical to what was required by his plays:

> At the first run-through of *The Woman* at the National Theatre I was astonished at the way the acting forced the play into the ground, buried it in irrelevant subjectivity. Much of the acting still belonged to the nineteenth century. The company

were acting emotions, hugging feelings to themselves gazing at themselves, speaking to themselves even when they shouted. They were private performers on a public stage, still part of the bourgeois theatre. How damaging it can be to an actor to spend years trying to pump emotions into the classics, years of reducing acting to funny voices and freak gestures. (Bond, 'Us, Our Drama', 9)

Bond's attempt to create a style of acting is perhaps best understood by Daniel Baron Cohen. Cohen was Bond's assistant at the National, working with Bond on *Restoration* at the Royal Court, and *Summer* at the National:

[Bond] was trying to create a socialist realism, the right gestures. Some actors are very insecure and frustrated and communication becomes tense when actors are thrown on their own resources. . . [Bond] also wanted to lose pomposity and ornamentation, but I don't think actors feel secure with the simplicity he is after. (Cohen interview)

Margaret Ford appeared in Bond's production of *The Woman* in two roles: as one of the three Trojan women with the plague and as Rossa. Ford observes: 'The point is [with Bond], he keeps on breaking stuff down until the bitter end and maybe that is where there are problems with actors' (Ford interview). By this, Ford seems to suggest that Bond distils an actor's approach to his character down to its essential social characteristics. Yvonne Bryceland, playing Hecuba, described how she needed to surrender herself intellectually but not emotionally. 'The only way I could work with him [Bond]', she recalled, ' was to say that intellectually I am at your mercy but emotionally and perhaps with my response maybe I have an instinctive response' (Bryceland interview). She was convinced that Bond should direct the first production of his own plays and felt that without Bond present she would have been unable to work:

There are certain kinds of actors who respond to him wholeheartedly and Edward gets splendid work out of them. He got terrific work out of some of the actors in *The Woman*, so much so that people still talk about aspects of that production and I think how can people say that he cannot direct his own work when this is a production they will always remember? (Bryceland interview)

What is needed in Bond's form of theatre are actors gifted with patience prepared to confront their own class position. Although Bryceland has said that ideological compatibility was not a require-ment, it may assist in the creative process: 'You do not *have* to be of any political persuasion, maybe it helps but I just think it relates to a certain generosity, understanding and caring about the issues he writes on. It is the human being [Bond] writes about.' (Bryceland interview.) In an interview, Peter Hall commented on the importance of class issues to an acting style:

I think [Bond] needs, like all great writers, good actors who are not self-indulgent, not sentimental and do not mind endorsing the issues even if they reflect badly on the particular character they are playing. . . I do not think an actor brings his class onto the stage, he brings his understanding of class issues. That is something different. (Hall interview)

Bond returned to the National Theatre as the director of *Summer* in 1982. Hall recalls that he thought *Summer* would be interesting in the Cottesloe. 'With *The Woman*, Edward [Bond] had proved he could direct' (Hall interview). Bond's repertory production of *Summer* opened in the Cottesloe Theatre of the National Theatre on 27 January 1982 and closed on 19 June having received a total of sixty performances.

The play's action occurs in an unnamed seaside holiday resort in Eastern Europe where Xenia, a former resident of the island, whose family owned the land during the Second World War, and her daughter, Ann, have returned for their vacation. Marthe, a former family servant, continues to live in the house and is dying from a blood disorder. She is cared for by her son, David, the local doctor. During the play, Xenia learns from Hemmel, a former German guard who is also holidaying in the area, that, as a child, she was a silent symbol of class and racial superiority and in her own way as responsible as the German she so obviously dislikes. As a result there are two main groups in the play – the oppressors (Xenia and the German) and the oppressed (Marthe and David).

A characteristic of Bond's production of *Summer* was simplicity in design. Both the set and lighting design reflected the play's starkness. Hayden Griffin's set was dominated by a stone wall at the rear of the stage which revolved for the scene on the island becoming the execution wall. The setting provided a functional metaphor for the play itself: a warm mixture of bright colours, reminiscent of a European villa. Pete Mathers, in an analysis of the production, includes a detailed description of the set:

> The high vertical walls were each interrupted, one by a door, the other by an opening. The back wall was topped by a steeply-pitched tiled roof. The roof was red, the tiled walls sand-coloured, the door green. Stage left, at the back, hung a cloth which evoked the Mediterranean sea and sky. The sea was a solid, linear blue, defining a straight horizon; the sky, spattered blue spots decreasing in density towards the horizon. (Mathers, 145)

The spareness evident in Griffin's set was emphasized by the lighting and the acting style:

> In my production of *Summer*, there were no blackouts in between the scenes. In fact, I like the lights to come up and the actors to become actors and walk off and then come on for their next scene as actors. I think the critics find that disconcerting. Someone dies on stage and then gets up and walks off. That seems to be saying something very beautiful and important about human beings. We can demonstrate to you the fact that other people die and suffer and then I, the actor, can get up and walk off the stage. (Bond, taped correspondence)

Bond believes this technique is representative of his theatrical method. However, some critics commented negatively on this directorial style. Milton Shulman or the *Standard* wrote that Bond 'managed to wreck one of the play's few moving moments by having the dead Marthe rise from her incumbent position to make an ungainly exit' (Shulman, 22).

Daniel Baron Cohen felt that the National's production of *Summer* should have been 'the perfect laboratory for acting.' In practice, however, the production was fraught with difficulties. Peter Hall recalls it as ' . . . not being a happy time. . . [*Summer*] did not have the euphoric energy of *The Woman*' (Hall interview). The most significant complication in rehearsals was the stylistic difference between Anna Massey's technique toward Xenia and that of Bond.

From the beginning of rehearsals, Bond made a distinction between the way Xenia appears and the truth that lies behind her character:

> Xenia is always giving gifts, always smiling-killing people. Its got nothing to do with her character or the character she was born with. I've written that little poem about how she got her character. She kept going around being good, being Lady Bountiful, but nobody was truly grateful. So she became frustrated, she became nervous and finally destructive, if you like, because she is a good woman. She was in the wrong situation. (Bond interview with Philippou)

His concern is not with showing Xenia to be a 'real' woman, but in exposing her *social* guilt, showing how she represents a certain 'class' and, as such, cannot help but reinforce the very image she so desperately wants to be rid of. As Bond maintains:

> I don't think we can talk about evil at all. People never begin evil. They may end up evil. They may end up infinitely corrupted but they always begin good. (Bond interview with Philippou)

Anna Massey's approach to the characterization of Xenia concentrated on producing a 'human' element. Massey observes:

> Xenia is a very interesting character, obviously representative of the right wing. In Bond's terms, and in mine, a bad person. But in writing her character he wrote a very much more complex person than he allowed me to play. If you *just* have the wicked witch you are writing for children – if you have the good Marthe and the bad Xenia, it is very black and white, you don't have interesting interaction. If you allow Xenia to have something worthwhile to say; that is, she is not absolutely bad, you must allow her to say them. Bond has included good things in her character because he is a good playwright as well as a strong Marxist. He wrote things which were much more interesting in her character than he allowed me to play. (Massey interview)

In an interview with *Plays and Players*, Massey suggests it was only as a result of Bond's direction that she emphasized Xenia's depravity:

[Bond has] written a very powerful argument for each side and the language was characteristically rich, but he couldn't bear to let my side score any points. (Massey, 'Across the Water', 12)

According to Massey, it was Bond's reluctance to have her appear as Xenia, carrying all her emotional baggage, which led to much of the conflict in rehearsals. In response to the criticism that he only wanted Xenia to appear as evil, Bond wrote to the editor of *Plays and Players*,

I am used to being accused of believing in concepts and encouraging practices I spend my creative life arguing against. . . I hope the text of *Summer* is itself proof that I would not connive at such crudity. Nor do I believe in 'evil.' Evil is yet another excuse – this time for our confusion and stupidity. It lets us off the hook. Evil may be forgotten but stupidity has to be paid for by all of us. Xenia is much more interesting than merely being evil. (4 August 1991)

Bond insists that there are no arguments that might excuse Xenia's actions: 'In fact I do not know of any powerful arguments in favour of massacring women and children, and there are none to be found in the play (Bond letter to the Editor). Bond clarifies the situation:

[Anna Massey] wished to show, at the end, that Xenia had a 'good soul' and that in some way that redeemed her. And to be fair, the way we usually teach acting encourages this false view – it is after all the way many people see life. Well Hitler liked dogs but if at the end he had left his money to Battersea Dogs Home the ashes of Auschwitz would not be diminished by one grain and he would not have been redeemed. . . The play's point is that the argument of the 'good soul' is a spurious convenience. (Bond letter to the Editor)

Instead of Massey approaching the role 'naturalistically,' Bond wanted an actor in the observation of her role, showing its social function and 'graphic sense,' within the whole of society.

In rehearsals for *Summer*, Bond emphasized two major requirements for actors: concentration on the play's issues and discipline. Bond maintained that audiences do not listen to an actor's voice, but rather to the workings of the mind. Consequently, he believes actors need to understand their character and pass on this interpretation to an audience:

> Another important thing is the head. . . It is quite extraordinary that actors can go through long speeches without thinking once . . . they do it by treating words as a form of music, or a form of sounds. They do not actually think. In my plays that is absolutely disastrous. (Bond taped correspondence)

Bond does not require actors to be relaxed during performance, instead he wants the 'alertness of the athlete and surgeon' (Bond taped correspondence).

Bond expressed surprise that German programme notes for a production of *Summer* in 1990 stated that '"inspite" of the recent changes in Europe the play was still valid because it dealt with the "eternal" questions of life and death' (Bond letter to Paparassiliou, 25 August 1990). Bond's opinion is that *Summer* is a play which becomes more relevant with the end of the Cold War and re-ordering of the European social structure. In a letter Bond comments: 'The changes do not alter the past – and the reappearance of Nazism and racism (did they ever go away?) in Europe are warnings' (Bond letter to Paparassiliou). The changes to Europe's social fabric in 1990 caused Bond to emphasize *Summer*'s continued importance:

> I consider that the recent changes in Europe make very little difference to *Summer*. What Marthe says about Xenia and her world remains true. The bourgeois standards by which Xenia lived were corrupting in the way the German makes clear. Changes in Europe do not bring the ashes of Auschwitz back to human life. Xenia was able to corrupt notions such as kindness and justice to serve her own (conscious or unconscious) ends and it doesnt matter to the dead victims of Nazidom whether their killers understood why they killed them: Marthe judges their deeds and not their intentions. Doing this has human dangers, but it is also necessary for humane reasons. (Bond letter to Paparassiliou)

Metaphorically, Bond describes his impressions of the Post-Cold War world and its relevance to *Summer*:

> As to the democracy of the new capitalist Europe: I should invite you to consider Adam and Eve sitting in their garden of Eden

covering their nakedness with figleafs; and in time they will be forced by starvation to eat their figleafs – whether it is starvation of the gut or the mind. I think we are going to live through a time of great effort, brilliance and decadence – and I think that *Summer* has a great deal to say about that, because the story of Xenia and Marthe is true. (Bond letter to Paparassiliou)

Ten years after the production of *Summer*, a play by Edward Bond was again staged at the National Theatre, but it was not directed by him. *The Sea*, directed by Sam Mendes, was performed in the Lyttelton auditorium between 12 December 1991 and 8 April 1992.

Set on the East Coast of England in 1907, the play examines the impact of Colin's death on a small village community. Colin's tragic drowning exposes the conflict between Mrs Rafi, the local grande-dame, and Hatch, the town draper and volunteer coastguard. Hatch believes that Colin's death and the survival of Willy, Colin's friend, from the shipwreck, confirm his irrational suspicions that the planet is being invaded by creatures from outer space. Colin's fiancé, Rose, is comforted by Willy whose attempts at rescuing Colin from the sea were unsuccessful. Evens, a recluse who lives on the beach, helps Willy to re-evaluate his world. And, in spite of their suffering over Colin's death, at the end of the play Rose and Willy leave the village together to begin a new life.

Bob Crowley's design was dominated by a turquoise cloth on the proscenium and fire screen. This screen was lowered prior to the play and during the interval. The set's side walls contained revolving flats downstage right and left allowing for the addition of scenery. Upstage the area was covered with stones to represent a beach. For the scenes in the draper's shop, a large 'L' shaped turquoise counter was set downstage which was replaced for the scenes on the beach by Evens's hut, a simple wooden structure with two stools in front and a bicycle alongside. Set pieces were also flown in: the front of Hatch's store and the windows for Mrs Rafi's drawing room.

According to some of the National's actors in *The Sea*, Bond had little effect on the production. However, Ken Stott, playing Hatch, observed:

As an author, Bond is bound to leave the work of directing to the director. But he was very helpful and gave us small insights, or rather big insights but in a small way. (Stott interview)

Stott mentioned one occasion in rehearsal for scene five when Bond suggested that Hatch should pause to dangle the scissors in the air as he was cutting Mrs Rafi's curtain material:

[This action] might seem small but it actually means an awful lot to an actor. It became a moment which unlocked a lot of frustrations in Hatch and allowed me to experiment. I used to go absolutely raving bonkers over the cloth but I have brought it back now and made it [the cutting of the fabric] more restrained. (Stott interview)

Sam West, playing Willy, provided a further example of Bond's influence in rehearsals:

Bond said that an audience should be able to hear an actors brain working. And so, with a scene like scene six, that we spent about ten three hour rehearsals on, we had about five different versions. We rehearsed it as a love scene or with Willy trying to cure her [Rose] with the typical aggression of a doctor. Then we came to the conclusion that they must be much closer because they shared more and this made them look at each other less. (West interview)

In a letter to the director, Sam Mendes, Bond makes some observations about the setting and offers a useful insight as to how Bond visualizes the play in performance.

There is a slight sense of the theatrical about them [the design photographs] . . . This becomes noticeable in the two interiors. If the figure of the woman in the drawing room is 5 feet six inches tall the window is about thirty feet tall. This is unlikely in Mrs Rafi's house. And the mullions would not support that amount of glass. The audience know, then, that they are being invited to connive at a level of theatrical reality which is socially unreal. The play works in the opposite direction: it states its social, factual premise realistically – and the fantasy is based on that. Its important to the play that the characters have great difficulty in reading their social reality – and this gives rise to the layers of fantasy and madness and illusion in the play. Taking the wrong direction (it should be reality-to-fantasy) disturbs the logic of the levels of reality for the audience. The problem is aggravated because the drawing room scene has a haberdasher's scene before and after it – which are intensely concerned with the curtains for these windows. . . The text even gives the size. The placing of these scenes is playing on the audience's awareness of the curtains. The text even specifies the size of the curtains. In the last of the three scenes the draper will try to cut the cloth to these dimensions. He will desperately try to be accurate at the beginning – pedantically exact: after all his life, profession and sanity depend on it. Later of course the tape measure is cast aside – and rage and fantasy take over. But he begins in reality. The audience wont be able to do this because you have visually lied to them: a concept (of design) will stand between them and the theatrical process. The audience may not be conscious of this – but it will be part of the way that they read and experience the scene. So the design, at this point, works against the actors. You understand that my objection isnt one of personal taste – or even opinion: it is one of theatrical logic and the way the play uses the levels of reality. The objects in this play (it isnt true of all plays) should be real. (Bond letter to Mendes)

Mendes adjusted the size of the windows for the production. Ultimately, responsibility for a play's theatrical presentation must lie with the director. However, Bond is a playwright intimately aware of the difficulties of producing his plays so, in assessing his work at the National, it is useful to consider his reaction to Mendes, the production and the National Theatre as a whole.

Bond has a mixed response towards Mendes and his work. As a director he describes him as presenting 'a very attractive package.'

And that is our society. 'Stand there, go there, brighten this colour.' It is just like designing a box of biscuits. . . I feel [this attitude] is a prostitution of the audience. (Bond interview, 22 December 1991)

However, Bond is quick to come to Mendes' defence with an example from rehearsals:

I remember the first time watching the cast assembling on stage for the funeral [of Colin]. They came on in this very simple way and it was rather moving. And I thought, 'Yes, that is what funerals are about.' He [Mendes] is very good at doing those big scenes. But he does something which is very strange. When he comes to the big scenes, that is when he takes the glitter away. He achieves the big effects by a greater simplicity. Now that is an ability and one asks why he needs to do it, what is he expressing, what need creates that ability? If you can have some faith in that need then I think he becomes interesting. (Bond interview, 22 December 1991).

Regarding the 1991–2 revival of *The Sea*, Bond does not consider 'adequate' to be 'good'. 'The play speaks, he [Mendes] does not stop it speaking but he does not help it to speak. The play speaks because he has not destroyed it' (Bond interview, 22 December 1991). It seems productions of his work that he has not directed are often seen to fail because the directors do not view the plays as Bond intends.

The reason why I want to direct my plays is that they are experimental without being obviously so. . . In order to write better for actors, I have to become part of their rehearsal process. If I want actors to be of a different sort, I have to get involved in the actual technique of creating it with the actor. I can't any longer be in the situation of nudging someone and getting them to relay the message. (Bond interview with Curran in Roberts, 74)

In addition, Bond's plays require an alternative approach to acting that depends on his close directorial involvement:

The plays are making new demands on actors – and I need circumstances in which I can work this out. . . The purpose of being on stage has to change and so does the nature, the object, of acting. And so does the text – which functions in new ways. (Bond letter to Stafford-Clark)

Some actors believe that Bond's involvement in the rehearsal process stems from an inability to release his work to actors and directors (Massey, 'Across the Water', 12). But this is not the case according to Bond who writes to *Plays and Players*:

When I direct or attend rehearsals of one of my plays I make one thing clear: I do not know how to play it. That is not my job.

The joy of the theatre is that the real secrets of a role lie in the performer not in the text – and I'm too selfish to give up that joy. All I can do is make clear the situations and their implications. If these are falsified there is a moral morass and interestingly, no drama. Surely an encouraging connection between drama and the truth! Yet our theatre is being destroyed by just such falsifications, and by directors who try to dramatise their way out of them by happenings, stunt lighting, coercive music and other effects that please and even stun but in the end stupefy. Effect-and-effect is replacing cause-and-effect. (Bond letter to the Editor)

Bond does not believe the National Theatre fulfils the aims it espouses. If they did, the theatre would have done more extensive productions of his plays. The National Theatre's programme states that the Theatre's chief aims are:

. . . to present a diverse repertoire, embracing classic, new and neglected plays from the whole of world drama; to present these plays to the very highest standards; to give audiences a choice of at least six different productions at any one time. (Programme for *The Sea* 1991)

Bond questions this idea.

The National are doing this play at the moment, which everyone agrees is a bad play but it gives an actor a good chance. That is the way the theatre will work. It is not that ability to describe the world which good theatre can do so that the world matters again to its audience, so that they can accept responsibility for their world and experience the happiness, the confidence of doing that. The National is just not on that level. (Bond interview, 22 December 1991)

So why does Bond allow the National to stage his plays?

You use whatever stages you can wherever they are, as a matter of common sense. You also try to infiltrate the ruling structures – the ruling cultural structures – with alternative contents: then even the structures have to react to this – accommodate it, partly incorporate it etc. Various strategies are open to them (the ruling structures) but you become, for them, a fact. (Bond letter to the author, 19 September 1991)

Clearly, as a director at the National Theatre, Bond needs a non-naturalistic approach to acting; a model that explores a character's social and political make-up. Bond requires actors to be engaged in the process of uncovering characters' actions, so that an audience will not be seduced by the actor in the guise of the character, but able to understand their political motivations. Instead Bond needs actors who understand and communicate the character's social and economic position. In this way, an actor approaching his work with a socio-economic perspective, will enable the audience to assess the character's political function. Bond's restlessness with theatrical reality is contained in an interview:

I sometimes feel cheated when I see an old woman on stage portraying an old woman. Well yes, I think to myself, I know you can do that. I want to know something else, I want to know something more. And at that moment I can only do that by working directly with actors. I haven't formulated that very clearly into a set of exercises or statements. I really can only state the problem. Take scene five from *Summer*, how are you going to act that? You don't want these people digging down into their psyche and getting more nervous and tense. You need something else. Imagine someone swimming in the sea and thinking they are drowning. What normally happens is that you get all these frantic gestures and that is what you get on stage. But the drowning man has his eye on the horizon. He sees where he has got to go. It's that eye on the horizon that really interests me. (Bond interview with Philippou)

The difficulty faced by Edward Bond is that in attempting to give shape to a theatrical form by directing his plays, his primary role as a playwright is threatened. Many European countries, especially France and Germany, welcome his work. But in Britain, as a result of his directorial intervention, his plays have been marginalized.

REFERENCES

Interviews

Bond, Edward. Interview by the author. 22 December 1991.
Bond, Edward. Interview by Nick Philippou. Undated.
Bryceland, Yvonne. Telephone interview by the author. 3 December 1989.
Cohen, Daniel Baron. Interview by the author. 19 June 1990.
Ford, Margaret. Interview by the author. 16 October 1989.
Hall, Peter. Interview by the author. 17 July 1990.
Henson, Nicky. Interview by the author. 6 June 1990.
Massey, Anna. Telephone interview by the author. 22 January 1990.
Stott, Ken. Interview by the author. 21 December 1991.
West, Sam. Interview by the author. 20 December 1991.

Unpublished Correspondence

Bond, Edward. Letter to the author. 19 September 1991.
Bond, Edward. Letter to the Editor of *Plays and Players*. 4 August 1991.
Bond, Edward. Letter to Mohsen Baraket. 3 February 1990.
Bond, Edward. Taped correspondence to John Lamb. January 1982.
Bond, Edward. Letter to Sam Mendes. 23 October 1991.
Bond, Edward. Letter to Vassilis Paparassiliou. 25 August 1990.
Bond, Edward. Letter to Max Stafford-Clark. 24 April 1990.

Publications

Bond, Edward. 'On the Red Floor Covering'. In *Bond Plays: Three*. London: Methuen, 1987.
Bond, Edward. 'Us, Our Drama and the National Theatre'. *Plays and Players*. October 1978.
Cohn, Ruby. 'The Fantastic Theater of Edward Bond'. *Essays on Contemporary British Drama*. Munich: Hueber, 1981.
Hay, Malcolm, and Philip Roberts. *Bond: A Study of his Plays*. London: Methuen, 1980. (Includes: Edward Bond letter to Tony Coult; Edward Bond, draft article for *Socialist Challenge*, August 1978).
Lewis, Peter. *The National – A Dream Made Concrete*. London: Methuen, 1990.
Mathers, Pete. 'Edward Bond Directs "Summer" at the Cottesloe, 1982'. *New Theatre Quarterly*. May 1986.
Massey, Anna. 'Across the Water'. *Plays and Players*. July 1991.
Peter, John. *Sunday Times* (London). 13 August 1978.
Roberts, Philip (compiler). *Bond on File*. London: Methuen, 1985. (Includes Edward Bond interview with Patricia Curran, 1 July 1979).
Shulman, Milton. *Standard* (London). 28 January 1982.
Young, B.A. 'The Woman', *Financial Times* (London). 11 August 1978.

6

Spread a Little Happiness: West End Musicals

Sheridan Morley

In celebrating, as we just about can in 1992, the first century of the British stage musical in its modern form, we would do well to remember the complaint of one of its greatest and most prolifically successful exponents, Noel Coward, who in a moment of uncharacteristic despair commented 'the only trouble with the British is that they have never taken light music seriously enough' (Coward, 'Preface'). To a lyricist and composer of his generation (he was born into a world of Gilbert and Sullivan just ten days before the last Christmas of the last century, hence the name Noel) it was a source of regular amazement and regret that his fellow-countrymen seemed through his lifetime to be getting less interested and/or confident in the whole notion of the West End musical as an indigenous art form, so that by the end of his long career Coward himself, that most quintessentially English of writers and men, was actually premiering his musicals on Broadway.

Since his death in 1973, the pendulum has of course swung back to the point where hit shows like *Cats* and *Phantom of the Opera*, *Les Misérables* **[Photo 7]** and *Miss Saigon*, routinely open in the West End and only later transfer to Broadway. But before accepting the convenient contemporary theory that the British musical only really found its dancing feet internationally with *Cats* in 1980, we would do well to recall that at least two English musical librettists, Guy Bolton and P.G. Wodehouse, were enjoying considerable Broadway success as early as 1917, and that the traffic across the Atlantic has in fact been two-way ever since. Long decades before Tim Rice and Andrew Lloyd Webber, not only Wodehouse and Bolton and Coward but Sandy Wilson and Lionel Bart and Antony Newley had all achieved hits in New York to rival those achieved by Rodgers-Hammerstein in London.

Admittedly, the British stage musical had never until the 1980s achieved on its home ground the dominance that its American counterpart had on Broadway: the musical remains without doubt America's greatest contribution to and achievement in the live theatre this century, whereas in Britain there still lingers a faint unwillingness to accord classic status to song-and-dance shows, hence the general reluctance to acknowledge the greatness of a musical like *Les Misérables* when it came from the stage of the Royal Shakespeare Company at the Barbican and indeed helped to pay for that stage over the next decade.

But what has changed in British musicals can be measured in economic realities: early in January 1986, when Andrew Lloyd Webber announced that his Really Useful company was to be floated on the Stock Exchange, that company was immediately valued at over £35 million largely on the basis of his own *Cats* and *Starlight Express*, since the earlier shows written with Tim Rice (*Evita, Jesus Christ Superstar* and *Joseph & the Amazing Technicolor Dreamcoat*) were the property of other managements. Clearly that valuation was also a declaration of faith in Lloyd Webber's future, and it was justified: in 1991, when he had added *The Phantom of the Opera* and *Song & Dance* and *Aspects of Love* to his catalogue, the PolyGram Corporation paid roughly one hundred million dollars for a mere thirty-percent share in his company. If you added up all the lifetime earnings of all other British stage composers in this century, the total would be unlikely to reach even a half of what Andrew Lloyd Webber is now worth.

What has also changed, of course, is the international record market: Lloyd Webber was, with Rice, the first to sell his shows initially on disc and only subsequently in theatres, and in that way theatre composers were at last able to share in the transatlantic and worldwide goldmine that had been opened up by such British pop composers of the 1960s as Paul McCartney and John Lennon. Such a goldmine was never open to Coward or to Novello, nor to any other British writer of musicals which predated the 1960s. But in the wake of the Beatles Lloyd Webber and his subsequent producer Cameron Mackintosh went on with Boublil and Schönberg's *Les Misérables* and *Miss Saigon* to franchise the British (or rather Anglo-French) musical across several continents, much after the fashion of Conrad Hilton or Colonel Sanders who had also discovered the all-importance of the logo and central packaging.

Even so, there has always been something subtly different about
the British musical at its most native: something that becomes
immediately apparent if one starts to consider what are commercially and internationally three of the most successful musicals
given a British setting. All three, as it happens, are the work of
a German composer and an American lyricist who was sent to
school in England at the age of thirteen by a millionaire shopkeeper
father who believed that no American ever spoke properly. One
of their three hits is set in a never-never Scotland, one in Covent
Garden and the third at the court of King Arthur. All are based on
quintessentially local material, carefully researched and reasonably
faithful to their sources, periods and conventions. Yet there is no
way that *Brigadoon, My Fair Lady* or *Camelot* could be considered
British musicals, despite the fact that the last two at any rate
opened originally on Broadway with all-British names above the
title. Something in their scale, in their approach to the original
subject-matter, in the big-band sound of their orchestrations, in
the tone of their dialogue, brands them as unmistakably American
musicals.

But if *My Fair Lady*, based by Alan Jay Lerner and Frederick
Loewe on Bernard Shaw's *Pygmalion*, designed by Cecil Beaton and
starring Rex Harrison and Julie Andrews and Stanley Holloway and
Robert Coote was still not a British musical, what is? To answer
that question, and to explain why an often underfinanced, critically
derided, small-scale and fundamentally nostalgic art form should
have exploded into the multi-national hits of the late 1980s, we need
to go back to the very beginning.

The precise identity of the first modern British stage musical is
still a matter for separate debate, but there can be no doubt that
it was Gilbert and Sullivan who made it possible. By the turn of
the century, 'Take a Pair of Sparkling Eyes', 'Tit Willow', 'We're
Very Wide Awake the Moon and I' and 'I Have a Song to Sing-O'
had been inculcated into the bloodstream of a generation of child
theatregoers from Noel Coward to Ivor Novello and Vivian Ellis; in
writing the first modern hit songs, and in writing them specifically
for the theatre, Gilbert and Sullivan had opened up the way to an
Edwardian era that was to be saturated with operettas and musical
comedies. In the years up to World War One, starting out from the
Royal Strand Theatre (where now stands Aldwych tube station) at
which in 1887 Fannie Leslie had introduced her 'musical comedy
drama' *Jack in the Box*, London was to celebrate one of its richest

orchestral periods. Not only were there the foreign imports of Franz
Lehar, Leo Fall and André Messager, all bringing across the English
Channel echoes of a European café and cabaret world to an audience
very few of whom had yet acquired the wealth or the means of
transport to find it for themselves abroad, but on home territory
Lionel Monckton, Paul Rubens and Leslie Stuart were all at the
height of their success: *The Quaker Girl, Our Miss Gibbs, Miss Hook of
Holland, Floradora, The Arcadians* and *A Country Girl* all served within
a very short time to establish the notion of the musical comedy as a
regular feature of London theatrical life.

But critics were still deeply suspicious of the new form: 'one of
the most curious examples of composite dramatic architecture that
we have for some time seen' wrote a critic of *A Gaiety Girl* (the 1893
show which was the first to describe itself as 'a musical comedy').
'It is sometimes sentimental drama, sometimes comedy, sometimes
almost light opera and sometimes downright variety show, though
always light, bright and enjoyable' the review concluded.

A Gaiety Girl, which toured America in its original London pro-
duction as early as 1984, was rapidly followed by *A Runaway Girl, A
Country Girl, The Shop Girl, The Pearl Girl, The Casino Girl, The Quaker
Girl, The Girl Behind the Counter, The Cherry Girl, The Girl Friend* (itself
wonderfully parodied by Sandy Wilson half a century later as *The
Boy Friend), The Girl From Kay's, The Girl From Utah, The Girl in the
Taxi, The Girl on the Film* and *The Girls of Gottenberg.* Then there were
the various *Belles (Belle of Mayfair, Belle of New York, Belle of Brittany)*
and the occasional *Maids* (mainly *of the Mountains*) and *Princesses
(Charming, Caprice* and the *Dollar* variety). Titles were not allowed
to vary much, and gradually an all-purpose plot began to establish
itself. This usually had to do with either royalty or millionaires in
disguise, misunderstood romantic entanglements, apparent betrayal
or sudden loss at the end of Act I followed by restoration and/or
reconciliation by the end of act two.

The arrival of the American musical in London ('they prance, they
bubble, they make rings of joy like a dog let loose in a field, they go
with a swing and a scamper' wrote Herbert Farjeon later) changed
forever the West End idea of what a night out with an orchestra was
supposed to look and sound and feel like, and when half a century
later *Oklahoma!* arrived, 'smelling' as the poet Carl Sandburg noted,
'of hay mown up over barn dance floors, stepping around like an
apple-faced farmhand and rolling along like a good wagon slicked
up with new axlegrease' (Quoted in Morley, 10) it was to make all

English musicals seem overnight about a hundred years out of date in terms of choreography, orchestrations, lighting, sets, costumes and action. British composers and producers alike went into a state of catatonic shock from which they only really began to emerge in the 1970s with the advent of Rice and Lloyd Webber and the rock operas.

But at precisely that moment, when on Broadway Stephen Sondheim had renounced the showbiz of both *Gypsy* and *A Funny Thing Happened on the Way to the Forum* for the more obscure and courageous barrier-breakers that were *Pacific Overtures* and *Sweeney Todd* and *Follies*, the feeling in Britain was that international success could only be achieved, on stage as on disc, with extremely simplistic and familiar material. Just because British musicals had been so deeply unsuccessful in the world market unless, like *Oliver!*, they dealt in Dickensian good cheer or, like *The Boy Friend*, in perfect period-piece nostalgia, Rice and Lloyd Webber fell back on such ready-made sources as the Bible (for *Dreamcoat* and *Superstar*) or the life of Eva Peron (for *Evita*).

It is not to belittle those hit shows (*Dreamcoat* has indeed recently returned in triumph to the London Palladium with Jason Donovan) that I would suggest they were not about anything or anyone that we did not already know; indeed it was precisely their quality of pre-sold familiarity which made them acceptable abroad and to the many Americans who make up theatre audiences in the West End. The selling of *Evita* did not start with the concept album; the selling of *Evita* started when Eva Peron herself made the Rainbow Tour of Europe back in the 1950s.

Equally, a musical like Willy Russell's *Blood Brothers*, which has now been running in the West End for as long as any of the Lloyd Webber's save *Cats*, has never really triumphed internationally simply because its contemporary theme, of the ravages of Thatcher economics, cannot be readily sold to someone who has not already seen it.

So the big hits of the British musical theatre, at least until the late eighties, were never about anything very much: *Cats* is a superb celebration of the poems of T.S. Eliot, and *Starlight Express* a hugely commercial roller disco, but neither has a plot which would occupy more than a line or two of printing on the back of a matchbook. That is why they work so well and so universally: they ask nothing of an audience beyond attendance at a certain theatre on a certain night. No language problems for foreign tourists, no demands of shared heritage or education, no cultural barriers to be stormed. If a musical is now to earn back an initial investment running at around ten million dollars, it needs to be an event: therefore the less a show is actually about, the better its chances of travelling the Atlantic.

This is not purely a local problem: as the scores of Sondheim have become more and more specialised, they have left the West End for the subsidised locales of the National Theatre and the Old Vic. What the commercial theatre sends across oceans are the easy spectaculars: New York gets *Starlight Express* and London gets another *42nd Street*. The fact that we could learn vastly more about America from *Merrily We Roll Along,* or that they could learn more about us from *Blood Brothers* or *The Hired Man,* is alas irrelevant to the men who do the financial estimates.

And the times again are a-changing as we embark on the 1990s: Broadway, emerging from a decade in which its homegrown musicals were decimated by a lethal mix of AIDS backstage and financial and real-estate crises along what was once the Great White Way, does at last seem to have recovered its dancing feet with *City of Angels* and *Grand Hotel* and *The Secret Garden.* London meanwhile, economically embattled by a fall in the tourist trade, has returned from such epics as *Miss Saigon* and *Les Misérables* to the small-scale revue format of *Five Guys Named Moe,* while the best and most intelligently lyrical of the Lloyd Webber scores, that for *Aspects of Love,* has ironically proved less successful commercially than the infinitely more self-evident *Phantom of the Opera.*

Flops like *Matador* have also indicated that a set and a score are still not enough, although the stage musical is oriented towards cinematic special effects in the manner of Steven Spielberg. With *Cats* still ascending to the Heavyside Layer by way of a space-lift that appears to be on permanent loan from *Star Wars,* it is the sets that have become the real stars – a danger foreseen by the late Kenneth Tynan in his 1962 review of an otherwise unmemorable Lionel Bart show called *Blitz*:

> It does, however, have Sean Kenny's scenery, and there are distinct signs that sets are now taking over. They swoop down on the actors and snatch them aloft; four motor-driven towers prowl the stage, converging menacingly on any performer who threatens to hog the limelight; and whenever the human element looks like gaining control, they collapse on it in a mass of flaming

timber. In short, they let the cast know who's boss. They are magnificent, and they are war. (Tynan, 119)

Thirty years later, it is clear that the war has been won, and not by the actors: Tynan's nightmare vision of a show 'in which the curtain will rise to reveal sets which advance in a phalanx on the audience and expel it from the theatre' (Quoted in Morley, 157) is not so far from what actually happened in *Time* and *Starlight Express*: all we need now is a set which can write the songs and applaud itself, and the cycle will be complete.

But what we have lost along the way is precisely Tynan's 'human element', although there are still certain causes for celebration, even as the musical stage gets polarised into tiny local cabarets or huge mid-Atlantic epics or nostalgia-fests. Musicals have always enjoyed a boom in times of recession: what was true for the Hollywood 1930s of Busby Berkeley has been proved true again by all the old singalongs that have thrived in London and New York during the eighties, and at the time of this 1991 writing, half the shows playing in the West End and on Broadway are in fact musicals of one kind or another. An audience that has trouble finding the money for its tickets also wants to see how that money is being spent, and musicals with huge sets and lavish costumes therefore fulfil an economic and escapist need. They also pose no real challenge: in the case of a revival, where one can actually go in humming familiar songs, the public can also be reasonably sure of what they are buying in advance at the box office.

It would be a brave theatrical prophet who could see in all of this any precise outline of future developments in the musical theatre, and I have never believed in the theory of the drama critic as racing tipster: as some audiences still want to put on their tap shoes and shuffle off to Buffalo to plug into a past that was only ever theirs on movie screens, and as other audiences demand ringside seats at space-age spectaculars, there is a third audience for the classics of Boublil/Schönberg, perhaps the only musical team outside of Sondheim still intent on shows which think while they are singing and dancing.

Shows like *Les Misérables* and *Miss Saigon*, indeed like *Assassins* and more romantically *Aspects of Love*, live not in the safe cushion of nostalgia but on the razor's edge, and in them might well lie the survival of the form as anything but trite. It might be better to end up with a slit throat from *Sweeney Todd* than a broken neck caused by looking back too far over one's shoulder at Rodgers and Hart. As Sondheim once noted, anyone can whistle.

REFERENCES

Coward, Noel. *The Noel Coward Song Book*. London: Michael Joseph, 1953.

Morley, Sheridan. *Spread a Little Happiness; The First Hundred Years of the British Musical*. London: Thames and Hudson, 1987.

Tynan, Kenneth. *Tynan Right and Left*. London: Longmans, 1967.

Part III

7

Breaking the Boundaries: The People Show, Lumiere & Son and Hesitate and Demonstrate

Lynn Sobieski

Neglected by British theatre critics and largely unknown to American audiences, The People Show [**Photo 8**], Lumiere & Son and Hesitate and Demonstrate have produced some of the most significant work seen on British stages during the past twenty-five years. Their particular form of performance, which challenges the role of text in production in order to explore the potential of theatrical imagery, is unique in context with most of British theatre which can be characterized in terms of its strong literary bias. Referred to variously as 'performance art', 'theatre' or simply as 'performance theatre', the work of these three companies has played a crucial role in the development of the British alternative theatre movement since the 1960s. During the 1980s and early 1990s, when drastic cuts in arts funding by the Thatcher administration resulted in the demise of countless fringe groups, the innovative work of The People Show, Lumiere & Son and Hesitate and Demonstrate has largely continued to flourish.

The year 1968 is frequently designated as the beginning of an era characterized by growing political awareness and activism. The coincidence of events ranging from the May student and worker rebellions in France to the American anti-Vietnam War demonstrations politicized an entire generation including artists and students. Thus, the socio-political eruptions were paralleled by the revitalization of artistic activity in both Europe and America.

Unquestionably, 1968 was pivotal in the development of the British alternative theatre. The Theatres Act, which was passed in September, officially ended the Lord Chamberlain's function as censor of British theatre. In London, the media began to give coverage to a theatre movement which it described as 'the fringe' in reference to the conglomeration of theatre groups which had developed in the middle 1960s on the fringes of the official Edinburgh Festival. The term 'fringe theatre' was used to categorize the proliferation of small groups and performance venues whose work characteristically challenged traditional social and aesthetic values. Its closest parallel in the United States is the Off and later the Off-Off-Broadway movements which emerged in New York City during the late 1950s and early 1960s.

It was in 1966, however, that a significant event occurred which was to have a major impact on the development of British fringe theatre – The People Show staged their first performance in the basement of Better Books in Charing Cross Road. Formed by Jeff Nuttall, the future author of *Bomb Culture*, the group was comprised mostly of visual artists who were interested in experimenting with the 'happenings' format. Concurrently, similar work with non-text-based performance was being done in the art schools of Bradford and Leeds by artists such as John Fox, Albert Hunt and John Darling. This network eventually spawned the work of both Welfare State International and, later, Hesitate and Demonstrate. Also during this time, London fringe artists were significantly influenced by the visits of several key American and French companies, including the Living Theatre, the Performance Group, the Open Theatre, the New York La Mama Company and Jérôme Savary's Grand Magic Circus from Paris. Some of these companies held workshops which trained key fringe performers such as Hilary Westlake, co-founder of Lumiere & Son.

The fringe companies which have been in existence since 1968 can be differentiated into three broad categories. The first category consists of experimental theatre companies such as the Pip Simmons Group, Steven Berkoff's London Theatre Group, Hull Truck and Freehold who challenged traditional theatrical conventions. Largely influenced by the visits of American companies such as La Mama Experimental Theatre Company and the Living Theatre, these British groups experimented with environmental staging, the relationship between performer and audience, actor training techniques and the process of creating theatre texts. The second category includes socialist political theatre companies such as Cartoon Archetypal Slogan Theatre (CAST), 7:84 and Red Ladder who gathered momentum during the anti-establishment revolts of the late 1960s and then aligned themselves in the early 1970s with the radical factions of the labour movement. Identifying closely with the struggle of the British working-class, they began creating theatre pieces committed to socialist change. Developing concurrently with the first two areas of work was a network of theatre companies including the People Show, Lumiere & Son and Hesitate and Demonstrate.

The work of these three companies can be characterized by a variety of critical factors which clearly distinguishes them from other forms of both experimental and conventional British theatre. The productions and the working processes out of which they are developed integrate most of the major innovations definitive of contemporary Euro-American theatre during the past thirty years. Their major mode of operation is to challenge traditional theatrical assumptions regarding the function of text, *mise-en-scène* (all theatrical elements of a production including acting, design, sound and musical effects among others) and audience reception in the performance event. Unlike most of British theatre, text, in the work of these companies, is displaced as the organizational element of the *mise-en-scène* in favour of a greater reliance on the visual and aural score as a signifier of meaning which is of equal or greater importance than language.

The productions of the People Show, Lumiere & Son and Hesitate and Demonstrate do not start from a basis in text, but instead develop from individual images, impulses, obsessions, ideas, objects, fictional literature and art works. Various theatrical elements, including design, music, sound, acting, choreography, imagery and words, operate on different tracks, but, unlike most of American postmodern performance, are often unified by a specific ideological theme. Performers never surrender their individual identity to that of a fictional character, but maintain a Brechtian distance which allows them to consciously exploit their own personalities as well as occasionally break the theatrical frame. The overall performance structure is precisely and tightly controlled moment-to-moment, bearing more resemblance to a musical score, which rarely includes language, than to that conventionally dictated by a dramatic text. The prevailing aesthetic of these three companies indicates a distinct departure from traditional, Aristotelian notions of narrative, character and dramatic action which results in an expansion of the spectator's role in determining the interpretation or meaning of the production.

This paradigmatic scheme raises a series of issues regarding definitions, the most significant being the issue of critical labels. Is there a descriptive term which sufficiently sets the work of the People Show, Lumiere & Son and Hesitate and Demonstrate apart from the rest of British avant-garde and mainstream theatre? The work of these three companies is often referred to by British critics as 'performance art' theatre, largely because of the experience of artists such as Jeff Nuttall and Geraldine Pilgrim in the visual arts movement of the 1960s and early 1970s. However, since the work has clearly become increasingly theatricalised over the past two decades, it is often characterized simply as 'performance theatre.' Still other descriptions are possible. Could these companies be labelled 'postmodern theatre' like the work of close American counterparts such as Robert Wilson, Mabou Mines and the Wooster Group? Or would Bonnie Marranca's term 'theatre of images' be more accurate? The most effective way of addressing the issue of definitions is to examine the artistic attitudes, working processes and representative productions of each company.

The most widely recognized of the fringe companies which have been in existence since the 1960s and early 1970s, is the People Show which began performing in 1966. The original members of the company were visual artists brought together by sculptor and jazz pianist Jeff Nuttall to stage a 'happening' involving motor bikes, fishing nets and very fat women in Notting Hill Gate, London. The People Show initially created performances involving found spaces and objects, subtly transformed into anarchic compositions which challenged the members of the audience to devise their own interpretation of the images. By the middle seventies, the group abandoned the 'happenings' format and became well-known for a distinctive theatrical style described by various critics as 'Dadaist,' 'irreverent,' 'atmospheric' and 'dreamlike.'

The working process developed by the People Show during the early years has operated virtually unchanged throughout the company's history. The ninety-seven People Shows produced during the past twenty-five years have had a variety of different starting points which always result, according to Mark Long, ' . . . as shows which are about the people performing in them' (Long). Typically the company begins working with each participating individual's current preoccupations. These may include ideas they have, objects they are interested in, actions which they would like to perform onstage, momentary obsessions, artwork which intrigues them or themes they wish to explore. *People Show No. 85, The Dentist* emerged because the group found an antique dentist chair about to be discarded on the street, whereas *People Show No. 84, The Bridge* was founded on a painting by Vincent Van Gogh.

After Long and the other People Show members, which have included throughout the years Chahine Yavroyan, George Khan, Alan Hill, Emil Wolk, Mike Figgis and José Nava among others, devise a provisional scenario, they begin to build the piece around a developing series of images and personae which are based on the individual quirks and personalities of the company members. The ensuing rehearsal process demands that the performers maintain creative spontaneity while constantly being aware of the evolving structure of the piece. The People Show operates as a collective and refuses to appoint a director, believing that the company's artistic vision is the province of the individual members and should never be usurped by the detached perspective of an 'objective eye.' Changes are often made during the run of a production, however, often at the suggestion of friends and colleagues who are trusted by the group.

Although People Show productions have generally given the impression over the years of being improvisational and anarchic, each is precisely scored with every image and action relating to an overall scheme. The company's productions often employ loose narratives, but aesthetic unity results from the interweaving of themes, both imagistic and ideological. Long, who admits to being influenced by the theories of Edward Gordon Craig, is adamant about the issue of unity. The elements of the *mise-en-scène* may appear to be randomly devised and functioning on different tracks, yet they are actually as particular and cohesive as the seemingly unrelated objects in a Magritte painting. Long equates the structural dynamic of the People Show's work to the intricate operations of jazz – a form of music characterized by syncopated rhythms, and which allows for carefully controlled improvisation within a very tight score.

The production which perhaps best exemplifies the artistic concerns and working process of the People Show is *People Show No. 79, The Hamburg Show*. The starting point of the Hamburg Show was the set which was conceived as a piece of sculpture composed of wooden uprights, pieces of corrugated iron and ropes with a dumb waiter in the centre. The result resembled an abandoned building site scattered with oil drums and various objects including an old gas meter. The set was designed to represent the two major levels of society, with personae from the upper strata performing at the top of the scaffold while the lower class operated underneath. After the set was completed, the next production element to be devised was the sound score which included police sirens, German *Lieder* music, roaring cars and airplanes, Tchaikovsky and contemporary disco music.

The show opens with a single light piercing through a chandelier made of broken bottles suspended from the scaffolding. As the light becomes increasingly brighter, other images are revealed including a naked woman hanging upside down, a body under a shroud, a bank of roses on a freshly-dug grave, a black woman weeping inconsolably and a golden throne room at the top of the set. According to Mark Long, these initial images were intended to indicate that something tragic has just occurred in the space inhabited by the lower strata of society.

After what seems to the audience as an interminable time, a man in a Commissioner's outfit climbs out of a garbage can, frees the woman from her ropes and clothes her in a costume which gives the impression of an absurdist housewife. She, and hence, the audience, are then led on a tour of the subterranean space as she dutifully cleans the glass chandelier with a feather duster. The hypnotic mood is suddenly interrupted by a blackout and the arrival in the audience of Emil Wolk as a clown-like man bearing planks of wood and a table and chair. Through a series of humorous confrontations with the audience, he manages to enlist their help in completing the set and building himself a platform on which he can sit.

As the audience is abruptly accosted by the smell of frying bacon, Wolk notices that there is action occurring behind a corrugated iron wall and proceeds to investigate. Suddenly the wall collapses to reveal an extraordinary scene – the woman who was earlier suspended from the set is now a working-class housewife making bacon sandwiches for a man in a tuxedo reading *The Daily Mail* and a man perusing the sports pages with a paper bag over his head. Another woman, costumed in silver strips, stands up and begins to rotate to the tune of Blondie's 'Heart of Glass', becoming, in effect, a human disco ball.

According to Long, images such as the bacon sandwiches, consumed regularly by the People Show when on tour, and the glittering ball, functioned as symbols of the lower classes, whereas those at the top of the scaffolding, including a gentleman sitting in the throne room playing with a model of the set, represented the upper strata of society. *The Hamburg Show* enraptured the audience through the creation of a poignant and ethereal atmosphere which was frequently pierced by moments of absurdist humour and clowning. The production effectively demonstrated the People Show's masterful control of the theatrical environment, including the design elements, the skill of the performers, and the precise juxtaposition of extraordinary images.

In recent years, the People Show's inclusion of more text and popular entertainment skills such as acrobatics in their work has met with a mixed reception from both audiences and alternative theatre critics, some of whom recognize the company's particular strength in visual composition. One exception to this is *People Show No. 92, Whistle Stop*, which enjoyed both critical and commercial success at London's Bush Theatre in 1987. The piece takes place on a fictionalized version of the Chattanooga Choo Choo in a reference to a genre of film best described as 'train movies', including *The Lady Vanishes* and *Murder on the Orient Express*. The loose narrative involves a young soldier, played by Mark Long, who is on his way to Russia, even though the other characters mistakenly believe the train is going to Tennessee. What follows is a manic romp through a British fantasy of American trains, complete with obsessive poker players, a torch singer, a transvestite, a passionate love affair and several murder plots, one of which is intended as revenge for Leon Trotsky's assassination. This bizarre pastiche is accompanied by American jazz, including blues numbers and Tin Pan Alley songs. The Company members themselves comprised the jazz ensemble, which has become an integral part of their work since the early 1980s.

People Show No. 97, Burning Horizon, which was staged in the fall of 1990, began from the starting point of music composed by George Khan. It was hailed by critics as a return to the style of production characteristic of the company in the 1970s and early 1980s, in which language was basically excluded in favour of an elaborate and surrealistic visual score. The company's continuing goal is not to promote a specific theatrical ideology or political agenda, but to explore situations which free the creative spirits and imaginations of the People Show artists. According to Mark Long, the sense of joy and celebration fostered when the People Show is working at its best, is what has made the company unique in relation to other British theatre and also what has accounted for its longevity.

Lumiere & Son is distinct from the People Show and Hesitate and Demonstrate in two ways: it uses a text in productions, written by David Gale, and rather than being collectively organized, is under the artistic leadership of director Hilary Westlake. Lumiere & Son began in 1973 when Gale, a writer with a background in literature and film making, met Westlake, a director who had been trained as an actress, and who had worked with the London La Mama Company. Both were extremely interested in visual imagery and both intensely disliked conventional theatre. Both were also fascinated with expressionism, surrealism and abnormal psychology.

Most of Lumiere & Son's pieces, particularly the early ones, are concerned with an investigation of subconscious forces which are manifest in social behaviour as extreme appetites, needs and actions. Westlake and Gale are not concerned with everyday reality, but prefer to explore various forms of madness and obsession. Lumiere & Son's shows have ranged from explorations of sado-masochism and homicidal mania to considerations of blind obedience and totalitarianism. According to a company press release: 'Our imagery has more affinity with dream and myth than "documentary reality", and consequently we tend to dwell on exaggeration, obsessions, fixations, illness, habits, rituals, customs and jokes.' Lumiere & Son's productions are often funny, but the comedy is always black, as in the case of the popular *Circus Lumiere*, which explores the dark side of clowning.

In devising a theatrical language capable of expressing the extreme forces lurking behind social masks, Lumiere & Son has rejected realism as inadequate in portraying human behaviour. Realistic British acting, in David Gale's opinion, reflects a 'grotesque' reliance on actors' vocal and physical mannerisms. Instead, Gale respects radical experimentation both in staging and in acting.

> I have a deep respect for anyone who experiments with stylization in theatre; it's so refreshing. Let's discard all of these curious, naturalistic languages. Let's discover instead a unique, theatrical language for each individual theatrical situation. (Gale)

Lumiere & Son's productions tend to favour an exaggerated expressionism, in which the various elements of the *mise-en-scène*, including language, movement and visual images, are highly styl-ized and function on a separate but equal basis in the production. Gale believes that conventional theatre, in its emphasis on realism, tends to place the text ' . . . at the peak of the pyramid with the design considerations low in priority.' Lumiere & Son's aim is to create a theatre in which the visual score in particular can be freed from illustrating the narrative in order to function as an independent signifier of meaning.

Even though David Gale writes the texts used by Lumiere & Son, even after he officially left the company in 1986 to pursue a career as a free-lance writer, the text is never the starting point of the production process. In earlier years, the process would begin with a thematic concern which was occupying David Gale; a good example is 1977's *Passionate Positions*, an exploration of the bizarre behaviour in individuals which obedience to absolute authority can produce. During the late 1980s and early 1990s, it was typically Westlake who formulated the initial idea. This vague theme is then explored through a series of improvisations with performers chosen because of interesting personal idiosyn-crasies. Westlake, who leads the improvisations, focuses on the physicalisation of emotional extremes which are indicated by the chosen theme. Eventually these exercises are choreographed by Westlake into a highly sophisticated movement score. The text is developed through the workshop process, with Gale incorporating quirks from the performer's individual personalities as well as ideas they contribute in terms of the theme.

The images are developed with the intention, according to Hilary Westlake, of ' . . . fleshing out the information being given in the text, as opposed to illustrating what is usually a very loose narra-tive.' (Westlake) Certain images, which in later years often appeared on a projection screen, are chosen to create a specific mood or atmosphere. An example of this is *Deadwood* and its abundance of Victorian icons in the set, on screens and in costuming. Others, for instance the non-naturalistic use of costumes in *Slips*, were intended to indicate hierarchies in relationships through echoing shapes and colours. Westlake maintains that her choreography is usually devised to explore the subtext implied in Gale's script. Yet she is insistent that ideological theme is ultimately the most important aspect of the production – the ideas obsessing Gale and Westlake are what unifies all the elements of the *mise-en-scène*. In *Special Forces: A Paramilitary Ballet*, produced in 1976, the highly

stylized movement score was choreographed to explore the theme
of compulsive obedience to authority, while the projected images
in 1987's *Panic* were designed to express manifestations of the
subconscious stresses involved in living in an urban environment.

A piece entitled *Passionate Positions*, performed in 1977, clearly
illustrates Lumiere & Son's preoccupation with extreme states of
mind and bizarre behaviour. In the publicity packet for the company, *Passionate Positions* is described as 'a play about heartlessness,
numbness and obedience.' According to Westlake, four characters
are introduced to the audience by a sadistic Narrator: one is a
clown who is a seeing-eye human for a blind, blood-drinking dog;
another demonstrates the indignity of a person with a rat stuffed
in his rectum; a character named Tension attempts to aggravate the
audience by smashing plates at irregular intervals; and the fourth is
called the Perfect Specimen, who, as her name suggests, is a flawless
individual. The four characters are mesmerized by the Narrator after
displaying their 'passionate' personalities to the audience. While
they are in a trance, the Narrator cuts out their hearts and offers
them to the audience. In order to retrieve their hearts, which are
real lamb hearts, the Narrator insists that the characters participate
in his play 'The Legend of Osiris the King' which consists basically
of a series of humiliating actions which they perform before the
audience.

Passionate Positions explored the boundaries of humiliation, obsession, perversion and servitude. It used both myth and direct confrontation to test the audience's tolerance of the extreme and willingness to participate in voyeurism. Gale is explicit about the theme
of the piece:

> It postulated that if you hold a position very passionately, you
> are always in danger of being knocked off of it and disarmed.
> It is more important, then, to have a broader view rather than a
> single conviction.

A production which typifies the collaboration between Gale and
Westlake is *Slips*, presented at the London Institute of Contemporary Arts in 1982. A surrealistic picaresque play, *Slips* featured both
a complex text and elaborate scenography which was produced
in collaboration with the Wimbledon College of Art. The piece
concerned a character named Mary and her interior restoration of
the various periods in her life. Gale has explained: 'I decided that

we'd trace the psychology of a young woman. The piece came to be about how memory works.' The inspiration for *Slips* came during a sabbatical Gale took in South America in 1981 when he found himself reminiscing about the various periods in his own life.

Slips is structured in successive sections corresponding to the most significant points in Mary's life as she remembers them: her birth, her early childhood, her girlhood, her adolescence and the present moment. Each period in her life is represented in a different genre in accordance with Mary's diverse associations. Gale and Westlake wanted the iconography for each section to be as distinct as possible. For example, in the birth section, Mary appears as a wooden doll, complete with head mask, which emerges from a large egg structure. The 'birthing' takes place in semi-darkness and is accompanied by deafening noise and billowing smoke. Gigantic figures in cloaks appear in the smoke and suddenly transform into four Victorian parents in an ornate and ghostly parlour. The Victorian images seemed appropriate for a childhood which Mary associates with repression and claustrophobia. The message of *Slips*, according to Gale: 'Our present is informed or deformed by the past. We must decide on the extent to which we want it to colour our view of things, particularly in terms of relationships.'

Lumiere & Son is not ultimately concerned with exploring the individual preoccupations of company members, as is the case with the People Show, but focuses particularly on the process of communication. According to Gale:

> Our work is not about a gothic inclination of an artist to dignify the 'backwaters' of his or her psyche, but to try to find points of contact between these 'backwaters' and those of the audience. We aim to challenge people's complacency and expose the complicated motivations for the things we do.

When asked what distinguishes the work of Lumiere & Son from other British experimental and mainstream theatre, Westlake maintains that the company's most unique aspect is its interest in devising different stylistic solutions to explore its preoccupation with relatively consistent thematic material. She indicates the diverse styles reflected in productions as varied as *Circus Lumiere* and *Deadwood* (1986), an elaborate spectacle produced in London's Kew Gardens. For that piece, which was inspired by the abuse of rain forests in England, the audience was led through a fantasy world occupied by exotic animals and Victorian men and women of leisure. Whereas the future of Lumiere & Son looks dubious owing to the company's loss of Arts Council funding in the spring of 1991, both Westlake and Gale plan to continue their careers in British theatre as freelance artists, exploring formal experimentation as well as contemporary themes.

Another company renowned for its formal innovation is Hesitate and Demonstrate, founded in 1975 by Geraldine Pilgrim and Janet Goddard, two graduates of the Fine Arts Department of Leeds Polytechnic. The company expired in 1986 due to financial reasons, yet Pilgrim has continued to work in British theatre. The training of the two women in the visual arts influenced their work from the outset. Text figured very little in their pieces which initially took the form of carefully planned 'events' performed in public places. The 'events' lasted only a few minutes and occurred amidst the routine activities of the chosen place. According to Pilgrim, on one occasion the two women shopped along a main street, elegantly attired, each carrying a lapdog under her arm. Finally the passersby began to notice that the women were actually carrying dead dogs which had been stuffed (Pilgrim).

Later on these street performances began to utilize a movement principle from which the name of the company emerged. Influenced by Edward Muybridge's photographs of human movement, the performers would hesitate slightly before they executed a motion as if deliberately demonstrating it to the audience. Another important element in Hesitate and Demonstrate's work which evolved during their first few years was the use of sound tapes. The tapes, created by John Darling of the People Show, included both classical and popular music as well as sound effects such as heartbeats, running water, animals and bird sounds and traffic noises. Very often the sound score served as the spine of the production, the element which determined both rhythm and atmosphere as it worked in juxtaposition to the visual images.

The working process which determined all of Hesitate and Demonstrate's productions was developed in the mid-1970s and adhered to throughout the company's history. Most of the preparation period was spent in discussion – only after the set had been built, the sound tape finalized and the image score devised, did the performers actually rehearse in the environment, usually only a few days before the production opened. The initial discussions between Pilgrim and Goddard usually concerned themes, words and images from favourite works of literature, which were often the starting point of the pieces. *Minutes*, produced in 1978, was founded on the poems of T.S. Eliot, while 1979's *Scars* took its inspiration from the works of the Bronte sisters. The work of artists was also discussed, including Magritte, Delvaux and E.L. Bellocq, whose photographs were the basis for 1978's *No Regrets*. Hesitate and Demonstrate's productions were also influenced by the personal histories of Pilgrim and Goddard. These included their relationships with families and lovers, as well as Pilgrim's middle-working class background and Goddard's experience as a member of the upper-middle class.

While the sound tape for the production was being created by Darling, the two women usually indulged in shopping trips to obtain objects and costume pieces which were to become part of the overall design. During this period of the work, Pilgrim typically kept a running journal of images and actions for the production, which would later be precisely coordinated with the sound score. Images were chosen for their atmospheric qualities as opposed to their expression of ideological themes, as is often the case with the People Show. The personae in each piece were not devised as fictional characters, but were based on each performer's own personality and experience.

As is the case with the People Show and Lumiere & Son, text in Hesitate and Demonstrate's productions does not function as the unifying aspect, and is often less important than the sound and image score in signifying meaning. Like Mark Long, Geraldine Pilgrim is adamant about the importance of unity in Hesitate and Demonstrate's work, but asserts that the company's work does not necessarily explore intellectual themes, but rather operates in terms of ' . . . an inner logic which, if clear to the performers, will be clear to the audience' (Pilgrim). The productions are generally structured around a surrealistic narrative which is not organized as a linear sequence, but which always culminates in a highly theatrical climax. Pilgrim maintains that Hesitate and Demonstrate's pieces, if all the visual and aural elements are precisely scored, could work without the presence of the performers.

Scars, produced originally in 1979 at the Liverpool Academy Gallery, was a piece based on the isolated lives and fantasies of the Bronte sisters, and also on Pilgrim's and Goddard's experiences at art school in Yorkshire. It was also the last production in which Janet Goddard participated with Hesitate and Demonstrate. The starting points of *Scars* were the research findings on the Bronte family by the two women and John Darling's sound tape, which included traditional Yorkshire brass band music, Wesleyan hymns, the music of Edward Elgar, moorland winds, the ticking of a Grandfather clock, a thunderstorm and the sound of dogs and owls. The intricately detailed set was comprised of a dozen tiny spaces which suggested the various rooms, spaces or situations in which the Bronte sisters conducted their insular lives. The result was a non-linear, surrealistic piece in which a collection of evocative images was held together by the mood of expectation, longing and immanent danger which is typical of Hesitate and Demonstrate's work. A *Time Out* critic wrote in early 1979, 'Like Robert Wilson, the group have poise . . . a tight, sophisticated, widely referential approach, essentially literary and imagistic, very much concerned with the visual potency of their tableaux . . . '

One of the most striking aspects of the production is the dream-like series of mundane activities rendered bizarre by the disassociation of the actions from any logical context. The spaces in which the activities were ritualistically performed suggested a variety of locales, including the Bronte's parlour in Haworth, a Gothic cemetery, an opera-house box, a neon-lit bar and a railway waiting room. A coal scuttle is emptied in the dark, a man at a dinner table is served paper which he consumes, a woman climbs under a funeral canopy to put on a death mask, another man serves ice-cream with exaggerated ceremony and three women pour afternoon tea by the railway tracks. All of these images evolved from the imaginations of Pilgrim and Goddard. The surrealistic operations of other images clearly echo the strange juxtapositions of Dali or Magritte. A pair of earrings is discovered inside a sandwich, a tiger-skin rug rears up to suffocate a bride, a woman in black sprouts a white, pre-Raphaelite angel's wing, and a silver salver is lifted to reveal a book. References to various cultural icons are scattered throughout the piece. *Scars* opens with Roy Orbison's 'Only the Lonely' played on the jukebox while the sultriness of Dorothy Lamour is recalled during a seduction scene played on a burning colonial veranda. Two lovers are furtively observed through French windows in a manner which refers to the films of Alfred Hitchcock and the nineteenth-century domestic details of the production clearly recollects the novels of Charles Dickens. The cumulative effect of the production on the audience was that of watching a kinetic painting, in which a hypnotic nightmare of Victorian repression is created through the

1. Almeida Theatre,
Desire by David Lan,
directed by Andrei
Serban, designed by
Richard Hudson, 1990.
Photo: Almeida Theatre

2. DV8 Physical Theatre, *Strange Fish*, Wendy Houstoun and Nigel Charnock, choreographed by Lloyd Newson, presented by Riverside Studios, London, 1992. Photo: Hugo Glendinning

3. Welfare State International, *Lord Dynamite*, directed by John Fox, commissioned b London International Festival of Theatre, 1991. Photo: David Haley

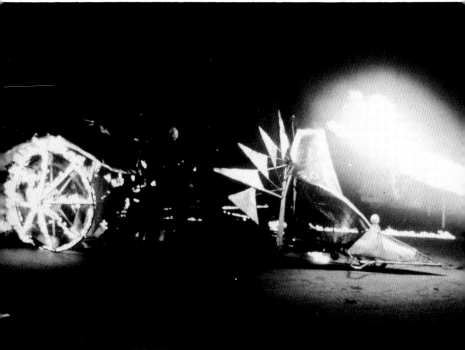

5. Gloria's production of *A Vision of Love Revealed in Sleep*, (*Part 3*) written and directed by Neil Bartlett with Regina Fong, Neil Bartlett and Ivan, 1989–90. Photo: Mike Laye

4. Tara Arts Group, *Government Inspector*, Antony Bunsee as Peter Singh Undarzi (Government Inspector) and M. Muraly as his servant Asif, directed by Jatinder Verma. Photo: Coneyl Jay

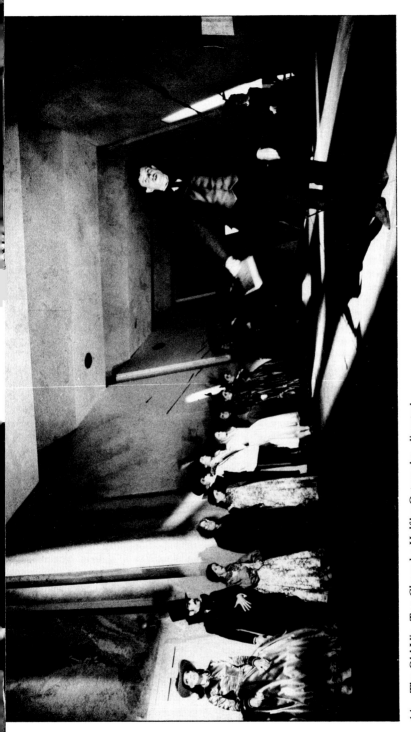

14. The Old Vic, *Too Clever by Half* by Ostrovsky, directed
by Richard Jones, designed by Richard Hudson, Alex
Jennings as the scoundrel. Photo: Simon Annand

fluid and precisely orchestrated interplay of images, sounds and actions.

The idea for *Goodnight Ladies*, perhaps Hesitate and Demonstrate's most successful production, evolved out of Pilgrim's fascination with Anna Anderson, the woman who believed she was Princess Anastasia of Russia, and her train travels in Europe after the Bolshevik Revolution. The company collaborated intensely on the piece, contributing images, paintings, movements and objects which were incorporated during the rehearsal process. Some of the found objects intrigued the company to the extent that entire scenes were constructed around them. An example of this is a scene which begins with a provocatively dressed woman rolled onto stage in a bathtub. Another scene involves a woman slashing open a red pillow with a dagger which she subsequently conceals in a large suitcase.

Goodnight Ladies, with its images of dark train journeys and clandestine encounters, was acclaimed by most critics as a finely crafted and evocative work and discussed in relation to such 'cloak and dagger' film classics as *The Lady Vanishes* and *Shanghai Express*. After this production, which was invited to be a part of the Public Theatre's 'Britain Salutes New York' festival in 1983, Geraldine Pilgrim continued doing freelance work in the style of Hesitate and Demonstrate, mostly in Italy, until Hesitate and Demonstrate officially disbanded in 1986 after a fire in a touring truck destroyed its property. Since then she has worked primarily as a designer in various British repertory theatres, but has plans to form a new company.

Reviewing the creative processes of the People Show, Lumiere & Son and Hesitate and Demonstrate, certain distinctions and similarities between the aesthetic principles and techniques of the three companies become clear. They can be differentiated mainly in terms of the inspirational foundation of their work, as well as by their individual approaches to the creative hierarchy. The People Show's productions are generally founded on the artistic possibilities of particular spaces, objects, actions and the personal preoccupations of individual company members. The work is developed by the collective, usually without the benefit of objective feedback from an outside source, whereas Lumiere & Son's productions are rooted in and shaped by the thematic obsessions of writer David Gale and director Hilary Westlake. Hesitate and Demonstrate's moving paintings emerged from the starting points of literature, legend and the personal experiences of Geraldine Pilgrim and Janet Goddard, who were largely responsible for determining the company's meticulous scenarios.

It is the factors they have in common, however, which make the particular form of performance shared by these three companies unique in relation to the rest of British theatre. Their work is distinguished by its tendency to rely on visual and aural images rather than text as the dominant elements of the *mise-en-scène*. This work also reveals the interest of company members in the aesthetics of modernist movements, especially Expressionism, Dadaism and Surrealism, which often juxtapose seemingly unrelated images. It shares with modernist theatre a tendency to unify all aspects of a production according to the particular style which best expresses specific thematic concerns. The work of these companies can be analyzed in terms of the dialectical relationships created between actual space, objects and behaviour and symbolic environments, icons and actions. The operation of the productions' formal elements can be examined in relation to musical structure, particularly in the employment of diverse rhythms, tempos and dynamics.

The People Show, Lumiere & Son and Hesitate and Demonstrate consider their company members performers rather than actors, who make artistic use of their individual personalities rather than surrendering them to fictional characters. The companies often incorporate elements from popular entertainment forms such as cabaret, carnival, acrobatics, folk festivals, music hall and circus. Their work reveals a conscious manipulation of cliche and genre, especially those found in film and literature, as well as an ambivalence toward the use of technology and its viability in live performance.

The work of these companies resists simple categorization. 'Performance art' is a valid term to identify performance as a medium for visual artists, but inaccurate in describing the productions of companies whose work has become increasingly theatricalised over the past few decades. Even though this work cannot generally be analyzed as containing plot or narrative in the conventional sense, the scenarios reflect a structure comprised of a distinct beginning, middle and end, which is not necessarily true of performance art. 'Performance theatre,' a description favoured by many British critics, is misleading, since all theatre can accurately be referred to as 'performance.'

Although postmodern theatre as a critical concept is of little interest to British critics and artists, some of its characteristics are useful in understanding the work of the People Show, Lumiere & Son and Hesitate and Demonstrate. These include the phenomenon of intertextuality, as evidenced by the dialectical relationship between text and visuals in Lumiere & Son's productions, and the semiotic interplay of parallel tracks of signifiers, exemplified by the juxtaposition of sound and images in Hesitate and Demonstrate's work. The productions of these companies often break the theatrical frame by calling attention to the fact that they are performance, which the People Show does by abruptly stopping the action to directly discuss the content of the work with the audience. Generally, however, the theatre created by the three companies has its foundation in the aesthetics of twentieth-century European modernism and film making, in the creative processes of 'happenings' and performance art, and in the devices of popular culture.

It would appear that no single term is sufficient to describe the work of the People Show, Lumiere & Son and Hesitate and Demonstrate. Their productions need to be examined and characterized individually, in both historical and aesthetic context. Yet the aesthetic anarchy of the People Show, the bizarre iconography of Lumiere & Son and the kinetic paintings of Hesitate and Demonstrate, have broken many artistic boundaries in contemporary British theatre and influenced the experiments of a variety of newer companies, including, Forced Entertainment and Station House Opera.

REFERENCES

Archival Material

Very little has been published on the work of the People Show, Lumiere & Son and Hesitate and Demonstrate. Most of my research materials were obtained in the archives of the three companies during the summers of 1989, 1990 and 1991. The materials included rehearsal journals, reviews, publicity documents, programs, administrative notes, correspondence with the Arts Council of Great Britain, photograph etc.

Interviews

Gale, David. Former writer for Lumiere & Son. Interview by the author, London, 22 January 1982.

Long, Mark. A founding member of the People Show. Interview by the author, London, 9 July 1991.
Westlake, Hilary. Artistic director of Lumiere & Son. Interview by the author, London, 15 July 1991.
Pilgrim, Geraldine. Director of Hesitate and Demonstrate. Interview by the author, London, 15 July 1991.

Productions seen by Author

The People Show
The People Show No. 75: The People Show Cabaret. London, March 1978.
The People Show No. 79: The Hamburg Show. London, January, 1981.
The People Show No. 82: Spaghetti: London, June 1982.
The People Show No. 92: Whistle Stop: London, February 1987.
The People Show No. 94: Farrago: London, July 1990.

Lumiere & Son
Passionate Positions. London, May 1977.
Circus Lumiere. London, July 1980.
Slips. London, January 1982.
Panic. London, May 1987.
Deadwood. London, July 1988.

Hesitate and Demonstrate
Minutes. London, April 1978.
Excuse Me. London, February 1980.
Goodnight Ladies. London, February 1982.

8

Diverse Assembly: Some Trends in Recent Performance

Tim Etchells

The artists I want to discuss are working through a number of contradictory traditions – essentially fine art performance, experimental theatre and new dance. My chosen range across these practices stems neither from their having merged into one (they haven't) nor from some desire that this should be the case, but rather from the presence here in the UK, as elsewhere, of a significant zone in which these disciplines meet. Whilst any level of crossover is partly a function of the funding and distribution systems, which are shared by these forms to a notable degree, it's also due to the intentional pluralism of form and context employed by artists. Not only are artists in these essentially transgressive forms moving across these three areas of practice, they're also, as a matter of course, taking influence and making links with many wider, more diverse areas of culture. From my position as an engaged artist (writing text and directing with Forced Entertainment Theatre Co-Operative since its foundation in 1984), and as a regular commentator on the field, I want to give a sense of what for me are some of the key concerns and common notions addressed by artists in recent years.

I

In light of post-modern identity theory, performance itself is re-framed – the assumption of roles, the conscious presentation or construction of self, the idea of the body as a culturally produced object, and the notion of ideal schizophrenics embodying numerous contradictory subject positions and impulses – have long, in a sense, been the acknowledged territory of actors, dancers and performers. Now that the bounds of performance have been re-drawn and extended through individuals, culture and the state, and since through this process, in the words of Susan Sontag, 'the notion of what is real has been complicated and weakened', it's true to say that performance is everywhere (Sontag).

For its own part identity onstage is now rarely a fixed point. More often, through actions, choreographies, or even speech the performers are seen as sharing a constituency of texts in which their own part or parts must be worked out, or in which their role is ever fluid – subject to play and to change. A prevalent idea is that both the character/performer and the stage are zones of possibility in which a number, or any number of contradictory things may lie, awaiting discovery. From this context conventions including verbal game playing, listing, obvious quotation of imagery or text, partial or flawed character representation, alienated delivery, mediated performance via video or PA systems, identical costuming, frantic costume-swapping or undressing, the construction of stage spaces with internal mirroring or echoing and the ceaseless re-arrangement of objects to produce fictions have passed into common performance language.

In this situation of continual flux the positioning of apparently or relatively real information, through text or action, has become a key way of creating both structure and meaning in the work. The nexus of non-narrative conventions touched on above is linked strongly to this issue of the real since in shifting from playing one possibility to playing another (or from one block via transition to another) there is often a gap, a space in between. Put simply, as performers move between tasks we see them, relatively speaking, undefined. In this in-between state they may be waiting, watching, setting up materials for another section or resting. These gaps may last a very long or a very short time. The gaps can be inserted deliberately (to disrupt a fictional or rhythmic continuum), or they may arise in a simple way from the tasks or activities at hand.

For works emanating from the real-time traditions of performance art or dance, such gaps help create a sense of a text-beneath-the-text, a sea of real presence, or of real-time work from which fiction can occasionally rise. As a principle however this tactic is not confined to works in the real-time or task based traditions. The positioning of relatively real information is an old theatrical one connecting, as it does, to aspects of ritual, to the conventions of plays within plays, asides, soliloquies and characters in disguise as well as Brechtian performance and the increasingly well established, though shifting, tactics of experimental theatre outlined above.

In their trilogy *Utopia* (1989) Claire MacDonald and Pete Brooks set two characters talking in a stage-set hotel room. The characters, called simply Man and Woman, never leave this location or do anything much, but rather they speak endlessly of Bishop and Adele, telling stories of them, defining their interests and lives, clearly using these linguistic doubles as a way of reinventing themselves and their own relationship, a way of moving beyond the solid, (more real) present time of the hotel room to some shifting dream-time of gardens, houses, cities and deserts. In *Utopia* the world is seen as wholly composed of language, language as the determinant of consciousness, language as an ideological battleground and, in a key shift from Brooks and MacDonald's earlier work in Impact Theatre Co-Operative, the culturally produced structures and often gendered oppositions of language can no longer be ducked by the supposed transcendence of action.

> In the second part of the trilogy we get the following exchange:
> MAN: She's the kind of woman who loves hotels.
> WOMAN: She met Bishop in a hotel.
> MAN: They were always in a hotel.
> WOMAN: In a hotel, telling stories, incredibly simple.
> (MacDonald)

It's an exchange that almost closes a circle, the most explicit of many internal echoes within *Utopia* and one that brings us deliberately close to the real situation of the theatre we are sitting in.

II

In 1986 we described a new Forced Entertainment performance as being 'understandable by anybody brought up in a house with the TV always on' (Forced Entertainment). It's a one-liner that applies equally well to many of our works and those of our contemporaries since the media space, as J.G. Ballard has written extensively, is a landscape that we live in, and, have to negotiate on both a concrete and a psychic level. Any contemporary sense of self is bound up with that landscape, inextricably, permanently.

Film and TV culture have informed new work in a number of ways, not least by providing a ready made collection of iconic genre narratives which artists can write both through and against. Film appears quoted, appropriated, reworked and pitched next to more personal material at many junctures – asserting time and again, amongst other things, that 'America has colonised our subconscious . . . ' (Wenders).

Impact's middle-period work theatrically approached film by focusing on narrative architecture, making the mythic visible by revealing structure, sometimes crossing narrative genres in unexpectedly revealing ways: in *No Weapons for* (1983) they made great play out of sexual mistrust and post-war images of predatory women by fusing the classic noir detective piece with a story about nuclear weapons testing in the Nevada desert. Here the traditional vampish noir heroines were also beings from outer space.

This obsession with the implications of specific narrative trajectories continues to be paralleled by use of film as a more straightforward image bank. In the eighties, from Impact (and latterly its remnants), from Rational Theatre and Hesitate & Demonstrate and later from Man Act, Forced Entertainment, Appeal Products, Dogs in Honey and others we saw work that unashamedly referred, at one level or another, to film as design, image, lighting and soundtrack source, often with the emphasis on elaborate and large-scale stage sets.

Steve Shill's post-Impact work is interesting here, not just because he continues to focus on narrative structure but also since his recent designs have left the large scale behind in favour of absurdly small, naturalistic sets, each representing the corner of a room. Lighting in these spaces is precise, filmic, evocative – streaming through windows or curtains, sliding through half open doors. The characters, often just a single man, appear pinned somehow in the tiny space and the action itself appears divided into shots, as one divides a film. On occasion the shots, some lasting a few minutes, others lasting only seconds, are drawn out of order from true narrative sequence so that linear time is disrupted. In *A Fine Film of Ashes* (1988) the mundane reality of the central character Michael, an estate agent, is plunged into disorder by his father's death – it's not long before the naturalism of location and event is also disrupted by developments of a much more dream-like kind.

Importantly in this piece and its successors the filmic realism is also held in tension by a series of more theatrical elements or presences. For one the black drapes beside the tiny set can't quite hide Shill's numerous entrances and exits and, more crucially, the room's painted floor-tiles end abruptly, as though cut in two at its edge. Within the performance Shill pays no attention to these slight deconstructions, but they do inform ones readings as he teeters on, and over, the edge of the fragile little world he's made.

The constructional tensions of the space are echoed in Shill's highly idiosyncratic but strangely paradigmatic performance style – a shifting balance of character detail and complete alienation; acting and speaking mostly like he's just woken up in somebody else's body, or as Michael says stiffly at one point 'Like I'm living my life about two feet to the left . . . just watching' (Shill).

III

In re-framing narrative, image, and design from the media culture, new work has tried to address the changes in our consciousness that shifting cultural forms have wrought. A chief factor in such change, especially as regards television, is the ubiquity of the fragment as a unit of informational exchange – everything's a soundbite now. To deal with this, works by Dogs In Honey and by Forced Entertainment have challenged, to some degree, the notion of a narrative continuum – instead it is almost disconnected images or scenes that slide across the stage in a way that seems both more musical and more devil-may-care than work from the previous generation. The neo-classical narrative structures, so carefully decoded by Impact seem to have slid further into oblivion now.

In 1974, before the remote control culture had really got underway, Raymond Williams wrote of the total flow of TV – its lack of the strong narrative closures and boundaries that other art forms have. (Williams) Now, with the remote in place, the TV is an endless montage of constructed fictions, constructed realities and occasional static, which is in itself endlessly re-montaged by every viewer, not only through channel hopping but also through the intersection, in their homes, of the TV image and their lives. With TV, after all, one can read, fight, wash up or make a phone call and still, consciously or not, keep track of what's happening on screen.

The effects of all this on our sense of narrative decorum were in evidence and under consideration in Forced Entertainment's *Some Confusions in the Law About Love* (1989) and in our subsequent work *Marina & Lee* (1991) [Photo 10]. Both works collaged and blurred texts from quite separate sources, sometimes appearing to create narrative and at other times setting up much more unresolvable collisions of image or form. In *Some Confusions* the performance of a British Elvis Presley impersonator, either acting out the demise of Presley or enjoying one of his own, is interrupted by a pair of jaded showgirls, by two 16th Century Japanese love-suicides dressed as skeletons, and by a babbling duo named Mike and Dolores who, via 'satellite link up' discuss the sex act they intend performing in Hawaii.

In *Marina & Lee*, with an eye on road movies and on the naively represented journeys of British pantomimes, the androgynous figure of Marina travels slowly across a neon-lit, flower strewn stage which she supposes to be a desert. As she walks she too is continually interrupted by scenes with little obvious bearing on her plight – kung fu fights, operas turning into adverts for Toyota, fragments of sex shows, TV thrillers, westerns and so on. Each time Marina stirs from resting in the corner of the stage it's as though she has accidentally arrived in the middle of the wrong scene, the wrong play, the wrong movie, the wrong life. The sense in this work, for us, is not that of complete story structures to be unpicked but of fragments to be dealt with, exorcised and rearranged – rearrangements which, on close inspection, are often contingent with the rather provisional and tenuous psychological construction of ourselves.

In the work of Dogs in Honey (formed 1985, based in Nottingham) the TV culture is even more to the fore and in both *Architecture for Babies* (1990) and *Blueprints for the End of the World* (1991) they repeatedly stage chat shows, quizzes, contests and formulaic magic acts which pertain not so much to some fictional narrative but to their own personal fears, dreams and whimsical desires. In *Architecture* the TV show format is broken on occasion for the performers to record video messages to their unborn children – a piercingly 'real' piece of mediated performance in a light, trashy studio world.

It's worth noting here a key complexity in working with appropriated media imagery in a performance field. Transferring imagery in this way is, of course, about giving it a new, more immediate presence. In live work an image seen many times on TV can, stripped of its familiar electronic mediation, shock us anew. Cru-cially however, this immediacy is balanced by another one, since in live work not just the image but the mechanics of its construction are inherently more present and visible than they will be in it's original form. The interplay of these twin factors – immediacy of presence and visibility of construction – is important not just in how new work approaches imagery from the media, but also to its engagement with other areas and concerns. What's important is the fluid, shifting nature of the relationship – the way an image and its doing/undoing lie in complex, undecided flux.

IV

The use of media-culture imagery in performance tends, somehow, to invoke its opposite – an underside of more intimate, more real autobiography and presence. However even in the most apparently straightforward uses of autobiography many artists seek to exploit its intimacy whilst simultaneously throwing it into question. In Dogs in Honey's *Sons of Bitchumen* (1988) **[Photo 6]** each performer breaks the fictional frame to recount some supposed truths about themselves – the truths, in the case of performer Stephen Jones at least, are constantly collapsing and the 'real' mementoes of his life which he shows us are knowingly and blatantly not genuine. It's clear from this that the whole notion of honesty, and the intimate utterance in a performance arena is highly problematic.

Bobby Baker (a fine-art-trained performer whose work is often seen in theatres) digs this territory very deeply. Her pieces *Drawing on a Mother's Experience* (1988–9), *Cook Dems* (1990) and *Kitchen Show* (1991) **[Photo 9]** lie somewhere between feminist autobiography, cookery classes, action painting and the eccentric British mono-logues of Joyce Grenfell. There's a constant balancing in the work between the sharing of secrets and the need to keep them, a constant and delicate sense that some things can't quite be explained – in the end we're aware not just of how close we have come to Baker in her honesty but also of how distant we remain – somehow she insists, through the work, that for all her telling, she can never be told. What Baker makes use of so brilliantly runs through the field of new work like a ghost – it's a crucial reserve, a privacy in public that's not remotely harsh, and perhaps, a quality quite new to these times.

In *Kitchen Show*, staged in her own kitchen, Baker presents a series of loosely connected thoughts or narratives each of which is 'fixed' in our minds with both a performed 'action' and a 'mark' that alters her appearance.

> When I get angry in my kitchen, I feel the need to do something violent to release the tension. Once I tried throwing a wine bottle on the floor, here, look you can see, but it made an awful dent . . . I think the best throwing action is to take a ripe pear and hurl it against a cupboard door . . . I choose a vinyl silk door because the pear washes off more easily. . . . (Baker)

She asks the audience to stand aside and with a shout she throws the ripe pear against a cupboard door with impressive force causing it to splatter. She 'marks' the 'action' by putting another pear in her breast pocket.

Anecdotes such as dancing whilst cooking alone, resting when the kids return from school, as well as Baker's chosen materials – margarine and dish cloths, tinned soup – all declare and simultaneously make us rethink their banality. For Baker the self and the past are things that must be constructed knowingly and re-valued in the present through a complex play of narrations, enactments and 'marks' made on the body. At this level her work is about domestic and biological landscapes as maps or indexes of memory. By the end of the piece she is transformed – an absurd, self-mutilated chart of her own narrations, her past and our new-found involvement in them.

Like Bobby Baker, the Gloria company, directed by Neil Bartlett, is concerned to pull into focus aspects of the culture which might otherwise be neglected. Their works *A Vision of Love Revealed in Sleep* (1989–90) **[Photo 5]** and *Sarrasine* (1990–91) both drew heavily on specific gay art traditions and on works by particular gay artists – *A Vision* used the story of Victorian painter Simeon Solomon, whose arrest in 1873 for cottaging led to disgrace, whilst *Sarrasine* intercut opera with pub drag and music hall, constantly re-making both the nature of the theatrical event and our sense of cultural divisions.

Crucial in Bartlett's work is the idea that one's contemporary self cannot be meaningful without a sense of the past; without a sense of precedent, history and context for one's actions and culture. Denied this, the gay community, or any other, is contained and rootless whilst the mainstream is left free to fix meaning. The situation Bartlett abhors is one where he's ' . . . told twice a year for the past ten years "you can't do your work here, there's no gay people in this town"' and where ' . . . gay performance art is considered difficult and *The Importance of Being Earnest* is not' (Bartlett, 'Getting Up').

In *A Vision* Bartlett intercut formally disparate material by and about Simeon Solomon with his own monologue of contemporary London gay life and with performances from drag queens Bette Bourne, Regina Fong and Ivan Cartwright:

> REGINA: Come, let us go forth and I will show thee a vision . . .
> NEIL: He took hold of my hand, dark against the wan air of the dying night, and he stood by me and he whispered in my ear. . . And I looked forward and I saw that the way before us grew dark in the night air and I said; I'm scared, I'm scared all the time, scared of losing my nerve, scared of losing my friends, do you know, I've walked this way home for years now but I'm lost, I'm lost . . . I don't know where I'm supposed to be . . . (Bartlett, *A Vision*)

Gloria's work plays confusion in the body as well as in the culture – in *Sarrasine* the central character is played by three people simultaneously, two men in drag and a woman, whilst in *A Vision* Bartlett spends most of the time naked, shaved of all body hair and powdered white from head to foot like a cherub in one of Solomon's paintings – the only thing that trips one up is the distinctly eighties moustache.

V

In *Dead Dreams of Monochrome Men* (1988) by DV8 Physical Theatre [Photo 2], based on the story of serial killer Dennis Nilsen, there is continual reversal and swapping of dance patterns, exchange of roles and inversions of power. This flux resides not in a kind of formalism, to which it may have a distant debt, but in a sense of an onstage community, through dance, informed by theatre, attempting to confront its own narratives, its own complicity, and its own pain. This notion of an onstage community pitching itself against a system of texts or images is prevalent in new work and the progress of the community in its task through the time of the performance is almost a contemporary version of plot. The onstage community, of course, is always a mirror for a series of wider ones, the audience at large, and for DV8 in *Dead Dreams* the gay community in particular.

DV8's work in the eighties also focused on notions of the body. Watching *My Sex, Our Dance* (1986) or *Deep End* (1987) one was struck by their obsessive essentialism – the desire to strip away the twin veils of decoration and technique leaving only the body in extremis. It's a desire that for all its implicit criticism of dance convention is as strongly located in a debate about identity. There's a constant sense in the work, which finds close parallels in theatre performance of the time, that what we are watching is the physical and psychological equivalent of peeling an onion – layer after layer pulled away until there's almost nothing left. The aesthetic of DV8 in these works is thus a kind of back to basics of the body, but again the project is not formal but determinedly social, metaphoric and engaged. The self here is elusive, located in the body and desire, but always shifting, disappearing, out of reach; the body observed, the body in struggle, the body blindfold, the body in exhaustion, the body thrown, the comfort of the catch, the fear of the fall, the rejection of the drop, the body itself as witness, the body as dead weight.

This questioning the idea of the body as an essential object can be picked up in a number of other works, not least through the prevalence of microphones, video, film and slides all endlessly masking, ghosting or transferring its immediacy of presence. In more theatrical terms in Forced Entertainment pieces from *200% & Bloody Thirsty* (1987) onwards, we've re-drawn the body variously as naive skeleton or ghost, augmented it with wigs or cardboard wings, and in other works used tacky rubber organs – breasts, penises and noses – in a quiet retake on the convention that stripping off is somehow getting more real.

Artist Gary Stevens and the group Station House Opera are both interesting to consider here since each places the body in performance as an unstable object amongst other unstable objects. In Station House (to whom I'll return later) performers are continually lifted, rearranged, shaped literally by their environments, or, as in the recent piece *Black Works* (1991), created as 'characters' only when fed detailed instructions for action over radio headphones.

In Gary Stevens' intellectual slapstick *Animal* (1989) the performers, moving in an environment of assorted cuddly toys, live a comical half-life; they are confused and frightened, constantly testing the edges of the world in which they exist, attributing feelings and character to objects that can have none, whilst never quite recognising themselves or each other for the living things they are. Says Stevens: 'Theatre still works on an archaic model that says where you have a speaking subject they know what they are doing, but to me the exciting thing is deconstructing the individual, to find a way of portraying people where they lose control' (Stevens, interview).

In an earlier work *If the Cap Fits* (1986–7), created by Stevens with Caroline Wilkinson, we see two performers trying to get a sense of who, or what they might be, agreeing only that: 'We came down the stairs, tip-toed bare-foot across the floor and now stand staring at each other in the dark. We try to figure out each others shape. It seems to be shifting and constantly changing . . . ' (Stevens and Wilkinson).

By the end of the piece, transformed beyond recognition by many layers of clothes and joined together in an outfit which blurs the edges of their bodies, they try to use objects as a way of marking their presence. Resting a table at an incline to represent the stage they add bottles to its surface to stand in for themselves. As the bottles repeatedly and inevitably slip off, Stevens addresses the audience in characteristic puzzled comic fashion:

> This goes on for half an hour! Ideally it should go on forever . . . with us having no recourse but to produce yet another bottle from an endless supply. We do not round off the action and exit with any grace but hesitate and stop awkwardly and arbitrarily. We stand exposed and naked. . . And stare at you with pleading frightened eyes. (Stevens and Wilkinson)

VI

With the self erased and slipping in this way it's no surprise to find the outside world in motion too. New work abounds with images of the city as a mutable presence, the experience of which is at the same time concrete and metaphoric. The city's clash of cultures, its blurring of territories, its organisation or lack of it, and its constant physical reinvention via building, demolition and re-use are all facts with which we struggle on a day to day basis as well as mythical and ideological indexes of larger social and personal battles.

New performance work is as rooted in the urban context of Britain's major cities as it is in the changes wrought by the media on our consciousness. The city's myths are those of transformation, collision, arrival, destruction, ruin, facelessness, fantasy and boundary-crossing.

In Station House Opera's performances *A Split Second of Paradise* (1985–6) and *The Bastille Dances* (1989) the steady workmanlike rhythms of the building site are conscious reference points, questioning our notions of timescale and event duration in both performance and the city itself. In both works we see groups of performers whose task is to rearrange hundreds of light-weight concrete blocks, creating a constantly changing architectural environment. In the words of Julian Maynard-Smith, director of the company:

> Architecture is usually thought of as something which exists outside of the people who inhabit it. [Here] . . . architecture becomes as intimate as clothing, a changing and individual expression of the protagonists character and situation. At one time it is exterior and monumental, at another close fitting and mobile. (Maynard-Smith)

The central image of the ambitious project *The Bastille Dances*, presented on the bicentennial of the storming of the Bastille, was the physical destruction of the Bastille itself and the appropriation of its stones – ' . . . only in revolution', wrote Maynard-Smith 'where the city walls . . . are demolished to make houses or cobblestones dug up to make barricades are the immediate materials to hand used in such a potent way' (Maynard-Smith). *Bastille Dances*, with some eighteen participants, was a durational performance that lasted five continuous days and nights, and included special heightened periods of performance each evening. It was staged, with a curious irony, beside the Royal National Theatre on the south bank of the Thames. Indeed, a good part of the interest in this decorative, almost whimsical and beautifully lit performance of building and work lay in its being presented within the real context of the city with its building sites and workers and its lives.

In an established tradition of such discrete, almost viral intrusions on the actual fabric of the city, Fiona Templeton's *You – the City* (1989) approached the interface between text, performer presence, audience consciousness and real places. In it one was led, as an audience of one, by a series of single performers, through a series of actual locations in the East End of London, starting at an office in the financial district by Liverpool Street Station and then on foot through Spitalfields Market and the Bangladeshi community on Brick Lane, by taxi to a set of high-rise flats, and then on, again on foot.

Barraged verbally throughout by a dense poetic text turning constantly on the word 'you', one was forever either invited, forced or seduced into making replies, trying to be in the scene or trying simply to watch it, making different senses of ones apparent relationships with the performers (some playing alienated and theatrical, others all filmic and intimate) and also of the apparent contingencies between text and environment. The old dialectical separations between inside and outside, fiction and reality, self and other, audience and performer, were here exploited and blurred, leaving the strangest sense that the city and oneself were now almost the same thing, a shifting network of narratives, places, touches, voices, lost puns, myths and intimacies (Templeton).

It's not far from here to the city as pure self-image, pure autobiography. This is the city which in our own (*Let the Water Run Its Course*) *To the Sea that Made the Promise* (1986) the characters named and renamed, more an index of their own decay or love than of any real place:

> WOMAN: They named it and renamed it every day, despite the bitter cold. They called it remarkable city, alphabet city, alphabetti city, New Milan and The Capital City of Britain.
> MAN: They sat up some nites and renamed it and their love grew as they named it: the city of spires, the Kentucky Fried city, the city of Elvis King, the exploding city, the city of joy.
> WOMAN: Part Three was more names for the Black City.
> MAN: In the dark they called it fuck city, shit city, blood city, sperm city, cock city, prick city, cunt city, twat city, bum city, arse city, shitty city, ridiculous city, stupid city. (Etchells)

VII

Two final things I want to pull out of the quicksand.

First a point about landscape or location. Jurg Woodtli, a promoter in Zürich, once praised a piece of our work because it so clearly came from a place. I think that's important because there's too much work that looks like it was born on the floor of some nameless, placeless Euro-Novotel. It's important because in all the work I care about it's an engagement with a particular landscape (literal, literary, cultural, mythic even personal) which seems to give it heart, and hate, and, in the case of Britain perhaps a certain kind of smallness and of melancholy. You can see the UK landscape in all the work of ex-Impact Theatre Co-Operative – from Brooks and MacDonald's *Utopia* with its cities and gardens, through Axis Mundi's *The Haunting Tree* (1988) with its roots in Walton's *The Compleat Angler*, through Heather Ackroyd's *Uses of Enchantment* (1989) on its stage of real grass, through Steve Shill's estate agent in *A Fine Film of Ashes* to the arid suburban marriage *The Little Theatre* (1991), and of course in Graeme Miller's *Dungeness* (1987) and *A Girl Skipping* (1990).

Miller has centered on the idea of memory contained in a place, not so much real memory as invoked memory. He said of Dungeness, the village on the coast which provided inspiration for his work of the same name: 'It is a marginal place, capable of evoking a disturbing sense of nostalgia, not a recollection of known memories, but rather, a profound recognition of events unknown and lives unlived' (Miller).

In his more recent *A Girl Skipping*, by attempting to transform time and space in a series of mutated children's games, the cast of five invoke a series of fragments – collective futures, pasts and dreamtimes all sharing innocence and its loss as a primary theme. Built on a sense of play both comically transgressive and almost spiritually transcendent *A Girl Skipping* is also very much concerned with the animation of space. It's as much about the ruined dreams written deep in its detailed reconstruction of a school playground (complete with puddles, faded paint lines, a drain) as it is about anything else.

I'm not talking about a UK landscape as a purely nostalgic invocation. I mean it more crucially in a very here and now way. In terms of our position to the US media empire, there is a need and desire by artists like Keith Khan to rewrite the landscape from a black viewpoint, and the need by Bobby Baker, and Annie Griffin and Neil Bartlett to remake the landscape for themselves and their communities, and the need by groups like ourselves, Dogs in Honey, Alison Andrews Company and newer groups like The

Engine Room, Reckless Sleepers, Pants, Blast Theory, Stan's Cafe, Bodies in Flight, and Index to work out and work through and work against the landscape of our cities, our sexualities, and our selves.

VIII

And finally, the last thought. At the end of her performance of *Moses* (1987) Rose English lies back on a four poster bed and closes her eyes. All through the piece she's been asking characteristic, rather grand Zen questions and making little jokes about whether we're going to see something truly remarkable in the theatre tonight, about whether the very big and the very small can be together in the same moment, about whether she or the little girl Dorothy who is her companion in the piece might ever get somewhere fantastic if only they try, and all through the performance Dorothy has been the perfect foil, the straight man, if you get what I mean, and never sure if the very big and the very small can be together at the same time and not quite sure if, by trying, they might get somewhere fantastic at all.

Anyway, near the end, English closes her eyes and lies back and Dorothy appears, beautifully, in a tiny little boat on a tiny illuminated stage set back in the performance space, sailing across between the red curtains, softly lit by the footlights. Only when the boat has disappeared does English wake up and ask of the audience if they have seen what she can only dream 'Did they get there ? Did they get there ?', she asks, all excited, as if she hopes they really did (English).

In short I want to put in a vote for transcendence, for escape into fiction. It can be quoted, problematized, self-doubting, incomplete. It can be like Julian Maynard-Smith at the end of Station House's *Cuckoo* (1987) suspended on a platform fourteen feet above the stage looking around like he's not sure how he got to this new place here or why, it can be like Lee, finally appearing to Marina after 'years' of absence in our own *Marina & Lee* – a long lost love returning, but only on video and dead, and in a false nose anyway, but he's still there for her and it still, really, is quite beautiful and it might even be love, or else a need for fiction and a dream.

REFERENCES

Baker, Bobby. *Kitchen Show: One Dozen Kitchen Actions Made Public,* a text of the performance with photographs, 1991. (Available from Artsadmin, 295 Kentish Town Road, London NW5 2TJ.)

Bartlett, Neil. 'Getting Up in the Dark', Steve Rogers Memorial Lecture, 1990. (Available as a video from Nottingham Polytechnic, Creative Arts).

Bartlett, Neil. *A Vision of Love Revealed in Sleep,* in *Gay Plays: Four.* London: Methuen, 1990.

English, Rose. *Moses,* unpublished performance text, 1987.

Etchells, Tim. *(Let the Water Run Its Course) To the Sea That Made the Promise,* unpublished Forced Entertainment text, 1986.

Forced Entertainment Theatre Co-Operative. *200% & Bloody Thirsty* publicity document, 1986.

MacDonald, Claire, and Pete Brooks. *Letters from a Hotel (Utopia Trilogy, Part II),* unpublished text, 1989.

Maynard-Smith, Julian. Notes on *The Bastille Dances,* unpublished, 1989.

Miller, Graeme. Interview by Lyn Gardner, *City Limits,* 30 Sep 1987.

Shill, Steve. *A Fine Film of Ashes,* unpublished performance text, 1988.

Sontag, Susan. *On Photography.* New York: Penguin, 1979.

Stevens, Gary and Caroline Wilkinson. *If the Cap Fits,* unpublished performance text, 1986–7.

Stevens, Gary. Interviewed by the author. *City Limits,* 9 Nov 1989.

Templeton, Fiona. *You – The City.* (Text published by Roof Books, The Segue Foundation, 303 East 8th St., New York, NY 10009.)

Wenders, Wim. *Kings of the Road.* A Wim Wenders film for Wim Wenders Productions, 1976.

Williams, Raymond. *Television, Society and Cultural Form.*

9

Experimental Theatre in Scotland

Alasdair Cameron

Philip Prowse, the distinguished designer and director and member of the triumvirate that runs the Glasgow Citizens' Theatre, once quipped that he only went to the theatre in London to keep *'au courant* with what is *deja vue'* (Prowse). Until recently this could have been dismissed as bravado; certainly not an accurate reflection of the state of British Theatre, as London had always been, indisputably, the centre of British Theatre. Anyone wishing to sample a whole range of new theatre work, or to experience fresh approaches to staging would have needed to stir no further north than London's Round House or further south than the Oval House. While it is true that some theatre companies like Impact or Welfare State chose to create highly-acclaimed work outside London, in Leeds and in the Lake District respectively, even they needed to show their work in the capital in order to secure funding and critical recognition. Very occasionally a company like the Royal Exchange in Manchester or the Glasgow Citizens' would forge a distinctive style which set it apart from the amorphous mass of 'provincial' theatres.

But, by the beginning of 1990, Prowse's *bon mots* had become the *mots justes*. The *dernier cri* in interesting and experimental theatre work was to be found, not in London, but in Glasgow. The reasons for the dramatic switch are clear. First, one the principal supporters of the Arts in London, The Greater London Council was abolished in 1986, with the result that over one million pounds a year in grants disappeared. At about the same time, property values and the cost of living in London soared, thus adding enormously to the cost of running a theatre or mounting productions in London. Finally, the government was applying a 'value for money' policy towards the arts and seeking to substitute private for public subsidy, both factors which discourage minority-interest experimental theatre.

By contrast, Glasgow in the 1980s provided a much more encouraging environment for the arts. The city had determined to rid itself of its long-standing reputation for grimness, and one strand in their strategy was through the arts. As well as setting a high value on the arts for their own sake, Glasgow District Council took the view that a prestigious and successful artistic life would bring economic benefits to the city. Accordingly, Glasgow invested heavily in its theatrical infrastructure and developed a generous system of funding. This policy was crowned in 1987 when the city was designated as European City of Culture for 1990, following Berlin, Amsterdam and Paris.

There are many features of the theatre programme surrounding Glasgow's year as European City of Culture which deserve discussion. Funding bodies like the Festivals Unit programmed and financially supported the special events associated with the year. These included venues like the Tramway and the Tron, organisations like New Beginnings and the Third Eye Centre, and individuals like Nikki Milican, all of which have been responsible for remarkable pieces of theatre. Much of this work was well outside the text-bound mainstream of British theatre. It was produced sometimes by visual artists, for whom the image is more important than the word, or by artists from abroad who reject the whole notion of fidelity to a text along with the traditional British practice of 'block it, learn it and get on with it' school of theatre production. Much of the most interesting work also crossed the rigid boundaries so beloved of mainstream British theatre and resulted from creative and liberating inter-disciplinary work between dancers, performers, visual artists and sculptors. Such innovatory and experimental work co-existed with the blockbuster productions, which are a seemingly necessary part of the Culture City remit, and the less spectacular, but equally valuable, continuing programmes of work produced by the Glasgow's own theatres.

John Myerscough's recent report, *The Economic Importance of the Arts in Glasgow*, vindicated the commercial and public relations aspects of Glasgow's policy for the arts. It concluded that though the arts make a small but significant contribution to the city's economy, the presence of a wide range of arts organisations makes it significantly more likely that firms will move to the city. A recent survey conducted for the Scottish Arts Council, has also shown that Glasgow District Council's policy of investing in the arts is popular with Glasgow's voters. Because of its political and economic importance, the city's arts policy has to have a high profile. This may mean a hugely popular Pavarotti concert or a visit by the Bolshoi Opera Company, but it is new and challenging work which is guaranteed extensive, positive and enthusiastic press and television coverage in which the city is discussed in the same breath as Paris or Berlin.

Confirmation of this came when the Festivals Unit headed by Robert Palmer with Neil Wallace as his deputy, was set up in 1987 to coordinate the cultural programme for 1990. Their first production, in 1988, was Peter Brook's *Mahabharata*. This not only provided the city with publicity undreamed of, as Brook's eight hour epic had no other performances in Britain, but with a new theatre, the Tramway. This was a former tram depot and Museum of Transport, which seemed to have all the features, not the least of which was an industrial past and the appearance of impending dereliction, which gives so many other prestigious European theatre buildings like the Bouffes du Nord or the Cartoucherie de Vincennes in Paris and the Mercat dels Flors in Barcelona, their special atmosphere. The main playing area is long and wide with a high glass roof which is usually boarded up and a rough pitted and plastered back wall set deep behind exposed red brick wings which can serve as a gestural proscenium arch.

The availability of theatre spaces other than Victorian theatres and black boxes is, in itself, a catalyst for experimentation and the exploration of new forms of staging and theatre. Mainstream Scottish theatre is even more conservative and text-bound than the English theatre, and the opening of the Tramway encouraged many companies to expand their horizons and plan productions on a scale they had hitherto never contemplated. The Tramway also gave Scottish theatre the opportunity to introduce new production styles into familiar material. The first to benefit from this was Wildcat Theatre Company whose production of *Border Warfare*, directed by John McGrath, used the ideas of Ronconi and Mnouchkine to illustrate 2000 years of Anglo-Scottish agit-prop history. Ronconi's free-floating platforms, some like caparisoned warhorses, conjured up the spirit of the middle ages, while eighteenth century political debate was brought alive by the use of Mnouchkine's techniques of direct crowd address and manipulation. Though the techniques were familiar on the continent, this was the first time they had been applied to a Scottish play and the result was a great popular success.

Partly because of its very rough and unfinished appearance, the Tramway is now perceived as a 'democratic' space, welcoming to everybody and less off-putting to those who normally avoid more traditional theatres. It also inspired many Scottish theatre directors to put into action plans which would have seemed impossible until the space became available. For example there was *City*, a huge community play which attempted to draw together performers from all over Glasgow. The project was coordinated by TAG theatre company; the text, called 'Malachie's Dream', was written by Tom McGrath and design and staging were by Neil Murray and Alan Lydiard. The cast of over two hundred performers and musicians, included many differently-abled actors, for whom the possibility of working on an equal footing with the rest of the cast was a source of great satisfaction. *City* was a journey through Glasgow's history from the dawn of time to the future. It used an expressionist vision of the eighteenth century neo-classical city for the past, a huge hospital ward for the present and for the future, outside behind the building, a 'Mad Max'-style waste ground full of rusting household appliances and lit by numerous fires.

In 1990 a second version of the play was performed on four sites scattered around the city, including the impressive Victorian Necropolis. The audience moved from site to site in buses and the event culminated, to the astonishment of other travellers, in the Glasgow's main bus depot. *City* may have proved to be over-ambitious in its aim of welding together all the very disparate communities which make up Glasgow, but it inspired some of these communities to create their own plays on a vast scale with some help from professional performers, writers, directors and designers. The tenants on a run-down housing estate called Ruchazie did just this in 1990 when, with the theatre company Fablevision, they turned a derelict block of flats into a set and used a whole street as a theatre, in an attempt to trace the post-war history of their community.

The Tramway also proved to be a stimulus for Communicado Theatre Company, a group whose much-praised work has mainly been based on classic texts like *Carmen*, but whose production style has always been inventively imagistic. They initiated the 1990 theatre programme with *Jock Tamson's Bairns*, a vast 'state of the nation play' built round the annual Scottish ritual of the Burns Supper at which a haggis is ceremonially eaten. In this piece the haggis was a decent Scottish 'new man', a questing artist who was also intended to represent the female side of the Scottish psyche. *Jock Tamson's Bairns*, the phrase means 'all God's children', was the result of a collaboration between the poet and playwright Liz Lochhead, the director Gerry Mulgrew and the artist Keith McIntyre. The play was presented by a devilish group of 'Bairns' or children, who would sometimes combine into a mob and sometimes act as individuals. The Bairns all had names like 'Clipe' (tell-tale), drawn from the memories of school of Scots over thirty, and part of the play was a litany of evocative Scots words from the backgrounds of this same generation, words which the majority of the audience also knew. The collaboration also attempted to examine the myths of the Scottish macho-male and his incapacity to create easy and natural relationships with Scottish women. The supper came to a cataclysmic and pessimistic end when the Bairns hunted and devoured their human quarry.

In 1991, Communicado also brought to the Tramway their adaptation of Robin Jenkins' metaphorical novel of regeneration, *The Cone Gatherers*, one of the very few pieces of environmental theatre Scotland had seen. The canopy of a West Highland pine forest was suggested by camouflage netting, there were clumps of pine trees set at intervals on a floor spread with real bark. The audience sat on logs on either side of the traverse playing space at one end of which stood the laird's mansion and at the other, the gamekeeper's cottage and a summer house. The director Gerry Mulgrew evoked the sounds and smells of the forest, created rainstorms using basins of water and staged a deer hunt with the actors playing both the hunters and the hunted. His production was imbued with a sense of menace and the heightened introversion of a small country estate trying to survive in wartime. As sometimes happens though, the effects outweighed the drama; character and plot, still central to Mulgrew's ideas of theatre, were lost in a display of vintage cars and bicycles.

Some of the same problems befell Bill Bryden's *The Ship*, the most spectacular site-specific piece of theatre specially commissioned for 1990. The play, a sentimental look at the decline of shipbuilding on the Clyde, was almost incidental to the staging. John Napier's set was the framework of the Queen Elizabeth II, the last liner to be built on Clydeside, and was constructed in one of the last remaining shipbuilding sheds on the Clyde. The acting area was

within the skeleton of the ship and the audience were physically
shaken by the laying of the keel, deafened by the riveters' hammers
and surrounded by the flames from welders' torches. Though the
script was thin, when a section of the set slid away and seemed to
be launched into the river at the end of the play, the audience was
treated to a moment of spectacle that no heritage centre presentation
could hope to rival and it was hard not to feel, with the shipbuilders,
a pride in the process of industrial creation on the Clyde and a
genuine regret at its passing.

The legacy of urban and industrial decline was also central
to other recent productions in Glasgow, in particular those of
the theatre group Brith Gof and the band Test Department both
individually and together. Brith Gof's *Gododdin*, which started life
in an abandoned car factory in Cardiff, came to Glasgow in 1989 and
gave the city a taste of Celtic theatre created without reference to the
London mainstream. *Gododdin* brought a taste of dangerous theatre
to the Tramway with its evocation of the last stand of a beleaguered
Welsh tribe, the seemingly indiscriminate hurling of trees, the
unleashing of huge quantities of water and the deployment by
the industrial percussion band, Test Department, of a vast array
of metal drums.

The guiding idea of *Gododdin*, to explore what it means to be
Welsh, was adapted by Test Department in 1990 to create *The Second
Coming*, a multi-media presentation of a text by the journalist Neal
Ascherson, which attempted to do the same for Scotland and the
Scots. *The Second Coming* was performed in another industrial space,
the St. Rollox Engineering Works, where Test Department combined the smell of oil, multi-screen projection and heavy industrial
machinery with a startling exploitation of the unusual perspectives
afforded by the forest of columns which supported the glass roof.
There were voices raised in protest at the nationalistic and, some
claimed, fascistic, overtones of some of the military drill, but with
the inventive use the twenty drummers made of the industrial
objects trouvé in the factory, allied to a thought-provoking and witty
script, the evening was an invigorating, if not a very comfortable,
experience.

Brith Gof have also brought *Los Angeles* and *Pax* to Glasgow.
Together with *Gododdin* they form a trilogy of pieces – past, present
and future – which predicted the saving of the planet by forces of
good which speak Welsh, the language of Heaven. *Pax*, the final
part, is undeniably impressive. It re-unites elements from the earlier

pieces, notably the use of trees, water, wind machines, powerful lights and magical descents from the ceiling. The playing space for *Pax* was the same factory shed used for *The Ship*. But where Bill Bryden had used industrial decline to indulge in nostalgia, Brith Gof raged at the destruction of the planet by industrial conglomerates. *Pax* was an opera with an ethereal score played by musicians who sat and sang in tall scaffolding towers which encircled the playing space. The cycle of plays culminated in the descent of the angels to wreak vengeance on the despoilers of the earth and to preach reconciliation between man and his environment. Using swirling mists, blasts of light, and songs of praise, the sheer force of the piece was physically shaking and a strikingly successful union of theatre, music and message.

Long before Glasgow's year as City of Culture, the main international arts event in Scotland, and in Britain, was the Edinburgh Festival. Unfortunately, Scottish theatre practitioners have, in the main, ignored Edinburgh's dramatic imports. In the autumn of 1989, however, the New Beginnings Festival gave Glasgow a taste of the benefits which native theatre could derive from the diverse events which such a festival brings. New Beginnings introduced to Glasgow some of the then Soviet Union's most interesting new theatre work and was notable not just for a prolonged exposure to the work of the Lithuanian director Nekrosius, but for the directors and actors from the Moscow Art Theatre's experimental Chelovyek Studio who worked with three Scottish actors on a production of Ludmilla Petrushevskya's *Cinzano*. Despite what to the Russians was the absurdly short, but standard British rehearsal time of three weeks, the play made a tremendous critical and popular impact. The three Scottish actors incorporated into their performances such standard European practices as acknowledging outside noises, in this case the trains rumbling past the theatre, and used them in their performances. The production also used such potent theatrical images as the central character shivering on the ledge of a high stained glass window – the theatre is a converted church – as rain poured down the windows lit from the outside. The productions of Nekrosius, an *Uncle Vanya* of palpable emotional turmoil and *Pirosmani Pirosmani* which utilised, with the genius of a Lubymov, a large window with wooden shutters and bentwood chairs, was an object lesson in how to shape theatrical images and create an atmosphere which is felt by the audience. The despair and melancholy of the painters wretched life was conveyed by the use of harsh bleak grey lighting and a large dirty shop-front with dusty windows placed centre stage. The windows were written and drawn on and the dust wiped into holes. Pirosmani's death was unforgettably marked by the ruthless piling up of a huge number of the bentwood chairs into an unsteady heap, like earth on a grave.

These new and very promising beginnings were coordinated by Christopher Carrell, at that time Director of the Third Eye Centre. The Third Eye Centre, in the heart of the city, had opened in 1975 and by 1990 its theatre and performance programme was under the much admired direction of Nikki Milican who had settled in Glasgow after a spell as a performer and then as Performance Director at the Midland Group in Nottingham. She is one of that very rare breed in British arts – an innovative producer. Milican provides more than just the money necessary to give effect to an idea. Through the Third Eye she provides what she calls the 'support structures', which enable experimental artists to develop their work. Milican explains her philosophy as follows:

> Collaborations enable the Third Eye Centre to build more creative partnerships between artist and producer and to improve the conditions under which the work will be undertaken. Given that our own resources cannot often match those of other producers, a prime concern . . . is to build support structures for artists, structures which, for the performer can be equally as important as project finance: the Third Eye Centre aims to offer a complete range of support facilities, providing rehearsal time and spaces, technical and administrative back-up, publicity, marketing and production assistance. (Milican)

It is in the commissioning policy of Milican and the Third Eye that Glasgow's new theatre policies are seen at their strongest and work at their best and most challenging. Unlike others with a similar role in the British theatre, Milican commissions theatre pieces rather than plays. She also takes exhilarating risks. Lloyd Newson of the dance company DV8 [Photo 2] remembers that before creating *Dead Dreams of Monochrome Men*, one of the great British successes of 1989, she told him, 'I want you to risk everything creating this'. She gives her artists no blueprint, just the chance to create and if necessary to fail, in an 'artist-friendly' environment.

Milican's commissions have ranged from the widely seen and much praised *Dead Dreams of Monochrome Men* and Neil Bartlett's

Sarrassine, to much more modest pieces like Bobby Baker's culinary performance art [Photo 9], which can include sitting on, and melting, a large bag of chocolate drops. What Milican offers her artists is time, space and money to develop their work. Ralf Ralf's production of *Dinner*, for example , which was eventually given its full premiere at Jacob's Pillow, was developed over a period of a year through the Third Eye Centre. This piece, colourful and fast moving, based loosely on everyone's need not only to eat but to eat in company, was a chance for a group of performers, who did not even have a common language, to work together using music and movement.

The success of her commissioning policy has been widely recognised, but Milican's concerns as producer go beyond performance, and she has encouraged interested members of the public to become involved in the creation of her commissions. This has been done by funding companies to undertake lengthy residencies in the city, opening rehearsals and workshops to the public, and even involving them in the actual productions. In 1990, for example, Simon Thorne and Philip Mackenzie, who the year previously had created *The Acts of Man* [Photo 12] for Milican's Man Acts programme, were invited to make another piece for a group of Glasgow men. *The Acts of Man* had been an exploration of a man's life from birth to death and the new piece, *The Sweatlodge*, explored some of the same concerns but on a more general and less personal level. This way of connecting with the local audience, but using professional actors rather than amateurs, was also used by Ralf Ralf in *Dinner* and Robert Lepage in *Tectonic Plates*.

The Sweatlodge used the idea of the male as peacock preening himself in sexual display, hiding his insecurities beneath smartly cut suits. The techniques used were simple and presentational such as repeated movement and the swish of the catwalk. Pop video techniques such as backlighting and swirling smoke created images of twenty be-suited men advancing on the audience through red clouds or waltzing gently together backlit through dry ice. The excitement conveyed by the performers, some of whom had no experience of movement work before the rehearsals began, justified this commission in social as well as artistic terms.

Many of Milican's commissions have concentrated on sexuality and sexual ambiguity, in particular gay sexuality and society's perceptions and distortions of it. These concerns lie behind the best known and most widely seen of Milican's commissions – Neil Bartlett's *A Vision of Love Revealed in Sleep* [Photo 5] and *Sarrassine* and DV8's *Dead Dreams of Monochrome Men*. No-one in the audience, even those who had seen some of the rehearsals, was quite prepared for the very physical assault of *Dead Dreams*. Against black walls were an incongruously domestic chest of drawers, a cold white functional bath and a vast mirror. Using these simple household icons the company laid bare the mass murderer Dennis Nilson's horrific but logical and carefully self-analysed life story. The four dancers threw themselves at the walls, suspended themselves from hydraulic meathooks and drowned in baths. At times dressed only in white underpants, they looked the audience straight in the eye challenging them to make simplistic moral judgements. They created persuasive images of loneliness and rejection but juxtaposed these with distressing scenes of the victims' failed attempts to escape by repeatedly trying to scale the high, slippery black wall. The subsequent success of the piece on television has made it widely known but the claustrophobia of that first performance in a tiny studio theatre was sufficient to persuade even the most die-hard cynic that there is no substitute for live, dangerous theatre.

Some of the best known and most widely performed results of the Third Eye commissioning programme, have been those theatre pieces undertaken in conjunction with Gloria, an umbrella organisation whose artists are known for their remarkable re-workings of familiar stories such as their dark dangerous and musical *Lady Audley's Secret*. Neil Bartlett in particular, has had a long association with Milican who in her time at the Midland group was the first to put money into his one-man version of *A Vision of Love Revealed in Sleep* which premiered in London on the Edwardian stairway in Battersea Arts Centre. The piece was later reworked and produced in a Docklands warehouse with pools of water on the floor and lit by candles; and subsequently was presented in a darkened Third Eye Studio glowing with Robin Whitmore's luminous frescos inspired by the work of the Victorian painter and poet Simeon Solomon. Bartlett's play drew pertinent analogies between Solomon's persecution for his homosexuality and the persecution he perceived the government of Mrs Thatcher to be indulging in, fuelled by a widespread ignorance of the causes of AIDS. The show was later extended to include the talents of several notable drag queens including Bette Bourne whose defiant personal memories achieved the remarkable feat of stealing the show from a naked Neil Bartlett.

Bartlett's next piece, *Sarrasine*, was one of the most remarkable pieces of theatre to appear in Glasgow or perhaps anywhere in 1990. *Sarrasine* was based on the short story of the same name by Balzac which had been highlighted by Roland Barthes in his influential essay 's/z'. The play however owed much more to Bartlett and the composer Nicholas Bloomfield who turned the intricate tale of sexual ambiguity, jealousy and revenge into a an all-enveloping sensual theatre piece. Giles Havergal once said that the real appeal of his very earliest productions at the Citizens' was the blood and the sex. (Havergal) Bartlett, a great admirer of Havergal and his productions gave *Sarrassine*, in addition to blood and lust, satisfying dollops of opera, mystery, transvestism and money.

Although the piece was first performed at the Edinburgh Festival Fringe where it opened at the Traverse Theatre, Bartlett created a special site performance for the Third Eye Centre. Nikki Milican had been one of the producers and provided one of the main sources of finance for the project. The stairs to the performance area were painted and stencilled with designs which echoed the architecture of the building by the Glasgow architect 'Greek Thomsom' whose classical revival work often has a distinctive acanthus-leaf decoration. There was an especially created foyer for the performance which transformed the audience into worshippers as desperate to hear La Zambinella as was the wealthy and mysterious American woman whose money had paid for this, his last appearance. The audience waited in a shabby anti-chamber, lit only by the orange street lamps of the real world outside, until the arrival of a taxi signalled that the evening's devotions were about to begin. Bartlett's restless pacing added to the tension but gave the audience time to note the dead leaves on the floor, the covered lamps, the litter of music scores and the mundane flask of tea for the musicians.

Rather bewildered and disoriented, the audience filed into the room where La Zambinella, who at this point was 260 years old, was to appear. The sound of heels on the stone steps heralded the mysterious American who entered in a shaft of bright light and proceeded to change into the 'robe gris et rose' which she had worn when she first heard La Zambinella sing thirty years before. As the lights became brighter, various elements in the set were revealed. At the front was a small stage with hooded footlights, empty champagne bottles littered the floor, heavy velvet swags hung from the roof and, in the dim half-light, far at the back of the deep narrow stage, there was a dimly lit painting of an androgenous figure.

Very slowly out of the dusty twilight a figure dressed in a heavy cape appeared. At first glance it seemed to be a venerable gentlewoman, an impression shattered with her first words, 'let them wait, let them fuckin' wait', when it became clear that the figure was neither gentle nor a woman. Over the next two hours this elderly vaudevillian Zambinella with her two alter egos – one played by a dancer, Francois Testory, the other played by Beverly Klein as a torch-song singer – slowly pieced together the story of La Zambinella, and provided a mocking commentary on it, usually in song. Although Nicholas Bloomfield, the composer and Musical Director, provided some wonderful delicate parodies of eighteenth and nineteenth century opera, his showstoppers were two raunchy music-hall numbers – 'It Took Me Ten Whole Days to Make Him Love Me' and 'Don't Give Nothing Away'. *Sarrasine* plunged its audience into a baroque labyrinth of cardinals, castrati, calculation, catholicism and crime. Just the kind of mixture prurient protestant audiences have relished from the Jacobean age onwards.

Sarrasine was an unusual attempt to create a work of art which made the audience an active part of the play. The daring structure strung together visual, literary, cabaret and musical theatre in a series of vignettes on a strong narrative thread. The production was witty and post-modern in its eclecticism, mocking and teasing in its explorations of the deceptions of appearance. This was most apparent in the costumes – black velvet for Beverly Klein and diamonds for Francois Testory. Bette Bourne as La Zambinella had elements of the costumes of her two alter egos in her moth-eaten velvet cloak which, like the good fairy in disguise in pantomime, was shed to reveal a gorgeous frock for her moments as a chanteuse. The only false note in the show was the attempt to overload the play with gay politics. Bartlett insists that as a gay artist his art is gay and political. But whereas the chilling repetition of 'young man, if you want to be happy be careful', with its dual warning against both queerbashing and AIDS, seemed an organic part of the world of Sarrasine, Bette Bourne's litany of offensive words for gay, though enlightening, seemed tacked on.

During 1990 the Third Eye Centre's saw attendances at its events rise 50 percent over the previous year's figures to 450,000. But the year was not just filled with special events, and their programme included annual fixtures like The National Review of Live Art. This is an intensive weekend of performances, lectures and installations which provide a platform for new work. For the last seven years, the National Review has been programmed by Nikki Milican who developed it into a showcase for new ideas in performance, always displaying a series of techniques which more mainstream theatre practitioners could use if they didn't fight shy of anything which smacks of non-verbal theatre. Performance artists in the main, because their background is usually art schools, tend to despise traditional theatre. This inevitably leads to the situation where the words in performance pieces are often their weak point just as mainstream theatre pieces can disappear under a load of verbiage through which a few sharp visual images could cut. Neil Bartlett is a rare exception to this; he is equally aware of the power of words and images and this helps to give his work its edge. Perhaps his awareness is heightened by his annual role as compere of the National Review in a Coco Chanel 'little black frock' and beads. Some idea of how the performance artists who appear at the NRLA can enliven mainstream theatre was provided by Richard Jones' production of *A Flea in Her Ear*, designed by the Brothers Quay, in which Rose English, who appeared at the 1990 Review in Glasgow, smouldered in a series of purple picture hats and brought to Feydeau her own brand of devastating eccentricity.

The National Review also uses a mixture of new performers and established artists such as Derek Jarman whose animated installation at the 1989 Review explored the relationship between sport, violence and homosexuality by juxtaposing Celtic and Rangers football strips, two male lovers in bed in a cage, police uniforms, pornographic images and homophobic tabloid headlines.

Indeed, it is often sexual politics which provides the National Review with its most fruitful field of exploration. In 1990, Fiona Wright's *Bride Kicks* used an 8mm projector to throw images of screaming, panic and questioning on to the stomach of a bride dressed in virginal white with Doc Martin boots peeping out from beneath its lacy hem. Lisa Watts' *Breadmaking* was especially memorable; a messy deconstruction in dough reminiscent of the 60s standard sexist performance piece in which a naked woman is pulled through paint leaving a print of her body on paper. Watts was dressed in full suburban housewife fig with a handbag full of dough into which she kneaded a lifetimes' domestic neuroses with her body and at the end left a satisfyingly gooey print on the wall of the art gallery.

The Third Eye's particular expertise was used to develop long term strategies in which new ideas could be explored, opened out, explained and incorporated into more traditional forms of theatre. The process is the very antithesis of the ad hockery of most attempts to influence British mainstream theatre. Their continuing programme of education and experimentation in Glasgow was given a unique boost by the 1990 theatre programme funded by the Festivals Unit which provided numerous satisfying syntheses of word and image and abundant alternatives to traditional theatre forms. There was, for example, the Wooster Group who brought a range of work from their most famous, *L.S.D. (. . . Just the High Points . . .)*, to their latest work-in-progress *Brace Up* based on Chekhov's *The Three Sisters*. Both shows revealed their mastery of the New York laid-back, dry-as-a-martini-at-the-Algonquin style which infuses literary texts and hi-tec gadgetry. Ingmar Bergman's *Markisinnan de Sade* showed how the poise, stillness and stylisation of Eastern theatre, eagerly sought by so many performance artists, can succeed in a traditional Western setting. Above all, and using similar ideas of theatre to Bergman's, there was *Deshima* – the Mickery Theatre's collaboration with New York director Ping Chong.

At the start of *Deshima* the audience was confined in a small closed box on hydraulic suspension like a hovercraft. This moved across the Tramway with many sound effects of travel until a curtain opened to reveal a stage with a conveyer belt floor backed by Japanese white-paper screens. Using oriental stylisation, almost never seen in British productions, *Deshima* made an imaginative link between Western, in this case Dutch, exploitation of the East and its revenge through Japanese acquisition of Van Gogh paintings for huge sums of money. A history of Dutch involvement in Java was interspersed with personal testimonials from the actors about the involvement of their families on both sides of colonialism and an ironic, stylised, commentary from a black American actor whose very presence added another dimension to this story of exploitation. At the end, the audience were again physically moved, this time into a Van Gogh painting which was brought to life with a clockwork train which crossed the horizon and the distribution of stuffed crows by the actors who also appeared as reapers. *Deshima* was able, by using a mixture of dance, projections, oriental theatre conventions, images and a spare poetic text to subject history and cultural relations to the kind of scrutiny in one hour which would take mainstream theatre, using a linear narrative and verbal arguments, at least a whole evening.

For a Scottish audience, perhaps most satisfying of all the imports, was Robert Lepage's *Tectonic Plates*. Using local actors to work on a text which had already been performed in various versions in Canada, Lepage and his company created a theatre piece which started from the premise that continents are in continual metaphorical collision. Using a specially built stage which had the audience peering down from scaffolding on to a huge pool of black water flanked by playing areas, the company unfolded narratives which seemed utterly fragmented, but were shown by the end to be circular, though worked out over hundreds of years. An ancient Scottish goddess, Skadi, wreaked revenge on a transvestite Canadian in a late night cinema in Greenwich Village, a double portrait of George Sand and Chopin was re-united in a New York diner; Alaskan men on the Oprah Winfrey show were linked to the diaspora of the Scottish Clearances and a Glaswegian drug addict in Venice. The pool of water was variously used to heighten the disturbing exploration of a father's incestuous love for his daughter, to reflect the Manhattan skyline, in reality piles of books with luminous spines, and for the projection of paintings. Nothing in Lepage's production, no prop or piece of set was there for mere decoration and everything on stage had multifarious uses. Tangible links between the theatre in Scotland and Quebec had already been established through Michael Boyd's translations of the plays of Michel Trembley presented at the Tron of Scots. These links however, were greatly strengthened by the enthusiasm which first *Tectonic Plates* and then performances of Lepage's *The Dragons' Trilogy* created amongst city audiences.

In the 80s and culminating in its selection as the 1990 European City of Culture, Glasgow took on a British and indeed a European role in theatre production and exhibition. Further, the city helped to nurture a new generation of British theatre artists. But now that the euphoria around 1990 has died down, the almost inevitable financial vacuum it has left is threatening this work. Though the final accounts have yet to be drawn up there are already casualties. The Third Eye has temporarily closed, to re-open late in 1992, after a rescue bid by the Scottish Arts Council, as the Glasgow Centre for Contemporary Arts. Many organisations, kept afloat by extra money made available in 1990, have closed and criticisms of the large sums spent on prestige theatre during 1990 are still simmering. But at least the Tramway remains.

Even though all around are voices prophesying doom, Glasgow's commitment to the new and the challenging in theatre remains, as does the city's policy of encouraging such theatre alongside the established and the traditional. Other cities are following Glasgow's cultural lead and while this is good for theatre as a whole, the city will have to work to maintain its position of pre-eminence. To compete in Europe costs money as well as demanding vision and though for one brief glorious year Glasgow showed what can be done, sustaining this dream exhausted both the city's coffers and its artists. But when the dust has settled and the questions have all been asked and answered, it should be more than a pious hope that 1990 will have marked the establishment of Glasgow's position at the 'cutting edge' of British culture.

REFERENCES

Unpublished

Havergal, Giles. A talk at the International Federation for Theatre Research Conference in Glasgow, August 1985.
Interviews and conversations with Christine Hamilton, Deputy Director of the Scottish Arts Council; Nikki Milican; Roberta Doyle, Press and Publicity Director of Scottish Ballet; Christopher Reece-Bowen, Press and Publicity Director Tramway; Neil Wallace, Director of Tramway; Alan Lydiard Artistic Director of TAG Theatre Company; Mary Brennan, Dance and Performance Art Critic of *The Glasgow Herald*.
Milican, Nikki. Quoted in an unpublished report on the Third Eye's commissioning policy undertaken in 1991.

Publications

Myerscough, John. *The Economic Importance of the Arts In Glasgow*. London: Policy Studies Institute, 1989.
Prowse, Philip. Quoted in Michael Coveney, *The Citz*, p. 120. London: Nick Hern Books, 1990.
Scottish Arts Council. The System Three poll on attitudes to the Arts in Scotland. Glasgow: Scottish Arts Council, October 1991.

10

The Welsh National Theatre: The Avant-Garde in the Diaspora

David Hughes

In September 1991 a booklet, *Export Wales*, was produced by Janec Alexander, theatre coordinator of Cardiff's Chapter Arts Centre. Its purpose was promotional and it was given wide distribution overseas. It marked an interesting reversal in the Welsh situation by ostensively defining a Welsh National Theatre made up of experimental groups. One cluster of groups, deriving from the Cardiff Laboratory Theatre (now The Centre for Performance Research), developed under the influence of Eastern European theatre practice, particularly the work of Grotowski and Barba's Odin Teatret. The influences on Moving Being, the only surviving group to gain high profile popularity from its inception, were the American postmodernists of dance, visual art, happenings and music: the artists grouped around the Cunningham Company, Cage, Rauschenberg, Johns and Cunningham himself. A cluster of movement- and text-based groups currently work in the space marked out by Moving Being, though perhaps not directly under their influence.

At the end of the seventies these two ground-breaking companies – the Cardiff Lab and Moving Being – stood out in scale and prestige in experimental Welsh theatre. Moving Being toured extensively the new circuit of university arts centres in Britain and to some extent in Europe, whilst the Lab Theatre's work was seen mainly in Europe. All the groups based at Chapter between 1972 and 1982 were situated somewhere on the continuum between Cardiff Lab's experimental physical theatre and Moving Being's mixed-media, visual-art-led performance art.

In the early eighties, both companies went through violent upheavals which left them split, but fertile ground for the emergence of a new wave of Welsh theatre – a phenomenon which Richard Gough, artistic director of The Centre for Performance Research calls, after Richard Schechner, schizogenesis. They develop by splitting apart. At that time Welsh experimental theatre was largely visual and non-verbal, text used as texture or for carrying information or to create atmosphere, rather than to develop character, situation and concepts. In the early nineties we see a re-emergence of the text, the writer and, rather than 'performers', conventionally trained actors. This is worthy of note because the situation in these experimental groups in their youth was one where it was a political gesture to be a 'performer' rather than an 'actor', and to reject the texts in favour of the living gesture and the resonant image which spoke at a more 'poetic' level than language was thought capable of doing. Richard Gough still holds to such a notion of theatre language although he is now making a case for the writer to create the kind of linguistic equivalent of the works of Magritte, Duchamp and Dali. A writing that does not call attention to itself as writing, but is of a higher, tauter, more bitter and precise order than that text which emerges from the verbal improvisations of actors.

This move to text might not seem to be a radical shift, especially as the visual and physical styles of the early years of experimentation in Wales are still strongly influential forces and besides, there were frequently textual elements in those early works. But now the discourse of these theatre-makers is full of the term 'play', not just 'text'. Most crucially, the current interest is in the possibilities of theatre text as spoken language. Whilst the formal explorations to find a new theatre language still inform much of the work, such concerns are not so universal as during the seventies and early eighties. Something has changed.

The informal National Theatre which these experimental groups constitute marks a re-location and displacement of the attempts by the conventional play-based theatre to create a building-based and classically grounded Welsh National Theatre. These experimental *Export Wales* groups have invested a great deal of time and ingenuity and integrity making work for and with the people of the rural communities and small towns. The more conventional contenders for the Welsh National Theatre crown thought of their rightful place as being something approaching the monumental luxury of the English

Royal National Theatre building; instead, after opening their productions in Cardiff or Bangor, they grudgingly took their watered
down versions of classic Welsh and English plays, with sets hastily
redesigned, to village halls and scout huts and small local theatres.
The Welsh experimental theatres, on the other hand, consciously
played to small audiences at Chapter Arts Centre, where most of
them were based through the seventies and early eighties, and it
was no compromise for them to work in small communities on small
scale projects, slowly building up trust, understanding, a shared
theatrical language and, most importantly, an openness amongst
their audience for new, unfamiliar theatrical and spoken languages.
Geoff Moore, artistic director of Moving Being, maintains that the
sense of being parochial to London is gone, and a new de-centred
model operates.

This independence from London was evident in the Welsh contingent of experimental groups at the Theatre and Nations conference
held in Glasgow in 1991. Mike Pearson of Brith Gof and Geoff Moore
both observed that the Welsh had nothing to fight for. Unlike the
Scottish who were still arguing the possibility of a National Theatre,
the Welsh were silent, realising that *they* were the Welsh National
Theatre, that the situation had, for the present, resolved itself, and
that plurality, diversity and a de-centred network of groups were
providing what a centralised monumental institution could not.
Indeed, in Wales there are two factors that have militated against
the practicality of such an institution reflecting nationhood through
a textual canon and a unitary, unifying language. The population of
Wales is scattered and culturally divided, its conurbations and cities
polarised between the Welsh speaking North and English South.
Cardiff, administrative capital, is not easily accessible to most Welsh
people. Wales is still a country of small rural communities grouped
around market towns.

The amateur dramatic, literary, poetical and musical cultures
have been rooted in the domestic situation – in the community,
the pubs and chapels – and there has been the feeling that there
is no place or need for a professional theatre. Amateur actors have
worked extensively in Welsh theatre and television whilst maintaining their lives as shopkeepers, teachers and clergy. And so it seems
logical that a theatre that would have some meaning in Wales would
be one also rooted in the lived culture of the community, not an
alien professional theatre simply making visits. Perhaps especially
in the work of Brith Gof, theatre has been made in places where

people work, worship and celebrate. Brith Gof have worked solidly since 1981 as theatre makers for the communities they served; and they have lived in the community alongside the clergyman, baker and pub landlord. Following the production of *Gododdin*, created collaboratively with the industrial, post-punk percussionists Test Department, Brith Gof have enjoyed something akin to cult 'rock' status.

This is the crucial difference in the work of the experimental theatres compared with the play-based attempts at making a National Theatre. Without being parochial or patronising, these practitioners have brought theatrical methods from all over the world to challenge and celebrate the Wales they live in. In so doing, they have not created the conditions for an imposed Euro-monoculture, but they have made the voice of Wales a resonant force in European theatre. A voice, it must be remembered, which is multiple, bi-lingual. Richard Gough sees his role as being to put Wales on the map by working with international issues, by taking Wales overseas and bringing to Wales the best of other cultures and theatrical practitioners. It is a successful agenda, and it has always been the case that if Barba or Grotowski were coming to Britain, one could be certain that it was The Cardiff Lab Theatre (or Centre for Performance Research) that would be hosting them. The Magdalena Project [Photo 11] continues the same agenda, but with an internationalist brief and a commitment to women in theatre.

Buildings, however, have been important in the development of this alternative theatre which has emerged as the cluster of dominant forms in Wales. Chapter Arts Centre was founded in 1972 in an old school in Canton. It provided a home for Moving Being and encouragement for the young students, Mike Pearson and Richard Gough, who formed Cardiff Laboratory Theatre there in 1974. In subsequent years Chapter was home for a host of experimental companies such as Reflex Action Theatre, Highway Shoes and Paupers Carnival as well as hosting residencies by the leading British and European exponents of experimental theatre and performance art such as Akademia Ruchu, Waste of Time, People Show [Photo 8], and Pip Simmons. When The Lab moved to the Gym in Chapter's school yard, that building became a key resource in Wales's cultural life. The Centre for Performance Research still occupies The Gym which is the base for all their work.

Throughout the life of Cardiff Lab, their performers worked with school kids at Llanover Hall, an educational facility near to Chapter.

Here many Cardiff adolescents came under the influence of the experimenters and went on to work with The Lab and in their own companies.

After a long co-production in Rotterdam in 1981, Moving Being's Geoff Moore returned to Cardiff with a sense that he needed a more adaptable space which he could fully inhabit, just as he had been doing for four months in Rotterdam's dockland. He found the derelict St Stephens Church in Cardiff's dockland. He converted it to a flexible performance space, and it is here that he has developed his work on plays, a necessity in one sense, deriving from the need to produce a greater volume of work to fill a continuous programme. It was here that the newest talent to emerge in Welsh theatre, Edward Thomas with his company, Y Cwmni, first had a chance to produce his fiery, rhetorical plays which re-create a Welsh mythology with the kind of ruggedness and muscularity he perceives in the myths through which Americans conceive and construct themselves.

The Welsh scene has consolidated to the extent that it can now proudly turn back to Europe and offer itself as a body of mature work by matured companies. But this sense of identity is plural. The work in *Export Wales* includes treatments of classic texts by Geoff Moore; a punk-inspired treatment of Tony Harrison's poetical theatre text *V* from Volcano Theatre (directed by Janec Alexander, a protege of the early experimentalists of The Lab); text-based plays from Y Cwmni and Dalier Sylw; dance theatre from Man Act [**Photo 12**], Paradox Shuffle, Earthfall and Diversions; large-scale song and music led spectaculars from Brith Gof; and contemporary music theatre from Music Theatre Wales. The Centre for Performance Research and The Magdalena Project are both difficult to characterise exactly as they are producers and promoters of performance works, and organisers of conferences, workshops and seminars.

The personnel and histories of these groups are closely interwoven, and tell an important story in the development of Welsh theatre from marginal experimentation to popular success and high profile, from creating work for a few people in a small studio to making large scale spectaculars and celebratory work for and with local rural communities.

Cardiff Laboratory Theatre has, perhaps, been the most significant influence on the current expression of Welsh theatre. The Lab started from the work of Grotowski making non-verbal, highly physically expressive and sparse pieces, each object multi-functional and having symbolic resonance. But whereas Pearson was a physical actor,

Gough was a visual trickster whose mentors are still Magritte and Duchamp.

The Lab's importance was not necessarily the work they themselves did as practitioners or promoters of events and workshops, but for their teaching and the crucial residencies which they hosted: amongst them Grotowski and the Wroclaw Laboratorium, Piccolo Teatro di Pontedera and Akademia Ruchu of Warsaw.

A particular watershed was the Odin residency of 1980. After presenting performances in Cardiff, Odin and members of The Lab set up in five rural communities across Wales. For Richard Gough this was important because it showed how exciting and relevant an experimental theatre could be. In the time honoured tradition of the prophet being unrecognised in his own country, the Odin company attracted a higher profile in Wales than the Lab itself had, not least because of their spectacular street events fashioned after the street carnivals of Italy and South America.

The rural projects were based on Odin's 'barter' system, where the local community trades their songs, poems and cultural artifacts with the company in return for the company's performance work.

Mike Pearson and Lis Hughes Jones, then still part of The Lab, worked on the Odin project in Lampeter, West Wales, and when they split from the Lab in 1981 they returned there making a series of performances in collaboration with the community and colleagues from theatre groups in Norway and Denmark, themselves off-shoots of the Odin Company. This split from the Lab gave rise to their company Brith Gof. They felt that the Lab's emphasis on world culture, on an universal theatre language, had caused them to be alienated from their own cultures, histories and mythologies.

From 1981–88 they were in Aberystwyth working extensively with students at the university's drama department, some of whom subsequently joined Brith Gof and went on to form their own companies influenced by Brith Gof's approach.

A key touchstone of their work is the presence of song, voice and music around which the action is built. A note on their *Pax* brochure declares them to be 'A Welsh Company', and that their commitment is to site-specific projects with local performers and musicians. Using the local language as well as Welsh and English. This combination of Welshness and inter-nationality clearly situates them as belonging to world theatre as much as their local community. Whilst drawing on the Welsh language, culture and history, they attempt to make a theatre which is as complex as the issues involved and which employs current technology that situates it within the spectrum of the experience of their audiences – a far cry from the hermetic world of Pearson's early work.

The Lab continued under the directorship of Gough after the split in 1981, and restructured itself as a permanent ensemble of mature performers. In 1984 this ensemble broke up and out of this splintering the Magdalena Project and Man Act came into existence to explore respectively women's role in contemporary theatre and man's role in contemporary society.

Originally a project of the Cardiff Lab, the Magdalena Project started out under the directorship of Gill Greenhalgh, to bring together women from all over the world with no common tongue or theatrical language. Their interest was in finding a complete physical, integrated technique and to answer questions such as 'How do you collaborate? Not just as a woman, but at all?' More questions followed as the making of work proved to be difficult within their loose structures. The next project was to find 'A woman's voice in theatre?' The question mark was important, as they were not sure what such a question could mean. Voice and text became major concerns of the project, merging in 'song'. Traditionally, in every culture, song was where woman could have a place, and the experienced and inexperienced alike could have access to it as a ground for work. The metaphor was resonant: woman finding her voice in the theatre and in life. Essentially, the group exist to promote the work of women in contemporary theatre. A broad brief which allows for many questions to be asked and hypotheses to be tested.

Man Act are Simon Thorne and Philip Mackenzie. During The Lab performance project *The Heart of the Mirror* in 1984, certain issues of gender, responsibility and culpability arose which the two men felt the group were not able to deal with intelligently and which, they feel, split the group. *Man Act*, which was the title of their first show when the company was officially formed in 1985, had been initiated as a study in 1983 whilst with the Lab. They decided they had to work in the arena of the male and find out what that meant. The particular starting point seems to have been a direct reaction to the form of Odin-influenced training which had become the basis of the Lab's work. Each member of the Lab company threw themselves, daily, into a rigorous personal training sequence. *The Heart of the Mirror* was throwing up questions of relationship and the two men wanted to work on a technique that they could share. Neither was a trained dancer, but ballroom dancing suggested a base from which they could work as an unit to train and to produce performance material. Like the Magdalenas who found song a convenient way in for a variety of women, Man Act based their physical language on the social dance. Although they refer to themselves as a theatre company, choreography is a key element in the process of making work.

One of the names frequently mentioned by the companies under discussion is the Polish Akademia Ruchu (Academy of Movement). They visited Cardiff at the request of the Lab in 1978 and were a profound influence on its members and on other groups working at Chapter as well as the workshop participants who came from all over the country. One of the groups, Reflex Action, took up Akademia Ruchu's notion of gridding the performance space as a visual cuing system for improvised performance.

Thorne, in Poland continuing his music studies, came into contact with Akademia Ruchu, and was, in turn, introduced to Richard Gough through them. Thus the connection was made which led to Thorne becoming a Lab member. Welsh based experimental theatre, it must be clear, has never been parochial, but is situated within an international nexus.

Man Act dissect the image of contemporary male macho iconised by the elegant Italian suit and the Cuban heel. Their work is ball-room dancing intercut with catwalk fashion parade intercut with two guys 'beating the shit out of each other' as Thorne puts it. But this characterisation does not catch the textual element so important in their work. Their early texts evoked a Beckettian world, but the problems of placing two characters without history on the stage led them to build more complete narratives. Consequently they have worked with two of Britain's leading new theatre practitioners on text-based pieces – Neil Bartlett and Steve Shill.

Since 1984 when this second split occurred, the Centre for Performance Research have continued as a multi-faceted organisation promoting cross-cultural performance projects, residencies, conferences, educational and training projects. As The Practice, the Centre also produces its own work. One month they could be working on a large-scale project with 60 artists from China's Peking Opera or Japan, putting it into a 2000-seat theatre. The next month they might be doing an intimate project with a small group from Poland presenting the work in a small church in North Wales to an audience of 100.

Gough wonders how experimental a company can be over 17 years of work. The pressure to create product necessarily leads to short cuts and known effects. He longs for the time when he can go into the studio on day one and not feel he has to produce something in the next six weeks. He reflects on the New York situation where you can 'pop into the Performing Garage and see a work in progress nine months into a working process. We've never created that milieu for ourselves.'

Questions of accessibility and presentability keep coming up, he claims, from those who are 'the self-appointed guardians of art in Wales.' Yet the facts argue forcibly for themselves: performed to children, or in a small village outside Madrid and in small communities in West Wales, shows such as *The Origin of Table Manners* by The Practice present no problems to understanding and enjoyment. The Welsh audience, through years of careful exposure to the terms of this experimental work and open to the surprises of new cultural influences, can understand in ways which are clearly difficult for those with entrenched views on what constitutes theatre. Despite his current interest in writing and fixed texts, Gough does not believe that one has to go through Shakespeare, Beckett and Pinter before being able to confront experimental visual theatre. Indeed, those models merely confuse the issue.

He now employs drama-school-trained actors because he wants to develop the use of character and narrative, but acknowledges that there is a necessary de-training and re-training that must go on with a new company of such actors, to balance his own poor theatre methods of training and composition with their more conventional experience.

With a wry laugh at himself he repeats the old axiom that all fools want to play Hamlet, and that he's interested in doing real plays. But this is his edgy manner of saying that he has a suspicion that 'we have things to say that cannot be said simply through images.' Perhaps what has warmed the Welsh audience to CPR's work is Gough's irrepressible sense of humour. Good theatre, he believes, should have the quality of a joke. 'But only the best joke, of course.'

If Cardiff Lab/CPR can be seen as the spawning ground for what is still largely an image-based theatre, Moving Being director Geoff Moore's work over the last ten years has opened the way for new writing and text-based theatre. Moore studied art, not theatre, and the first five years of the company's life, to 1974, was spent at The

Place in London. At that time Moore was exploring a territory marked out by the convergence of three precursors:

> Rauschenberg spoke of operating in 'the gap between life and art'. Godard's films had obliterated the distinction between dramatic narrative and abstract ideas, between high and low art, between culture and politics. And the musical collage compositions of Cage and Berio were like the sound-track of the world passing through your head. They were all artists for whom the formal limits of a given discipline no longer existed.

If The Lab's work was cross-cultural within the world of third or experimental theatre, Moore's cross-over was between media (projection, film, visual image, installation) and forms (dance, theatre, film, rock culture).

McLuhan's tag that the medium is the message was part of a move to displace the criteria for how meaning was conveyed. The play couldn't possibly 'contain the fluid transmuting present age', says Moore. This led to a distrust of 'the play' and 'the writer'. What was needed was the live gesture, group expression, the spontaneity of improvisation, a medium that had to be open ended, able to function with the direct energy of rock'n'roll. In 1970, London's *Time Out Magazine* said of him:

> He draws on a wide range of texts – from Aristotle to the Underground Press – to give up a jumble of reflections of the world we live in; ideas, sentiments are juxtaposed, quite arbitrary, as they surely hit us every day. No explanations, just weird and wonderful sights and sounds.

There were problems for Moore in his compendium method. The stage was full of 'hip' people, but there was always the problem of acting. Acting he felt was a form of lying, a belief based on the dullness of much bad live theatre. To say something articulate, he felt, it could not come out of those lumbering things (plays and actors). Beyond cutting text up like film, beyond irony, information and a certain articulateness, he didn't, he confesses, know much about text. His current position is that there is something in what a playwright does in creating human utterance in the ways that Handke, Müller and Shakespeare have done. His project is to find a form of acting that is authentic, for now, not just rhetoric and not just part of an old vocabulary of gestures, which can address what writers are writing and have written. He believes in the notion of the accrued wisdom in classic texts and that the theatre is still the place for people to meet 'around the fire place of a text that can be stretched high and low and they can come into direct confrontation with that text'.

His work always contains some dancers, he can't ever reject that, he says, but admits to work which is less visually interesting. He repeats the current truism that the image can be ambiguous, and language, he feels can be made less ambiguous.

Moore also rationalises his return to text and play, and the same impulse in his Welsh contemporaries, because there are things to say – general issues of politics and ecology are important; and in the context of the Welsh language issue, there are things to say about Welshness, about being in Wales. But this is no parochial stand-off. Moore rightly points out that the companies in *Export Wales* are extremely cosmopolitan and they are all concerned with finding a voice for Wales in Europe, a voice constituted by a long history of dialogue with European theatre practitioners. The Welsh voice these companies are striving for is a voice in dialogue, a voice asking questions, not one which simply talks to and of itself, but a voice that gives some authentic utterance to the plurality of the nation.

Moore's interest in Heiner Müller reflects his interest in the political theatre and the theatre of dream images registered in Müller's dual connection with Brecht and Robert Wilson. And also that Müller's work reflects the sense that a socialist principle cannot be perfected in the world. Having grown in the naive atmosphere of the summer of love (the company was formed in 1968) and the sense that anything was both possible and allowable, Moore also seems in older age to have come to the position of wanting to ask more profound questions, not to take the easy answers, not even to believe that there are any easy answers.

Moore's Mabinogion project, based on the Welsh folk legends of the Mabinogion, are part of a series of works literally giving voice to a small nation 'still struggling to define itself.' The project was an important development for Moving Being. It was the first opportunity for the company to work with the Welsh language and to collaborate with Welsh speaking writers, actors and musicians. From its first showings at Cardiff Castle it has become a living popular cultural event. *Gwrthryfel/The Rising*, illustrates another context for Moving Being's integration with its environment, rather than being an international touring company simply based in Wales where funding in the early seventies was up for grabs. The project began with texts and documents given over to the company by Cardiff University's ex-Professor of History, Gwyn A Williams. Workshops with Aberystwyth University students provided the context for Moving Being's visit to that bastion of Welsh Folk culture, the National Eisteddfod. A bilingual script was then developed.

Through Youth Theatre projects, Moore has made St Stephens and his work accessible to the newest generation of young people in Cardiff, and in the final production of *Gwrthryfel/The Rising* the setting became a modern day Merthyr classroom and so the central actors were played by this new emergent generation of theatre artists.

The Welsh situation is and has always been a question of language. Not simply the Welsh language, but the language of theatre. Assumptions about the language of theatre, the orthodox language of the well-made play, have foundered in Welsh culture. It is the companies' striving to find new languages, hybridizing their theatrical and cultural forms, which have emerged as having the voice which Wales seems to understand. Perhaps it is precisely this split of tongues that provides the ground for such an acceptance and openness. Perhaps it is the Welsh 'hywl', that ecstatic delivery of the non-conformist preacher akin to speaking in tongues, that binds them, the sense that the fire with which something is said is as important as what is being said. This would certainly be true of the rhetoric of Welsh politicians and its effectiveness historically. The work discussed here is multi-lingual – theatrically, culturally and linguistically. This Welsh theatre does not simply speak to and of itself.

REFERENCES

Promotional and documentary material (including quotes from publications) produced by the companies mentioned.

Interviews with the following carried out by the author in Cardiff in November 1991:

Alexander, Janec. Theatre Coordinator, Chapter Arts Centre, Cardiff.

Gough, Richard. Artistic Director, The Centre for Performance Research, Cardiff.
Pearson, Mike. Co-Director, Brith Gof, Cardiff.
Russell, Maggie. Project Associate, Magdalena Project, Cardiff.
Thomas, Edward. Artistic Director, Y Cwmni, Cardiff.
Thorne, Simon. Performer and Co-Director, Man Act, Cardiff.

11

LIFTing the Theatre: The London International Festival of Theatre

Claire Armitstead

In 1981 the London International Festival of Theatre (LIFT) pushed its way into the international festival circuit, a poor but determined relation of Avignon and Madrid. The festivals it has staged every two years since have raised a strong and idiosyncratic voice. LIFT has braved political indifference, critical antagonism and public prejudice to establish a biennial meeting of unlike minds. In doing so, it has helped to move the markers of British theatre away from its traditional textual patriotism towards an acceptance of different ways of doing and seeing.

It has achieved this through an extraordinary range of strategies – from enlisting business sponsorship for the building-blocks used to construct the Bastille in the heart of the South Bank, to unleashing a party of Catalan pyromaniacs on the usually sober reaches of Battersea Park.

Danger has been a fact of life for the LIFT organisers since the festival was conceived and it takes many forms, from the regular, protracted panics over funding, to eleventh-hour confrontations with the safety inspectorate and the unpredictable risk that, as happened in 1989, a hot summer could combine with a transport strike to demolish precariously budgeted audience numbers. Founders Lucy Neal and Rose Fenton meet the squalls with a self-critical rigor which has enabled them to capitalise as much on mistakes as successes.

The first lesson predates LIFT itself, going back to their student days in 1978 when they were offered a chance to contribute to a theatre festival in Portugal. They hurriedly set up a University drama company and mugged up a staple of the radical home repertory: David Hare's portrait of Chinese revolution, *Fanshen*. As Rose Fenton says:

> We rather patronisingly thought it would be politically relevant, but it couldn't have been a worse choice: text-based, dramatically dull, when what we were seeing from other companies was spectacle and shows that communicated by visual impact. (Fenton)

Within months Neal and Fenton – by then graduates to waitressing – were enthusing to doubtful theatre managers about the potential of an international festival in London. They met with little encouragement for an idea which, the old hands pointed out, meant luring people to foreign shows in foreign languages in the notoriously difficult summer season. They persevered, and the pockets of support they did receive were substantial enough to go ahead with a festival budgeted on £5 per performer per day. In 1981, at a total cost of £110,000 they played host to 10 companies from as far as Malaysia and Peru.

The reception ranged from sceptical to ecstatic, proving that, if there were prejudices to overcome, there was also a hunger in London for something outside the regular theatrical diet. As the director Ronald Eyre pointed out, there had been random visits by foreign companies, but there had been no sustained commitment to international theatre since Peter Daubeny's World Theatre seasons at the Aldwych came to an end in 1973 (Eyre).

Responsibility for maintaining an international presence had since then fallen to a scattering of enlightened individual directors. The British Council had the money to send British companies abroad but had no budget to honour exchange visits. Visiting Arts, set up by the British government in response to the Helsinki Agreement to honour reciprocity, had a budget in 1981 totalling £77,000. It gave £5000 of this to LIFT, in the biggest single grant it had made. The Arts Council was hamstrung by its own constitution, regretfully explaining to the LIFT organisers in 1981 that international theatre did not fall within its brief.

Neal and Fenton represented enthusiasm coupled with a discriminating intelligence that guaranteed a certain standard. Their media profile – of two bright young things batting around the world between children – has remained part of LIFT's personality,

although in 1991 they preside over a £700,000 enterprise with a distinguished and committed board of directors, and an increasingly expert staff. The disadvantage of this image is the inference that they are not quite serious; the advantage is the licence it gives them to chip away at preconceptions. If LIFT says circus is a form of theatre then it will be debated and attended as such.

The first LIFT opened in July 1981 on a budget nearly a third of which had been raised from private donations. Its largest and sexiest event was the Brazilian show *Macunaima*, which was presented at the Lyric, Hammersmith, by the Grupo de Teatro Macunaima of Sao Paulo to a reception of delighted surprise. Audiences queued around the block for the four-hour comic epic, which used spectacle, music, parody and the body beautiful to chart the highly equivocal progress of a national folk hero, and by inference a society, from jungle to city. *Macunaima* was a raw and charismatic explosion of cultural consciousness, even if in European performance terms it was not particularly original. As Michael Coveney wrote, 'It is as if the Third World has engaged in cultural collision with the European idiom of Max Ophuls, Fellini and (expanding the boundaries just slightly) Hal Prince' (Coveney, 1981).

It was quite different in both its ambition and achievement to the state of the art contribution of the Dutch Werktheater, with its moving 90-minute documentary of gay identity, or to the state of the nation presentations of the festival's two Polish contributors. One (the student-based Teatr Provisorum) revealed a dual reverence for the politics of the shipyard and the art of Jerzy Grotowski; the other (Theatre of the Eighth Day, newly emerged from a period in the political doghouse), anatomised a society split between Catholicism and Communism through a splatter of apocalyptic images. One of the most memorable involved a cascade of pink plastic piggy-banks fought over by the inhabitants of hell. Even those who were unaware of the precise significance of the pigs came away moved and amused by a symbolism that straddled the divides of language, politics and culture with a succinctness that text-based theatre would be pushed to match.

Annexed, almost accidentally, to the festival proper was a small collection of street performances. 'We gave £500 to two people to chuck it together', says Neal. Yet this strand of performance in public places has proved one of LIFT's most productive and most directly challenging to theatre's ivory towers. Urban Sax's 30 foil-clad French saxophonists might be dismissed for Gallic pretentiousness, but they made the most stunning entrance of 1983, abseiling down the walls of Covent Garden's Piazza, and contributed an undeniable buzz. The crazed Catalans of Els Comediants did that and more, with a pyrotechnic extravaganza in Battersea Park which has been likened to standing in a box of fireworks and watching them go off. Ten thousand people gave themselves to the exorcism of *The Devils*, running and shouting in a participatory frenzy as the sparks rained down on them in a magnificent, orgiastic release from the normal restraints of life, expression and imagination.

Those who witnessed *The Devils* were given an unrepeatable experience, if only because of the clamp-down on fire regulations in the wake of the Bradford football stadium disaster in the same year (1985). The need to re-adapt to such developments in public or bureaucratic consciousness has, of necessity, played an important part in LIFT's developing identity, not least because of their financial implications.

The timing of the festival's launch placed it at a turning point in attitudes to public sponsorship of the arts. The election of a Conservative government in 1979 had signalled the start of a sustained attack on public spending by all levels of government. The Greater London Council (GLC), a staunch supporter of the first three festivals, had been abolished by 1987.

A mix of individual local boroughs and undertaker quangos became responsible for honouring the GLC's commitment to the arts. Not only did London lose the benefit of a single authority with an explicit commitment to entertain Londoners but it had to contend with a new devolutionary zeal from the Arts Council, articulated in its 1984 report, *The Glory of the Garden*, which argued for a greater regional spread of resources.

The theatre, in common with other arts institutions, spent much of the decade tightening its belt and turning its artistic directors into sponsorship-seekers. New plays became smaller in scale and there were fewer of them. The Roundhouse, a magnificent converted railway engine shed in North London which in the seventies had been the home of music and theatre spectacles, closed its doors in 1983 blaming inadequate funding and leaving London without a venue appropriate to the sort of work that Peter Brook was doing in Paris at the Bouffes du Nord and elsewhere across the world. (Brook, who has a totemic significance for British internationalism, has twice negotiated with LIFT to bring his company to London, first with *The Mahabharata*, and then with *The Tempest*. Both times he went to Glasgow instead, because London simply could not provide the right venue for him.)

Through ingenuity, professionalism and a remarkable ability to communicate the excitement of its ideas, LIFT has actually done rather well from the changes. In a time when money has been short, it has brought two valuable functions under one administrative and financial umbrella. It has imported to Britain work of a character not usually seen in the capital. In doing so, it has been able to represent the work of a community of British performers as part of a European tradition of spectacular, visual work rather than as oddballs clanking around the fringes of the British mainstream.

A central part of its strength has been its ability to anticipate and respond to developments in the theatre itself. In the mid eighties, internationalism began to become fashionable, forcing LIFT to re-examine its own function. Glasgow's Mayfest became an important international event which was firmly and productively rooted in a particular community, while the National Theatre began its own international season, hosting high profile ensembles like Steppenwolf of Chicago or Peter Stein's Schaubühne from Berlin. Clearly it was vital for LIFT to establish a complementary role, while refusing to be seen as a second division, promoting work that was not good or important enough to make the South Bank.

Michael Morris, an independent producer and former theatre director of the Institute of Contemporary Arts (ICA), admits that a couple of years ago he would have questioned the need for LIFT to continue. 'But now they are being much more pro-active. They're not just taking what's going on but are creating, commissioning and giving back to the marketplace' (Morris). His point is exemplified by *The Bastille Dances*, by London-based Station House Opera. This contribution to the 1989 festival took the form of a perpetually reconstructing model of the Bastille formed from 8000 breeze blocks on the South Bank. Day and night the blocks were shunted around, sometimes frenetically and at other times slowly and sleepily. It played to conventional audiences who turned up at given performance times, but also to anyone who happened to stroll along the South Bank, munched sandwiches, took photographs or simply looked on in bemusement. Lucy Neal comments:

> As a puzzling event it was fine but if you wanted to take it further
> I believe it was a very fine example of the way performance artists

are able to tap theatre in a way that the theatre itself, because of the restrictions of the constructs around it, isn't able to do. (Neal)

In scale, vision and character, *The Bastille Dances* belongs to a tradition of visual arts-oriented theatre the discussion of which has largely been limited in England to a specialist press catering for arts practitioners. Its inclusion in a programme that also included classical drama meant that it could not be so easily categorised. As Michael Billington wrote:

> On one level, it is a reminder, since many of the performers are dressed as artisans and sans-culottes and since tableaux of familiar events emerge out of the breeze-blocks, that the French Revolution was a form of street theatre. But it can also be taken as a metaphor, heroic or cynical depending on your point of view, of the process of the French Revolution. . . . Is it really theatre? Since it is directed . . . aesthetically controlled, lit and costumed, the answer has to be yes. (Billington)

The choice of a location cheekily close to the National Theatre represented an intrinsic challenge to traditional theatre values, at the same time illustrating the importance of finding the right venue.

Just as it has been said that the most important job of the play director is the initial casting, it can be argued that correct siting is the single most challenging and creative task confronting the festival organiser. Both involve an imaginative investment capable of making or breaking the finest product. LIFT's own experience has taught it that you cannot put a Jamaican women's show in a predominantly white venue like Islington's Almeida Theatre and expect issues to take precedence over aesthetics. The patois politics of *Fallen Angel and the Devil Concubine*, contributed to the 1987 festival by Jamaica's Groundwork Theatre, fell on deaf ears in Islington. Yet in Brixton Village, its metaphor of two old women learning about racial harmony from co-existence in a huge and crumbling colonial mansion besieged by young thugs, was eagerly embraced by an animated audience.

On the other hand, the siting of Pirandello's *Six Characters in Search of an Author* in the baroque splendour of the Brixton Academy dance hall, complete with its skewed dance floors and its

proscenium model of the Rialto Bridge, gave an altogether appropriate twist to the work of the maverick Russian Anatoli Vasiliev:
the rough little scaffolding theatre, in which he insists on touring
his work, sat forlornly in the belly of this elaborate whale – a theatre
within a theatre, outside which the actors loafed, in full view of
their audience, awaiting their entrance cues. The venue, in this case,
became as much a part of the play as costume or props.

Where Vasiliev's Brixton visit had a self-conscious appropriate-
ness, with the incidental benefit of luring London theatregoers to
an area too often stigmatised as a riot zone, other choices have been
dominated by a more down to earth impulse to make connections
between art and its environment. LIFT's infiltration of the city has
been astute and varied, ranging from behind-the-scenes initiatives
to forge links between its business and diplomatic communities
to more conspicuous occupation of its heart for art's sake. Julia
Rowntree, since 1986 the development director of the festival,
is a creative fund-raiser whose strategies have involved a deep
understanding of the place and its people. One strategy has involved
flying chefs in from the countries of participating companies to wine
and dine potential sponsors, while giving them a chance to make
diplomatic and business contacts. To get Station House Opera off
the blocks, she devised a sponsorship scheme inviting firms and
individuals to 'buy' a breezeblock, at £10 for a 'Sans-Culottes',
£100 for a 'bourgeois', and £1000 for an 'aristocrat'. This simple
scheme had the triple role of raising money while providing a useful
publicity gimmick and giving a number of people who might not
otherwise have done so a reason to go down to the South Bank and
see the work in progress.

Her 1991 money-spinner – a conceptual model of the theatre in
which £5000 makes you an 'angel' while £25 secures a place in the
'gods', and the £355,000 received in grant money is acknowledged
as 'bricks and mortar' – takes the idea a stage further: it shows
patrons as part of a continuum which stretches from performer
through performance to the people who watch or pay for it.

The Scottish performer and poet Fiona Templeton made a similar
point from a different perspective with her contribution to LIFT
89, *You – the City*. Starting by appointment at a firm of City
accountants, audiences of one – 'You', identified by a pre-arranged
password – were taken on a two-hour mystery tour that took
in houses, a church, and the streets themselves. This was the
city as you had never seen it before – a hectic, uncomfortable,

inquisitorial place in which insignificant corners yielded furtive busy-bodies: a consumed consumer, a meterless cabbie, armed with questions, speeches and accusations. Tom Lubbock captured the feeling of intrigued uneasiness provoked by the work: 'The experience is immediately reminiscent of other occasions where intimacy is artificially induced: therapy, prostitution, fortune-telling, being button-holed by a loony' (Lubbock). *You – the City* began in Manhattan, and has since played elsewhere in Europe, but its relationship with its environment is such that each different location produces an essentially different show.

Various companies, from Welfare State [Photo 3] to Bow Gamelan, have homed in on the river Thames as a part of London's identity, reflecting its social and economic history as well as providing an inspiring habitat for performance. Bow Gamelan's LIFT 87 project *Offshore Rig*, set on an island in the river and watched from barges by its audience, is rated among the best of the company's work, not simply because it forced them to work on a bigger scale than ever before, but because of the way it anchored their imaginations to a particular bit of land with a particular history and particular practical problems.

In his introduction to the catalogue to Edge 90, a pan-European presentation of performance arts, Oliver Bennett pointed out that art had both a commercial and a 'missionary' value.

An international audience, both in person and via the media, can mean much to local councils and companies, even if it is invisible public relations for the future. . . . The attitude of the art worker, in this set-up, can become that of the missionary, righteously disseminating art values in hostile, underdeveloped places. And for others, the impulse can be benign and pedagogical, a Fabian legacy hinting at the notion of improvement and instruction. (Bennett)

His opinion is echoed in the 1990 *Local Futures Report* of the Henley Centre for Forecasting, which warned:

In Britain, Glasgow has become a city of culture; Birmingham the city with a big heart. In these cities too, there seems a general enthusiasm for the values of urban life in their local form. Surrounding London, there seems to be no such buzz, no such appetite for the future, no urgency attending the discussion of

its identity. The image lacks shape, confidence, daring. The city
lacks a champion. (Henley Centre)

It was in a conscious effort to 'champion' the city that LIFT
devised its 1991 programme of site specific work, Lifting London.
Once more the river was much in evidence, as a challenging (and
available) venue; but there was also a strong missionary flavour to
a programme of commissions which included collaborations with
tenants of a newly refurbished South London council estate and
with the large homeless population of what has been dubbed
'cardboard city'.

LAPD Inspects London represents a particularly timely attempt to
embrace a sector of the population that has nothing going for it. The
expertise came from the Los Angeles Poverty Department, whose
director John Malpede has dedicated himself to working on street
level in the United States. The project raises a number of thorny
questions about the value and role of theatre: Why, for instance,
should homeless people bother to take part? Why should anyone be
interested in watching them? Is their inclusion in an arts programme
an act of genuine and useful conscience or of patronising and woolly
philanthropy; worse still, of voyeurism? Will this brief moment of
attention leave them better or worse off once their audience has
gravitated, as it inevitably will, off the streets and back into the
art houses?

There is something in the English character that shies away from
such earnest consideration of the ground-level ethics of the arts.
Yet the potential returns of this sort of community link-up can be
seen in more conventional terms through the youth musical *Project!*,
once again led by an American concept of the social role of theatre.
Project! came from Chicago to the Theatre Royal Stratford East in
1987. This beautifully preserved Victorian theatre crouches on the
side of a dual carriageway in one of London's poorest areas. It was
the home of Joan Littlewood's Theatre Workshop in the 1950s and
has since specialised in theatre that reflects the ethnic composition
of the surrounding community. The musical, a *West Side Story* for
the 1980s, originated from the huge Chicago estate of Cabrini Green.
It told with a gutsy honesty of a population 'depraved on account 'a
they're deprived.' The essential difference from *West Side Story* was
that this was a group of young people who had been given the
confidence and the resources to tell their own story. So enthusiastic
was the reception, and so strong the recognition, that it spawned a

similar youth musical in Newham.

An acknowledgement of the different populations that a capital city encompasses is imprinted on the developing character of the festival which, as far back as 1983, began to identify three distinct, though overlapping categories of audience. London's ethnic minorities, concentrated in areas such as Brixton or Newham represented one historically neglected tranche, accessible to the right show in the right place, publicised in the right way. But there was also a large floating community of arts practitioners, eager to experience, explore and discuss; and, in some ways most elusive of all, there were the mainstream, once-a-month theatregoers who had to be convinced that the event they were being offered was the one they had to see.

Michael Morris argues that LIFT has yet to prove itself at the big theatre box office. Its venture into the Old Vic, with two classics from the Katona Jozsef Theatre of Budapest: Chekhov's *Three Sisters* and Gogol's *The Government Inspector*, was a critical triumph but a financial disaster. Whether sidetracked by the hot weather, or daunted by the thought of watching classics in foreign languages, the Old Vic regulars were conspicuous by their absence, dragging box office receipts down to 28 per cent. Yet those who braved the shows saw classical theatre at its most vigorous, accessible and – in Gogol's case – relevant, with world class acting and direction and a razor-sharp political intelligence. Far from throwing the duped worthies into panic, as Gogol himself intended, the real inspector arrived in the final scene to be casually assassinated in a lift – a complete change of meaning that involved virtually no tampering with the script.

While the Katona Jozsef languished, Garry Hynes' Abbey Theatre revival of a 1961 play by Tom Murphy, *A Whistle in the Dark*, sold out at the Royal Court – a testament to the traditionally successful partnership of the Royal Court and LIFT, but also to the entrenched views of London audiences for whom the Abbey Theatre represents the safe face of internationalism. It was a fine revival by a major theatre of an old (and dated) play, which represented Fenton and Neal's faith in the director rather than any urge to evangelise for the Abbey or rediscover the work of Tom Murphy.

Its inclusion in the LIFT programme could be seen to exemplify what detractors of the festival have seen as a deliberate eccentricity of programming: a refusal to go out with the shopping trolley and come back with pre-ordered goods. Michael Morris admires Neal and Fenton's refusal simply to represent the state of the art. 'There are certain shows that every festival takes, and they are under a lot of pressure to programme them' (Morris). Neal and Fenton argue that there are often more mundane reasons for conspicuous absences, such as the availability of particular companies in July. They point to Peking Opera's Royal Court visit of 1985 as an example of conspicuous success at the main theatre box office.

But they have an undeniably principled attitude to their work, which stems from a sense of piecing together a great world jigsaw puzzle of performance. Major companies will always have a place in that puzzle, though not necessarily a predictable one. In programming for LIFT 91 the world famous Maly Theatre of Leningrad (which became St. Petersburg before before the company arrived) they insisted on partnering the vintage, and well-travelled, *Brothers and Sisters* with a less well-known piece, *Gaudeamus*, improvised by the younger company members. They were using the shopping trolley to carry unfamiliar goods.

They fiercely resist 'folk' theatre as politically and culturally retrogressive out of its context, yet they are prepared to put festival money into commissioning new work based on traditional forms. In 1987, for instance, they commissioned the young Nigerian choreographer Peter Badejo to put together a piece of dance theatre incorporating disparate tribal styles and disciplines. Such commissions carry an inevitable risk. The resulting work – *Kufena* – was not wholly successful, losing its bold satirical insight in a melange of different dance styles. But it provided a badly needed forum for a number of disparate performers from different areas of the country. It also contributed to LIFT's passionate and vituperative discussion between the various black groups at the festival, about the role of theatre in the establishment of a community identity.

The diversity of work like *Kufena* and *A Whistle in the Dark* points to LIFT's acknowledgement of the need continually to challenge the preconceptions of its audiences, whether that means the Euro-American focus of performance circles, or the more obviously reactionary equation made by many theatregoers between theatre and the text.

The stir created in 1983 by the assault of the Compagnia de Collettivo of Parma on Shakespeare was such that Terry Hands, director of the Royal Shakespeare Company, is said to have responded with a relieved memo to his company that they represented no threat. Yet here was Prince Hal as a motorcycling mobster and Hamlet in blue jeans, the very ordinary hero of a tragic farce that threw text out of the window but could not be faulted for concept or performance and could not even be dismissed as disrespectful. The productions were not gratuitously anachronistic, but represented a skilful annexation of classical theatre to the contemporary consciousness, challenging the British theatre establishment in its own front garden. As Michael Coveney wrote, in a spirited defence of the Collettivo:

> Once you translate Shakespeare into any language, the shock of a new idiom and rhythm allows for almost any further liberty. The point only remains as to how responsibly and creatively that shock is exploited. (Coveney, 1983)

Effectively, then, the Collettivo's work is to be considered on equal terms with any other foreign language interpreters of Shakespeare.

At least, in audience terms, the Collettivo had Shakespeare as a reference point; but what of *The Dancing Deer of Manipur*, a delicate dance drama from a restricted area of India, which used its own form of allegory to tell of the repression of its people and the destruction of its environment? And what of the Spanish performer Alberto Vidal who spent the 1985 festival caged up in London zoo beside the pumas and orang-utans, one specimen of *Urban Man*, complete with newspaper, typewriter and gawping onlookers.

What, for that matter, of LIFT's 1991 courageous and provocative programme of commissions from British artists working at the tip of the avant-garde. One of them, the irresistible Bobby Baker, invited 25 people at a time to her own home [Photo 9] to sample her unique blend of visual and performance art, which is formulated around her identity as an artist and mother. Baker's work is funny, acute and mouthwateringly accessible, using household implements and food to create a colourful canvas of her own everyday life, but it is not the sort of work that in England is reviewed as, or attended as theatre.

The danger is that the exoticism of this sort of experiment elicits an amused indulgence without challenging basic attitudes to the theatre itself and without convincing funding or sponsoring bodies of the importance of investing in its future. It is in the nature of such work that it has a high failure rate, both aesthetically and critically, and that pseuds and second-raters abound as well as the genuine innovators. It badly needs the sort of discriminating protection that

LIFT's commissioning budget allows. It also needs the affirmation that is given by the opportunity to work, and be seen at work, in an international context.

Lois Keidan, an Arts Council officer who has helped with the LIFT commissions, is convinced that the festival has succeeded in forcing a significant shift of perspective through its championship of an area of theatre that is disqualified by its very size and ambition from most other platforms. (Keidan) The Arts Council has recently put aside a sum of money for cross-disciplinary work, carefully redesignated from 'performance' to 'live' art. The Gulbenkian Foundation has started a fund for outdoor events, citing many LIFT shows in its original proposal. Robert Lepage, the fashionable young Canadian director, whose visually thrilling *Dragons' Trilogy* was a hit of LIFT 87, was invited to take his latest show *Tectonic Plates* into the National Theatre.

LIFT itself has grown and matured into an institution with an influence which extends beyond the London theatre scene. Its £700,000 budget is still small compared to those of most other European festivals, but it has become adept at making the money stretch. The 1991 programme reveals a concerted attempt to extend its influence through co-productions with individual venues and through regional touring of LIFT shows. The £151,000 it receives in grant money from the Arts Council, which will continue for three years, is an acknowledgment of its achievement and its need for stability, even though the withdrawal of another, London-oriented, funder – the London Boroughs Grants Scheme – has more than offset the gain. Rose Fenton and Lucy Neal will mount another campaign and, doubtless, another festival. Julia Rowntree will continue to look for angels. They admit that, for people who like their art clearly packaged and labelled, LIFT can be irritating:

> It comes in odd shapes, which some people can't stand, but we see ourselves as alternative in the best sense of experiment, creativity and fostering an alternative perspective. We argue that's what sheds light on things. (Neal)

To its detractors, probably the most irritating feature of the festival is the restlessness of its vision: just as its audiences are beginning to adjust to one beam of 'alternative' light, LIFT is busy punching new windows in our monumental preconceptions about the theatre.

REFERENCES

Interviews

Fenton, Rose. Three interviews by the author, February–April, 1991.
Keidan, Lois. Interview by the author, April, 1991.
Morris, Michael. Interview by the author, April, 1991.
Neal, Lucy. Three interviews by the author, February–April, 1991.

Publications

Arts Council of Great Britain. *The Glory of the Garden*. London: Arts Council of Great Britain, 1984.
Bennett, Oliver. 'Edge 90: Art & Life in the Nineties', *Mediamatic*, Vol. 4, no. 4 (Special issue), pp. 169–71.
Billington, Michael. *The Guardian*, 20 July 1989.
Coveney, Michael. *Financial Times*, 6 August 1981.
Coveney, Michael. *Financial Times*, 10 August 1983.
Eyre, Ronald. 'Introduction to LIFT', *LIFT '83* (London International Festival of Theatre Programme), 1983.
Hare, David. *Fanshen*. First performed by Joint Stock Theatre Group at the ICA Terrace Theatre, London, 22 April 1975.
Henley Centre for Forecasting. *Local Futures Report*. Henley: Henley Centre for Forecasting, 1990.
Lubbock, Tom. *The Independent*, 5 July 1989.

Part IV

12

The Electronic Media and British Drama

Martin Esslin

I

Contemporary British drama in all its diversity and continued vitality cannot be divorced from the general background of the cultural landscape of the country as a whole: and of the factors which must not be overlooked in this context is the part played by the electronic mass-media in shaping the consciousness and the life-style of the people in the British isles. More than most other European countries perhaps, the British are an indoor people, an Englishman's home being his castle, as the oft-repeated cliché has it: and the rise of the mass media has, if anything, reinforced this tendency.

The renaissance of playwriting in Britain, which is usually dated from the opening of John Osborne's *Look Back in Anger* in May 1956, has brought to the fore an astonishing number of important dramatists. One of the factors that led to it, was undoubtedly the opening up of the educational ladder, by the Education Act of 1945, to talented young people from social classes that had hitherto been barred from institutions of higher learning. But another, perhaps equally important element that played a part in setting this 'new wave' in motion, was undoubtedly the immense influence of the electronic media – radio and television – and their availability as an outlet for the production and diffusion of drama.

By what was perhaps no more than an accident of history, Britain was spared, at least initially, the linkage between the mass media and advertising, which has turned radio and television into cultural wastelands in the United States.

When radio first became available as a medium for entertainment after World War I, programmes, both in the USA and the UK, were originally provided by the manufacturers of sets who felt they had to give their purchasers something to listen to. In 1922 the British radio manufacturers formed a co-operative, the British Broadcasting Company, the first general manager of which was John Reith, the son of a Scottish Presbyterian minister.

As programmes grew more ambitious and costly the question of how they were to be financed became ever more pressing. In the United States advertising provided the answer. In Britain the puritan Reith felt that this would put the most important new cultural medium of the century into the wrong hands, and so he devised the concept of the public corporation – a body set up by a Royal Charter and entrusted with the monopoly of broadcasting. The Sovereign was to appoint its 'governors', for fixed overlapping terms. This 'board of governors' would be independent of political interference and empowered to raise an annual 'licence fee' from all households operating a receiver. The board (which in fact *is* the British Broadcasting Corporation [BBC]) is charged by its charter to use the medium of broadcasting for 'information, education and entertainment in the national interest'. (In Canada the CBC, modelled on the BBC, does not have the right to a licence fee and is financed by direct government grant, which increases its dependence on the government.)

The BBC started operating under its new charter on 1 January 1927. Thus, from the very beginning, the maximising of audiences never was the sole – although still a very important – objective of British broadcasting. The spread of cultural values, the raising of taste, the diffusion of important works of art, the fostering of new talent, were included among its aims under the general heading of serving the national interest.

II

By the time the BBC was constituted as a public body, drama had already become an integral part of its programming. After much debate whether plays would make sense without the visual element, the first 'reading' of a play – Shakespeare's *Twelfth Night* – took place on 25 May 1923 and proved an immediate success. The first play specially written for radio followed on 15 January 1924. It was by the Welsh novelist Richard Hughes (1900–1976) and called

Danger. Hughes had solved the problem of the absence of visuals by setting the play deep down a coal-mine, starting at the moment when an accident extinguishes all lights, so that the entire action takes place in total darkness.

By the time Val Gielgud (1900–1983), an older brother of Sir John Gielgud, took over as head of the radio drama department on 1 January 1929 – a position he held for thirty-four years, until April 1963 – the technique of the production of radio plays had made vast strides. Plays were broadcast live (recording techniques were still too primitive) from an array of different, acoustically sealed studios, so that orchestral music and different acoustic milieus could be blended and cross-faded effectively. And the actors no longer merely 'read' the play, but moved their positions and had developed techniques of subtle characterisation and vocal expression.

When World War II broke out in 1939 and greatly restricted the mobility of the population in the black-out, radio drama reached its highest peak of popularity. Val Gielgud had created a permanent company of radio actors when the department was (temporarily) moved out of London to avoid German air-raids and these actors (among them Gladys Young, Marjory Westbury, Norman Shelley, Carleton Hobbs) who commanded audiences of up to twelve million on the weekly 'Saturday Night Theatre' became the country's most popular stars.

The art of radio drama had also considerably developed. Among those who first recognised its potential was Tyrone Guthrie (1900–1971) who worked as BBC radio drama producer in Belfast from 1924–1926 and wrote some of the earliest radio plays to exploit the medium's possibilities. As he put it in the preface to a volume containing three of his radio scripts:

The microphone lacks the glamour and physical magnetism of the stage, but lacks also the too, too solid flesh. Because its pictures are solely of the mind, they are less substantial but more real than the cardboard grottoes, the calico rosebuds, the dusty grandeur of the stage; . . . . more real because the impression is partly created by the listener himself. From the author's clues the listener collects his materials, and embodies them in a picture of his own creation. It is therefore an expression of his own experience – whether physical or psychological – and therefore more real to him. (Guthrie, 81)

Guthrie was one of the first to develop action entirely within the consciousness of the principal character. His best radio script, *The Flowers are not for you to pick* (1929), takes place in the mind of a drowning man, who re-lives his frustrated life.

The first radio play in verse – *The March of the '45* by Geoffrey Bridson, a pioneer director as well as writer – dates from 1936. During the war the poet Louis MacNeice (1907–1963) joined the BBC as a writer-producer and contributed a long line of poetic radio plays, many of them in verse. In the preface to the published version of *Christopher Columbus* (first broadcast on 12 October 1942, with music specially composed by William Walton) MacNeice affirmed his belief in the place of poetry on radio:

> For man, we should always remember, is born poetic. Hence the predominance of nursery rhymes in the nursery and of poetry in all early literatures. Poetry, in this one sense at least, is more primitive than prose; it was easier on the ear and less strain upon the mind. That is why radio drama – not because the medium is new but because of its primitive audience – might reasonably be expected to demand a poet's approach. And poets on the whole seem more at home on the air than novelists, say, or essayists. (MacNeice, 10–11)

Among MacNeice's many radio plays the undoubted masterpiece is *The Dark Tower* (1946 – with music specially composed by Benjamin Britten) in which he used the theme of Browning's poem 'Child Roland to the Dark Tower Came' to create a powerful image of the artist confronting his destiny.

This and others of MacNeice's verse plays were, as he had pointed out, designed for the mass audience of radio. Yet the then director-general of the BBC, William Haley, felt it was unjust that radio should not be able to cater for an elite audience as well, an audience that could be given the most select intellectual fare. The result was the creation of the 'Third Programme' (to supplement the two established national networks, the 'Home Service' and the 'Light Programme'), on which nothing was to be too highbrow, and intellectual and artistic excellence the sole criterion, regardless of the size of the audience. It opened on 29 September 1946 and has to this day (renamed Radio 3) remained one of the principal sources of experimentation and creativity in drama and music in Britain.

The 'Third Programme' created an opportunity to commission

new works from leading experimental writers and poets. Also, because there was no limitation of length on this elite network, which operated without any fixed programme times, it became possible to broadcast plays uncut and to revive many that could not have hoped ever to get back onto the stage. This opened the way for a rich repertoire of European classics and Elizabethan, Jacobean, Restoration and Victorian drama, quite apart from full-length performances of the plays in the standard repertoire with the best and most famous actors.

Radio drama thus assumed a threefold function:

First, it provided a continuous stream of popular entertainment with adaptations of crime stories and classical novels, soap opera type serials and light comedies and thrillers.

Second, it acted as a medium for the wider diffusion of stage drama (most of which needed very little adaptation to overcome the lack of visuals). Apart from popular West End or Broadway successes, this included productions of the classics, and, not least, translations of important foreign plays that would never have had a chance of reaching the English-speaking stage. By being able to commission translations, BBC radio drama made a number of important plays accessible in English. Ionesco's *Rhinoceros*, for example, had its world premiere on the Third Programme in an English translation before it was performed on the stage in Paris; the translation of Max Frisch's *Andorra*, originally commissioned by the BBC, reached the stage at the National Theatre in London and subsequently Broadway.

Thirdly, and most importantly, the BBC's radio drama department devoted itself to developing the new art form of radio itself, making use of the medium's unique ability to dramatise the workings of the mind, and present internal monologue, dream and fantasy with a greater immediacy and impact than the stage or the screen could ever hope to achieve. A radiophonic workshop was created which provided electronically treated sound effects and became a pioneer in the development of electronic music. Experiments in stereophonic and quadraphonic sound followed. A whole new field – the marrying of poetic words with specially adapted sound was opened up.

Writers like Samuel Beckett and Harold Pinter were in the forefront of the many playwrights and poets who made use of the potential of radio. Beckett's first radio play *All that Fall* was broadcast by the Third Programme in 1957. It was followed by *Embers*

(1958) and *Words and Music* (1964). Among Harold Pinter's early works *A Slight Ache* (1959), *A Night Out* (1960) and *The Dwarfs* (1960) were commissioned by the BBC. John Arden's first dramatic work *The Life of Man* (1956) was written for a radio play competition. Tom Stoppard wrote some of his earlier plays for BBC radio and has continued to produce some of his best work for the medium (see Stoppard).

The long list of prominent playwrights who earned their first spurs in radio includes Robert Bolt, Alun Owen, Bill Naughton, Willis Hall, David Turner, Joe Orton, James Forsyth, John Mortimer, Henry Livings, James Hanley, Alan Ayckbourn (who was on the BBC staff as one of its radio producers in Leeds for many years) and Caryl Churchill, to name only some of the best known. Among the poets who were persuaded to write radio drama are Henry Reed, Ted Hughes and Peter Redgrove.

A writer who did his best work for radio was Giles Cooper (1918–1966) whose mordantly witty and eerily frightening radio plays far surpass his stage and television work. He was a master of the implied visual effect which could be hilarious, as, to give but one example, in *The Disagreeable Oyster* (1957), when the hero, or anti-hero, Bundy (who is represented by two inner voices that portray his mind split between his desires for respectability and for adventure) having been stripped by a mob of angry women, finds refuge in a nudist colony and enters a room filled with 'the discreet murmur of voices and, as a permanent background, the tockety-tock of ping-pong being played' thus instantly evoking the ludicrous image of large numbers of naked people playing table-tennis (see Cooper). Giles Cooper later also broke through into the live theatre: it is surely significant that one of his plays *Everything in the Garden* was adapted for the American stage by no less a playwright than Edward Albee.

III

After sixty years of continuous development British radio drama, although it has, of course, lost the large mass audience to television, still remains extremely vigorous. It uses all the refinements of modern technology, including stereophonic and binaural sound, electronic music and some ultramodern studio equipment. Its output is larger than ever – some 1500 productions a year – produced in London and regional centres at Bristol, Birmingham, Cardiff, Manchester, Glasgow and Belfast. It receives hundreds of unsolicited scripts every month. All these are read and returned; promising writers are guided and encouraged, those with the greatest potential are invited to radio writing seminars.

The BBC's radio drama department is thus a veritable nursery of writing talent. Although, on the average, only about two percent of the scripts received are ever of a standard that can be broadcast, some fifty new playwrights receive their first production each year on BBC radio. And many of these progress to television, the stage and the cinema.

The BBC's radio drama thus plays a vital part in fostering new dramatic writing talent and providing it with the practical experience of highly professional acting and direction. Compared to the production costs of the stage, television and the cinema, radio is an extremely inexpensive medium; the vast output of the department presents new writers with wider opportunities than any other medium could hope to offer.

The 'public service' concept underlying the BBC's original ethos also includes the notion of serving the nation's writing talent. Owing to the unique range of the BBC's radio drama output and the availability of such a large body of material to a public including young people of potential talent, it is no coincidence that the generation of playwrights of the new wave were born around 1930. They were the first to have grown up in a world in which so much drama was freely available. A generation of young people who came from social backgrounds previously not often exposed to drama, became familiar with a great body of plays broadcast by the BBC. When asked what made them want to become playwrights or actors, quite a few replied: 'By the time I was fifteen I had heard most of Shakespeare, Ibsen, Shaw and Chekhov on the radio'. How many talented young people of rural or industrial backgrounds in previous generations perhaps never even discovered their taste or ability for dramatic writing!

IV

The BBC also was the world's first broadcasting organisation to have started a regular television service, as early as 2 November 1936. This development had been preceded by years of experimentation. The first experimental television broadcast of a play actually took place as early as July 1930 when Lance Sieveking (one of the great pioneers of radio drama) directed a test transmission of Pirandello's *The Man with a Flower in his Mouth*. In the early, pre-war phase of British television, plays written for the stage were produced live from the studio. After each act there was an interval to allow viewers to relieve themselves until a bell recalled them to their sets. With the outbreak of war in September 1939, BBC television ceased operating, as it was thought that its transmitters might be used as directional beacons by German aircraft.

The service re-opened after the war on 7 June 1946, but did not achieve true mass penetration until 1953, when the broadcast of the coronation of Queen Elizabeth II led to the mass purchase of television sets. But as television became a genuine mass medium, the BBC's monopoly of television in Britain could not be maintained.

In 1955 a Conservative government introduced a rival commercial system. However, the legislation under which this new system operated was heavily influenced by a study of the worst aspects of American television. The commercial companies in Britain are under the control of a separate authority and obligated to broadcast a fixed proportion of culturally valuable material. Their licenses are reviewed at regular intervals in the light of their performance and some who have not fulfilled these obligations have lost them. Advertisements can only, by law, be broadcast in 'natural breaks' between programmes, they must be clearly separated from programme material, and the amount of advertising is strictly limited in time. Even more important, from the point of view of televised drama, was the existence of the BBC and its traditions which, from the very beginning, set standards with which the commercial companies had to compete. As a result the drama output of the commercial network (the fourteen regional companies network their more ambitious material) compares favourably with that of the BBC.

In 1982 a second commercial channel was added to BBC1, BBC2 and the existing commercial network. This Channel 4 is organised on a different basis from that of the first commercial network. It has no production facilities but commissions its programmes from independent producers as well as the existing commercial companies. It has thus become an important stimulus for independent film-makers and documentary producers. Many of the films it has commissioned, which constitute its drama output, have also become world wide successes in the cinema.

V

Drama, in a multitude of forms, thus plays an important part in the output of British television. The cost of television drama is very high compared to that of radio drama, but is still less than the production cost of a feature film. On the other hand an increasing amount of British television drama is now being produced on film.

There is, of course, a proliferation of reruns of cinema films on British television, as well as a large number of American serials, situation comedies and mini-series. On the BBC channels these products look infinitely better than in their home environment in the US, for they run uninterrupted by commercials. *Twin Peaks* or *Dallas* can develop a positively classical sweep towards a climax and peripeteia. Even on British commercial channels the interruptions by clearly separated advertisements tend to subdivide American material into a neat two or three act structure.

And, of course, there is still room for locally commissioned and produced popular as well as 'serious' drama. It is the existence of the latter which constitutes the unique feature of British as against US television. Both the BBC and the larger commercial companies (Thames and London Weekend Television in London, Granada in Manchester, Yorkshire TV in Leeds) make use of the best writing talent in the country for the production of dramatisations of novels and original plays specially written for the medium.

There is hardly a major dramatist who has not, in the last thirty years, contributed to the substantial body of this literature. Merely to cite some of the best known produces an impressive list: Beckett (*Eh Joe!, Ghost Trio, . . . but the clouds*), Pinter (*The Collection, The Lover, The Tea Party, The Basement, Langrishe Go Down*), Arden (*Soldier, Soldier, Wet Fish*), Stoppard (*Professional Foul*), John Mortimer (*A Voyage round my Father* and a long series of *Rumpole* episodes), Peter Nichols (*The Gorge*), John Osborne (*A Subject of Scandal and Concern*), John Hopkins (whose tetralogy *Talking to a Stranger* [1966] became one of the first television classics), David Mercer (*Let's Murder Vivaldi* and large body of other outstanding television drama), Trevor Griffiths (the Bill Brandt series about the life of a Labour M.P.), David Hare (*Licking Hitler*), Howard Brenton, Alan Bennett (*An Englishman Abroad*), A.E. Whitehead (*The Man who fell in love with his Wife*), Simon Gray (*Death of a Teddy Bear*), Michael Frayn – to name only some of the most important writers.

All these playwrights have also achieved prominence with their stage work. There is, however, also a considerable number of writers who concentrate on television and have thus become less prominent outside Britain. Among these are Dennis Potter, Colin Welland, Hugh Whitemore, Julia Jones, Nemone Lethbridge, Jeremy Sandford, Ken Loach and Mike Leigh. Here too the list could be prolonged quite considerably.

VI

Television, being essentially an unending stream of entertainment available on tap at any hour of the day, favours the epic, serial format which by its recurrence at regular times, structures the amorphous flow and forms the audience's listening habits. Hence the immense appeal of soap-operas, situation comedy, detective, police and thriller series, the dramatisation of long novels, and the arrangement even of plays designed to stand by themselves in series under generic titles like 'Play of the Day', 'Love Story', etc.

In British television drama these different genres are well integrated. Some of the best writers have adapted novels from Dickens and Trollope to Henry James, Robert Graves and Evelyn Waugh; some of them, like John Hopkins, have helped to create police-series such as the famous *Z-Cars* which injected a high degree of realism into what had been an anodyne form of moralistic kitsch about goody-goody bobbies (and greatly influenced American series that sprang up in imitation); even situation comedy in Britain has been, at times, on a fairly high artistic and intellectual level, one need only remember *Till Death us do part* or *Steptoe and Son*, which led to long-running, if somewhat debased American imitations in *All in the Family* and *Sanford and Son*. The leading soap operas, Granada's twice weekly *Coronation Street*, which has been running for decades, and the BBC's *East Enders*, attain a very respectable level as compassionate and sympathetic pictures of working-class life. This is by far most popular form of television drama in Britain and regularly reaches an audience around twelve million, which is to say that it is watched by about 25 percent of all adults in the United Kingdom.

Audience figures for 'single plays' (as the serious drama that tries to stand by itself is referred to in the professional jargon) are much lower than they were in the seventies. One of the reasons for this is the appearance of the fourth channel, which fragments the audience; but there has also been a spectacular upsurge in the sale of video recorders which enables the audience to make its own programming. The recent introduction of satellite television on a commercial basis, and cable television, as yet not very far advanced in Britain, adds a further factor. Whether satellite and cable can contribute their share to the fostering of creative drama remains to be seen. There has also been a certain drop in the quality of the plays being written – the creative upsurge of the fifties, sixties and early seventies seems to have slackened. The emphasis on intimate details of working-class lives tends, all too often, to produce a stereotype of atmospheric episodes from the world of not very interesting individuals. Thus there is, at present, something like a crisis in the field of the 'single play' which makes some observers fear for its continued presence in the schedules.

It must also be taken into account that whereas the first generation of the playwrights of the 1956 renaissance of British theatre had grown up in a world where most of their experience of drama came from radio with its strong component of 'classical' drama, the younger wave of playwrights has grown up in an entirely television dominated milieu, where the prevalent fare was, in spite of some high-level 'single plays' and series based on good literature, dominated by the cheaper kind of soap opera, sit-com and police shows. The effect of this on the writing of plays for the stage shows itself in a very much more fragmented structure of short scenes and a loss of the more solid principles of construction. And whereas the dramatists of the earlier group still mainly aimed at establishing themselves in the media so that they could then break into the live theatre, the lure of the easy way to fame and wealth by writing for television and the cinema now makes success on the West End stage, and even less so in the subsidised theatres, less alluring.

In this respect the situation in Britain is getting nearer to that in the United States where the absorption of writing talent into mass-produced television material has such a devastating effect. Nevertheless, the existence in Britain of the much stronger publicly-financed media of radio and television continues to provide a means for playwrights to earn a decent living without selling out completely. So long as the availability of slots on radio and television remains in the background, they are able to work within the parameters of the avant-garde fringe and pub theatres, or within subsidised theatres like the RSC, the National or the Royal Court which have shown a growing willingness to open their doors to new playwrights.

It remains to be seen whether the ominous changes that may be looming on the horizon will enable this situation to continue. The future of the BBC and the manner of its financing is a subject of violent political debate, the advent of national commercial radio channels (up to now commercial radio was strictly kept on a local level) and the proliferation of material on satellite and cable television channels may well drastically reduce the opportunities for serious dramatic material, which is far less cost-effective than other forms of broadcasting like pop-music or talk and game shows.

But whatever the future may hold, it is an established fact that radio and television have played an important role in the rise of the most vigorous period of dramatic writing in the history of the British isles since Elizabethan and Jacobean times.

REFERENCES

Guthrie, Tyrone. *Squirrel's Cage and Two Other Microphone Plays.* London: Cobden Sanderson, 1931; quoted in James Forsyth, *Tyrone Guthrie,* London: Hamish Hamilton, 1976.

MacNeice, Louis. *Christopher Columbus. A Radio Play.* London: Faber & Faber, 1944.

Stoppard, Tom. *The Dog it was that died and Other plays.* London: Faber & Faber, 1983 (includes Stoppard's early short plays for radio together with his latest radio play); his earlier radio plays are in *If you are Glad I'll be Frank.* London: Faber & Faber, 1969; *Albert's Bridge.* London: Faber & Faber, 1969; and *Artist Descending a Staircase and Where are they now? Two Radio Plays.* London: Faber & Faber, 1973.

Cooper, Giles. *Six Plays for Radio.* London: BBC, 1966.

13

The Playwriting Profession: Setting Out and the Journey

Theodore Shank

Playwright Howard Barker says there is a kind of promotion system for playwrights in Britain. They begin on the fringe – perhaps in London at the Bush Theatre or Upstairs at the Royal Court or in Edinburgh at the Traverse Theatre – and if they do good work and develop a reputation, they are promoted to the main house at the Royal Court Theatre. If that goes well, the natural impetus, he says, is either toward writing for television or moving on to the Royal National Theatre or the Royal Shakespeare Company which are the premiere flagships of the culture. However, very few playwrights manage to follow this simple formula. The roads to success as a playwright are various. While it is impossible to describe the typical training and development of British playwrights, the opportunities available and a few selected case histories will suggest how some playwrights became playwrights and how they survive in a profession of severely limited opportunities.

The first theatrical experience of an incipient young playwright living outside of London might be to see a performance by a touring company. A youngster might see a production by Welfare State International [Photo 3] and even become involved in working with the company during a residency. When Welfare State arrives in a community it is much like a circus coming to town. They usually set up out doors in parks, soccer fields, tents, shopping malls or other public places. They construct props, large puppets, masks, lanterns and banners culminating in parades and performances. It is easy to see how such excitement, contrasting with the drabness of an industrial town, could inspire a teenager to devote his or her life to the theatre. Or a young student might see a performance of a new play by Paines Plough which tours throughout England and might even participate in a playwriting workshop – perhaps led by the playwright or the director of the touring production. While most productions of the Royal National Theatre do not tour, special touring shows are produced which are intended to interest ethnically heterogeneous audiences. In the last few years young people have seen Lorca's *Blood Wedding* set in Cuba and performed by a cast of predominantly black actors directed for the National Theatre school tour by Yvonne Brewster, head of the Talawa Theatre Company. And they have seen Jatinder Verma's productions of *Tartuffe* and *The Government Inspector* [Photo 4] presented by Asian actors [see Verma essay]. Other early theatre experiences might be on a school trip to one of the regional repertory theatres or to London or Stratford-upon-Avon. A young student might have been lucky enough to be attending Dartington Primary School in 1992 when Adrian Mitchell was in residence writing a play with the students which was then produced.

The National Youth Theatre has been in existence for more than 35 years, and it is estimated that over 20,000 students aged 14–21 have been involved in their courses and productions. The organization is based in London but have toured productions throughout Britain and to several countries abroad. They accept students from throughout the country who participate during school holidays. While there is no specific training for young writers, the improvisation courses provide some pre-playwriting experience. The success of the organization has been such that there is now also a Scottish Youth Theatre and a Welsh National Youth Theatre.

Except for possible peripheral involvement with a theatre company such as Welfare State or as a participant in one of the Youth Theatres, the first theatrical training a future playwright is likely to receive is at a university of art college. Some students, who subsequently became playwright-director-designers of their own companies studied visual arts at a college such as Leeds or Dartington. Geraldine Pilgrim and Janet Goddard, who founded Hesitate and Demonstrate [see Sobieski essay], studied painting at Leeds where they came under the influence of John Fox, the founding director of Welfare State, and John Darling, who had worked with both the People Show [Photo 8] and the John Bull Puncture Repair Kit. Both Fox and Darling, of course, have visual arts backgrounds.

On the other hand, playwrights with a strong verbal interest, who work in the more traditional way of writing scripts which are staged by others, typically attended universities where the emphasis of their studies was more often philosophy, languages, history or literature rather than drama. In part this may be so because drama programs were comparatively rare and were made increasingly so in the eighties when budget cuts resulted in several departments being abolished. Specific training in playwriting is even more rare, with most such instruction being informal.

Advanced education of future playwrights is concentrated in four or five universities. Playwrights born in the twenties and thirties most often attended Oxford, Cambridge and Manchester in that order of frequency. A few, including Harold Pinter, Ronald Harwood and Ann Jellicoe attended professional acting schools (RADA and Central School of Speech and Drama) instead of university. Some, such as Edward Bond, Shelagh Delaney, Michael Hastings, Mustapha Matura, Tom Stoppard and Peter Barnes, received only secondary educations.

Among the younger playwrights David Edgar, Mike Stott and Peter Flannery all attended Manchester. Terry Johnson and Louise Page received degrees from Birmingham where their interest in playwriting was doubtlessly encouraged by David Edgar who had become Playwright-in-Residence. Resident playwrights are the principal means by which students receive specific training in playwriting. While a few other universities are represented – Howard Barker studied History at Sussex, Snoo Wilson has a degree in English and American Studies from the University of East Anglia, and James Stock has an MA degree from Exeter – a majority of future playwrights attended Oxford or Cambridge, most often the latter. Oxford, for example, was the university attended by Caryl Churchill, Christopher Hampton and David Mowatt. Cambridge is the alma mater of Howard Brenton, Steve Gooch, David Hare, Dusty Hughes and Steven Poliakoff.

Cambridge has a reputation as the 'RADA' for directors' even though all of the training available there is extra curricular in productions produced by the drama societies. The same is true of Oxford where in 1989 the Cameron MacIntosh Visiting Professor of Contemporary Theatre was established to promote the study and practice of contemporary theatre. In addition to paying the expenses of the professorship held so far by Stephen Sondheim, Ian McKellen and Alan Ayckbourn, the fund allocates support to producing organisations at Oxford. Professionals work with the students on productions and younger students learn from more experienced ones. After all, Peter Hall and Trevor Nunn, later artistic directors of the Royal National Theatre and the Royal Shakespeare Company, were active in the Cambridge drama societies and upon receiving their degrees their skills and accomplishments were such that they immediately began working professionally.

Other opportunities available to young writers are courses and festivals sponsored by theatres and other organizations that are assisted by grants from the Arts Council of Great Britain, Regional Arts Boards and corporate sources. There is the National Student Drama Festival, principally sponsored by the *Sunday Times* and the BBC, and *The Guardian* Student Drama Award which bring professional attention to the best student work. There is also the Young Writers Festival of the Royal Court Theatre which has had success in finding young playwrights with less formal education. Another source of training is made possible by The Arts Council which offers a maximum of £2000 per year to help companies organise skills workshops which are conducted by experienced writers. Several theatres, including the Royal Court in London, the Traverse Theatre in Edinburgh and the touring company Paines Plough, have used these funds effectively.

ARTS COUNCIL OF GREAT BRITAIN

There can be no doubt that the Arts Council of Great Britain and its regional affiliates have done the most to foster playwriting in the country. If the commercial theatres of the West End are an indication of what theatre in Britain would be like without the Arts Council, we must be extraordinarily grateful to those responsible for the continuing existence of the Arts Council. Playwrights would hardly survive writing for live theatre if it were not for the Arts Council. Howard Barker, perhaps the most profoundly reflective and prolific of the younger mature British playwrights says of the Arts Council:

> I must be the classical example of someone who has been wholly sustained by state funding. I've been very much supported by that always. The state has patronized me and I'm wholly dependent on it. That's a pretty poor income, I might add.

While he is somewhat over-stating his dependence on such subsidy – he has written plays for BBC Television (unproduced) and he receives royalties for productions at home and abroad – there is no doubt about the importance of the support provided to Barker and many others by the Arts Council either directly in the form of bursaries or indirectly through theatres.

The total grant to the Arts Council for 1992–3 was £221.2 million. Roughly 35 percent of this amount went to the Scottish Arts Council, the Welsh Arts Council, and ten Regional Arts Boards. Another £18.9 million was awarded directly to the Royal Opera, the Royal Ballet, and the Birmingham Royal Ballet. The remainder was divided among the various Panels: Dance, Drama, Literature, Multi-Disciplinary Arts, Music, Touring and Visual Arts. The two theatres with the largest grants were the Royal National Theatre (£10.89 million) and the Royal Shakespeare Theatre (£8.26 million); and both theatres were awarded additional money to support their touring programs (£200,000 and £540,000 respectively). By contrast the English Stage Company at the Royal Court Theatre received only £840,000 and Paines Plough £143,500.

In 1992–3 £310,000 of the Drama portion of the Arts Council budget went toward the several 'Schemes for Writers and Theatre Companies' which assist playwrights directly and theatres on behalf of playwrights. Theatres which receive annual grants in excess of £185,000 from the Arts Council and other public funds are expected to offer at least one commission from those funds. Other theatres may apply to the Arts Council for funds to award commissions. Theatres must pay the playwright no less than the minimum prescribed by the Theatre Writers Union (£3800 in 1992) and the Arts Council provides at least half of this. About 100 commissions are awarded in a year. Also available on application are Resident Dramatist Attachment Awards to provide a writer with the opportunity to become directly involved in the work of a theatre. Approximately 25 of these awards are made in a year. In 1992–3 the award was £4000 for a six-months residency which could be extended for a maximum of two additional six-months periods. The theatre is expected to offer a commission for the play written during a residency and, if produced, the playwright receives a royalty of 7.5 percent of total box office income. Charles Hart, the Arts Council officer in charge of theatre writers' schemes points out that a residency 'helps put the writer into a seat of power being right there in the theatre. We also don't expect the theatre to use the

writer to read plays on the cheap' (Hart). Theatres can also apply for funding on behalf of playwrights for second productions of plays, to commission a translation, to engage experienced writers, and to offer workshops to aid 'the skills development of inexperienced playwrights or the further development of established writers' (*Arts Council Schemes*).

Awards which the Arts Council makes directly to playwrights are in the form of bursaries to support a playwright or for translations. These are normally for £3000 and no more than £5000; they cover no particular period. Charles Hart explains the requirements.

> Anyone who has written three works for the stage (not neces-sarily produced) can apply, but the percentage of success is low. Often these go to experienced writers who want to get off the commission treadmill – writers who want to write something for themselves. (Hart)

Howard Barker is one of the experienced playwrights who has benefitted from bursaries. They, together with commissions, have helped make it possible for him to write for live theatre with little other income.

With the increasing development of the European Community and Britain's involvement, Hart thinks there may be some changes in the way writers are supported. In France, he says, writers are given production money so they have some leverage when they ask a theatre to produce their plays. There is also the possibility that British writers will be able to apply for support from other countries and vice versa.

In 1991 the Arts Council made an important change to accommo-date the work of some artists who do not fit into the traditional categories. A program called New Collaborations was formed with a budget for the first year (1991–2) of £200,000 and increased for the second year to £350, 000. According to Lois Keidan, the Arts Council Coordinator for the program, there was a dual need for the new program. First, some worthy work, some which might be considered the *most* worthy in terms of new expression in the arts, was not being funded by the existing programs because they were not considered to be within their province. A second impetus for the creation of a New Collaborations program was a report on ethnic arts commissioned by the Arts Council (Keidan). In his report Michael McMillan, a black writer, concluded that the traditional categories of art used by the Arts Council were Euro-centric thus leaving out many artists with non-European heritage (McMillan, 6–7).

While the Drama Department of the Arts Council had seen its purview to be broad enough to include the work of experimental companies in which writers, visual artists and musicians collaborate – companies such as Welfare State, Lumiere and Son, Hesitate and Demonstrate, and the People Show [see Sobieski essay] – the New Collaborations program provides an additional source of funding for the exploration of cross-media possibilities.

TRAVERSE THEATRE

Edinburgh's Traverse Theatre is one of those small theatres where a fortunate playwright might receive his or her first production of a play. In 1992 the Traverse Theatre moved into a new building which is probably the only purpose-built theatre erected in Britain during the second half of the twentieth century to be devoted to new playwriting. Its two performance spaces seating 100 and 250–300 are intended to carry on the policy of producing new work which was initiated in 1963 by its founder, Jim Haynes, and has endured under the direction of Chris Parr and others. The recently-appointed artistic director, Ian Brown, is continuing the tradition of presenting premieres of British plays, especially Scottish, and British premieres of plays from abroad.

Ian Brown sees the mission of the Traverse as serving primarily new Scottish playwrights. To help them develop he has successfully applied for aid from the BBC Television in Scotland to finance Inter-course, a playwriting course for new writers. The five-month course was taught by the Traverse directors and working playwrights in Scotland. Some of these plays were then presented in the autumn festival. The theatre also receives about 500 unsolicited plays each year which are read by a Reading Committee which meets every 4–5 weeks. While this may result in only one play a year which the theatre produces, Ian Brown believes it is worth devoting energy to the reading of these plays by way of encouraging young writers.

Most of the plays produced by the Traverse come from commissions awarded to playwrights whose work they know and from referrals by agents. There are about ten commissions out at any one

time. When a commissioned play comes in and it has been read by
Brown and other staff members, they talk with the writer about it
and arrange for a private reading. A company of actors will spend
at least one day working on it.

> These workshops vary depending on the what is needed. Some
> plays need scenes worked on so the writer can re-write. It's
> very important to hear what the actors have to say – 'This
> doesn't work because'. It's very important to have actors who
> can try out scenes in different ways and can make suggestions.
> (Brown)

There are several production formats for those plays chosen.
There are mini festivals of staged readings, there is a new play
festival in which about six plays of an hour or less are fully
produced and presented on double or triple bills, and there are
individual productions of longer plays.

The Traverse finds itself in a unique position with respect to
Scottish playwrights because the two largest theatres in Scotland,
the Lyceum in Edinburgh and the Citizens' in Glasgow, present
very little new work. 'That is a real problem', says Ian Brown,
'because writers have no place to progress to after the Traverse.'

> So the Traverse comes under pressure to present writers who may
> have outgrown the theatre – writers who should have moved to
> larger stages. I'm ignoring the older generation of playwrights
> because I don't have enough slots. I feel my job primarily is
> to present newer writers, to nurture them. I can't deal with the
> older writers.

Such a writer is Glaswegian Tom McGrath whose first production
was at the Traverse in the 70s. The Artistic Director, Chris Parr, gave
him a commission and was very helpful in guiding him.

> The Traverse was of key importance to me – more so than
> Glasgow. Edinburgh gave me a chance to be in a foreign place.
> In Glasgow they could hardly accept that I might have some-
> thing to say. Also the internationalism of the Traverse and the
> Edinburgh Festival is very important because of the perspective
> it gives you.

PAINES PLOUGH

Paines Plough, founded in 1974 by director John Adams and play-wright David Pownall, has held fast to its objective of presenting new plays by relatively unknown writers. Anna Furse, who became artistic director in 1990, refers to the company as the leading touring company specialising in new theatre by new writers. Their publicity warns that 'without staging the voices of today, there will be no theatrical development tomorrow'. The company performs throughout Britain and internationally visiting some twenty cities per year.

Although they fully produce only two or three plays per year (all premieres), they have a greater impact on new writing than that suggests. They organize writers workshops, offer special training courses in writing for the theatre, present readings of new plays, offer playwriting residencies with the company. The company also does residencies in schools, theatres and community organisations. Some of these activities receive funding from the Arts Council of Great Britain in addition to their basic annual Arts Council grant (£143,500 for 1992–3). For several years they have also received support from the stationers W.H. Smith Ltd in support of the W.H. Smith/Paines Plough Writers' Roadshow consisting of workshops, rehearsed readings, talks and discussions with members of the company while on tour. These are intended for young, potential writers who may have had little experience, but are also attended by some more experienced writers.

Anna Furse says, 'We are interested in developing the concept of the writer. We should be at the cutting edge of what is the playwright's place in the world.' They see the workshops as a means of urging writers to the edge. The company have organised workshops for writers which focused on new feminist theory, on music theatre, on black writing (in cooperation with Black Theatre Cooperative), on writing by and for disabled people (Creating Ripples) and a workshop conducted by artists experienced in visual theatre, dance and music. There are also playwrights who meet regularly under the auspices of Paines Plough.

The company advertises for the submission of 'scripts from writers everywhere – produced or unproduced, beginners and experts.' Each script receives a written report from their Script Reading Panel and is considered for the company's season of rehearsed readings of new plays by professional actors and directors. In these readings the emphasis is on the process and audience feedback to the writer. So as not to discourage theatre artists whose interests are not primarily verbal, the company accepts 'treatments' for dramatic works which may be importantly visual, physical or musical. According to their publicity,

> PAINES PLOUGH is committed to writing as part of a total theatre. Musicians, dancers, as well as designers, actors and directors work together with the writer towards the most consciously THEATRICAL results. We avoid naturalism. We are devoted to the survival of live theatre as distinct from TV, film and radio drama.

Among the playwrights Paines Plough claims responsibility for helping to develop are Terry Johnson, Heathcote Williams, Jonathan Gems, Dusty Hughes, Doug Lucie and Louise Page.

ROYAL COURT THEATRE

The English Stage Company at the Royal Court Theatre has had a longer history of producing new plays and in various ways promoting, encouraging and helping playwrights develop their abilities. An Arts Council appraisal team in 1989 called it 'the major new writing theatre in the country' and noted that the larger of its two theatres, seating 405 in the three tiers currently used, 'is the only auditorium of its size principally producing new work' (Arts Council Report).

The company's dedication to new plays began in 1956 under artistic director George Devine who produced John Osborne's *Look Back in Anger* and has continued – principally under the direction of William Gaskill (1965–72), who opened the small Theatre Upstairs in 1969, and Max Stafford-Clark who took over the directorship in 1979 and is expected to remain until 1993. The Court has accumulated such a history of accomplishments, having produced the early works of Arnold Wesker, John Arden, Edward Bond, Ann Jellicoe, Joe Orton, David Storey, David Hare, Howard Brenton, Caryl Churchill and Timberlake Wertenbaker, that serious attention is paid to each new playwright introduced there. With the opening of the small Theatre Upstairs, the Royal Court increased their potential for producing new work. It is the special quality of the Royal Court that someone like Wertenbaker can, in eight years, go from being an unknown with a play in the Theatre Upstairs to second and third plays in the larger theatre to being recognized internationally.

The Royal Court finds unknown playwrights through the 1500 scripts they receive annually in the mail. Max Stafford-Clark says it is unlikely they would produce any of the unsolicited plays, but the theatre forms relationships with the most promising of the writers and may commission plays from them. Typically commissioned plays receive feedback from members of the staff and might go through several drafts followed by a reading and, perhaps, by production in the Theatre Upstairs. Stafford-Clark describes the process by which all plays are evaluated. Every Friday morning there is a script meeting chaired by the Literary Manager of the theatre and attended by several staff members including Stafford-Clark, the Writer-in-Residence, the director of the Young People's Theatre, two young directors invited as guests, and perhaps others for a total of about nine. A chart is maintained listing who was there, the ratings, and other information.

> We discuss all of the plays that have come in and we rate them with a particular code. PU means 'production Upstairs', C means 'meet the writer', N means 'no', X means 'over my dead body', and so on. . . . Also on the chart is information on what's in the larder. There are the plays completed for downstairs, plays that are scheduled for downstairs, plays we know people are working on and plays commissioned that we know people intend to write for us but haven't yet started. And we have the same information for the Theatre Upstairs.

A productive way of discovering promising young writers is through the Young Writers Festivals. Stafford-Clark believes that his theatre must be open to amateur writers.

> You must be able to respond to a play written by a taxi driver or somebody from a council estate in Bradford such as Andrea Dunbar [a young writer who died of a stroke in 1990 at the age of twenty-nine] . . . . writers who haven't necessarily had secondary educations.

Rather than simply hoping such writer will send a script to the Royal Court, directors and writers and tutors journey into various regions of the country and offer workshops. The playwrights are encouraged to write toward a certain deadline and those plays are favourably considered for a Festival. These Festivals are fostered by the Royal Court, but are dependent upon local interest. 'So, for example, we would get in touch with the theatre in Plymouth, tell them what we want to do, and ask for their help. We might ask them to provide us with six actors for the day.'

The Royal Court has also explored ways of bringing writers from other media into the theatre. In 1990, following the political upheaval in Eastern Europe, Stafford-Clark conceived this simple structure:

> We sent original Socratic dialogues and plays by Havel, which are very much based on Socratic dialogues, to a number of key thinkers and writers – people like the Bishop of Durham and a scabrous columnist for the *Daily Mail*. We asked each of them to write a play 30–40 minutes long – a two-hander. We commissioned 16 and 9 or 10 came through.

The results were staged under the collective title, 'May Days' using both theatres. Media attention was good, critical response and attendance were poor. In the end Stafford-Clark realized 'you can't create a playwright by effort of will. The Bishop of Durham is a master orator, but you don't transform him into a playwright simply by involving him in the program.'

In 1991 the London International Theatre Festival used the 'May Days' concept for a series of short plays Upstairs at the Royal Court. In this instance, however, each play was accompanied by a longer play which remained constant – Ariel Dorfman's *Death and the Maiden* which subsequently moved downstairs to the larger theatre and received an Olivier Award in 1992.

The Court has about 30 plays under commission at any one time. While there are writers such as Peter Flannery and Caryl Churchill who prefer not to have commissions so they can decide on the best place for their play when it's finished, most writers welcome the commitment of a theatre. The theatre has an intention of producing the plays they commission. In practice, however, says Stafford-Clark, they perform only about half of them.

> There was a period early in my regime when we made a commitment to produce every play commissioned. In retrospect that

was a mistake as it led to us doing plays that didn't advance that writer's reputation and didn't do the theatre any good.

Although commission rates may vary depending upon the stature of the playwright, they are intended to be commensurate with the RSC and the National. Upstairs the commission in 1992 was a standard £4000. In the larger theatre downstairs commissions vary from £5000 to £8000, half of which could be an advance against royalties.

Nurturing writers is important, says Stafford-Clark, but it is also important to produce mature contemporary plays.

It is important that we keep the loyalty of senior writers and not allow them to graduate to [the National Theatre's] Olivier or Lyttelton or the [RSC's] Barbican. Partly it is financial and partly the standards become higher. If you see a new Caryl Churchill play along side a play by a new writer you are setting a standard for the younger writer. And it is important to nurture the senior writers. The history of the Royal Court is littered with the whale-like corpses of writers from previous generations washed up on the shores of Sloane Square.

A workshop process is used in the preparation of some plays. The process, previously used by Stafford-Clark and William Gaskill when they directed the Joint Stock Company, may begin before the play is written and is potentially very helpful to the playwright in developing the script. Caryl Churchill's *Serious Money* (1987) was to deal with the complicated world of finance which acquaintances had warned they would never understand. The three-week workshop period began without a script but with the determination to penetrate the secrets of the City. Stafford-Clark explained how they went about it.

The actors went to the City and talked with stock brokers, with people on the floor of the Futures Exchange and they reenacted those interviews every evening to each other. An actor would take a particular story from the *Financial Times* that seemed impenetrable – like chocolate going up in the Ivory Coast. They would follow that story through the next day about transport subsidies being withdrawn by the French Government so you could see that the price of chocolate was going to go up so chocolate would be a good futures to buy. I think the workshop helped Caryl write the play.

The workshop for Wertenbaker's *Our Country's Good* was different. The play was to be based on Thomas Keneally's novel *The Playmaker* and they couldn't research the world of convicts going to Australia in the eighteenth century in the same direct way. But again the research helped to penetrate that world and give a sense of its emotive qualities and some of it ended up in the script.

For example, an actor researched the technique of hanging – how the body weight had to be commensurate with the drop so as to avoid pulling the head off. Too short a drop wouldn't do the job. The problem is set out in the novel and more fully explored in the play. Another actor was given a map of eighteenth-century London and told to walk over Suffolk Bridge to Drury Lane seeing what he would have seen two hundred years earlier. He was then able to describe to the others more vividly what it would have been like.

ROYAL SHAKESPEARE COMPANY

The RSC is known as a company which produces the classics, especially Shakespeare, but the leadership there – Artistic Director Adrian Noble and Executive Producer Michael Attenborough – believe the production of new plays in their program to be indispensable. It is important, says Attenborough, to audience, actors and directors. 'A company that is merely examining antiquity and classics could become stilted or stultified, stagnant, without being enriched with what comes from contemporary writing.' In practice, new plays have been presented in four of the five performance spaces of the RSC (three in Stratford-upon-Avon and two in London). Because these spaces vary in configuration and size, it is possible to put each new play in that space which best suits it in terms of its spacial demands and the anticipated audience interest. The theatre which most often has originated new work is the Other Place at Stratford which seats 220. Plays which opened there and subsequently transferred to London and elsewhere include Pam Gems' *Piaf* and Christopher Hampton's *Les Liaisons Dangereuses*. Some of the other writers whose plays premiered at The Other

Place include Edward Bond, Howard Brenton, Nick Dear, David Edgar, Peter Flannery, David Rudkin and Peter Whelan. Many of these plays transferred to the 200-seat Pit in London the following season.

There are several other benefits offered a writer who works at the RSC. First of all, the writer becomes part of a company with a group of actors who know each other and have worked together. You could argue, says Attenborough, that such a company saves two weeks rehearsal. And the RSC offers the number of actors and facilities that encourages the writer 'to paint on a larger canvas'. The writer needn't worry about cast size; in fact, the RSC is not interested in plays which could be produced by a less well-endowed theatre. Because the company specifically focuses on the classics, taking on plays with poetic language and complex textual challenges, the writer gains an understanding of the relationship between language and emotion, language and ideas, language and the audience. Attenborough says that the dialogue of Peter Flannery's *Singer* and the non-naturalistic form of the play was inspired by Flannery having seen everything in the Swan Theatre at Stratford and seeing the way non-contemporary texts work. Because the aim of the theatre is for actors to return over a period of time and become really fine classical actors, they bring to a new play a range of skills and understanding which an actor who had been doing only new work would not have. From the company's point-of-view there is a marriage between the textual rigor of classical work and the contemporary vision of contemporary work. Hopefully, the contemporary vision will help the classical work as well. Actors who do both can make classical work feel contemporary (Attenborough).

Attenborough believes it is important to integrate writers into the company. He points out that unlike other workers in the theatre, playwrights are typically 'out workers'. Until their play is in rehearsal, their work is done away from the company. The RSC leadership wants writers to have the social opportunity of being part of the company and, for example, offers them transportation and accommodation to Stratford where they can spend time with the acting company which typically stays together for a two-year cycle.

It is possible for a playwright and a director to explore potential projects in the rehearsal studios. Gregory Doran, who had worked as an assistant director at the RSC, wanted to explore with some of the RSC actors the narrative form of Homer's *Odyssey*. The playwright

Derek Walcott was invited to work on it with the group. The work culminated in a production which opened at The Other Place at Stratford in 1992.

In the case of the young writer James Stock, who became a playwright in resident during 1992 with the help of a Thames Television Theatre Writer award, he was free to work on whatever interested him. 'We hope', says Attenborough, 'that at the end of twelve months we will have a play from him that we want to do.'

> He's a relatively inexperienced and raw writer. I hope he'll spend a lot of time digesting the work going on around him. It's not our responsibility to tell him what kind of playwright he should be. Fundamentally, you enable them to write the play they would have written anyway. I think you develop scripts by eliciting from the writer as clearly as you can where the writer wants to go. Help the writer try to articulate what he or she wants to achieve. Then advise them by helping them achieve it. What are you after? What's the play about? Where do you want to go? What do you want to achieve with the play? Where's its heartbeat? Then I can say, 'If that's what you want to achieve, I think you're achieving it there and not there for the following reasons.'

Attenborough believes the point at which a director is assigned to work with the playwright is very crucial. 'If you bring in a director too early, they can limit the range of the work because they are already beginning to see how they want to stage it. Equally, if a play is too fully developed and the director has strong views, the writers eyes can cross in confusion.'

ROYAL NATIONAL THEATRE

John Burgess, the Associate Director of the National Theatre Studio and Literary Manager for new work at the National Theatre, has an even stronger hands off policy with respect to writers. 'I don't believe in developing new writers,' he says, 'I believe in supporting them. I believe in giving them money. I believe in giving them opportunities.'

> If you're in the field of anything new, you have to allow it to be whatever it needs to be. The point about new talent is that if it

is new, it's not like old talent. I regard my self as a director, and I see my literary manager job as a non-job – standing out of the way or being on the right committees to promote the writing. But some people feel a need to justify the job by doing a lot 'now alter Act Three'. I can't imagine John Arden being a better writer for a story conference. What's wrong with *Sergeant Musgrave's Dance* no story conference will cure; and what's right with it no story conference will produce.

The National Theatre Studio, which Burgess helped found in 1984, is a unique organization. The building in which it is housed is given rent free and it is funded by private money raised by the National Theatre. The building does not meet fire regulations for theatres, so there are no public performances, only presentations to invited audiences every month or so. As there is no need to make money, this is not a problem. The Studio has two functions: one is to run classes for the actors of the National Theatre, the other is 'to bring on' new writers and directors.

Burgess looks for young writers in many places. He used to work at the Royal Court and see the plays presented by the Young Writers Festivals and he looks at the best plays from the playwriting program at the University of Birmingham. Sometimes these young writers are offered commissions. More recently, they have been attached to the Studio where they become part of the community, free to attend rehearsals and other activities of the Studio. They are given an office and a typewriter and expected to show up for work every day. They are given a playwright tutor to whom they show their work once or twice a week and talk about problems. For this younger group and more experienced promising writers, the Studio may organize an unrehearsed reading so the writer can hear the work. Or a play may be given four-weeks rehearsal with a National Theatre cast and performed once or twice for people from the National Theatre or other theatres. The play might end up being produced in the National's small Cottesloe or even in the large Olivier Theatre or another theatre might decide to produce it. Burgess says that Sarah Daniels' *Neap Tide* would not have been produced in the Cottesloe so soon had it not been for the Studio. And *Trackers* by Tony Harrison would not have gotten on without the Studio. It was created in the Studio to go to the Delphi Festival in 1988. Then it was presented in the Olivier.

The National Studio has also fostered group playwriting projects.

Black Poppies was developed by a group of black actors who began by interviewing black soldiers and then edited the transcripts and performed it. Subsequently it was adapted for television. Burgess had used the same process earlier at the Royal Court resulting in the play *Falkland Sound*.

Most of the new work presented on the three stages of the National Theatre does not come from the Studio, it comes from offering experienced writers direct commissions for new plays, adaptations and translations. In any one season since the artistic directorship has been taken over by Richard Eyre, approximately half of the productions consist of these premieres and half of classics and revivals of more recent plays. This is an increase over the years when Peter Hall was Artistic Director and only about one-third of the productions were premieres.

There is no question that playwrights are most anxious for their plays to be produced by the National or the RSC. These theatres offer the finest facilities available, some of the most skilled actors and directors, nurturing and, compared to the commercial theatre of the West End, an openness with respect to serious subject matter and style. The not-for-profit theatres all pay roughly the same for commissions and residencies, but if one's play is presented in one of the larger theatres of the National or the RSC there is a chance that additional royalties will make it possible to survive without another job or without writing for TV or film.

ARRIVAL AND SURVIVAL

The means are various by which playwrights get a foothold in the theatre so as to practice their art and survive. Many able ones give up or are attracted to other media; some really prefer the other media. David Farr, the twenty-one year old who received *The Guardian* Student Drama Award in 1991 seemed headed for film even as he accepted the award. Others have doggedly held on to a profession in live theatre despite the difficulties. And some such as Alan Ayckbourn, Caryl Churchill and David Hare have been able to earn more than a survival income. Others, despite skill and productions, lead a rather precarious financial existence.

In addition to the Arts Council support, a playwright might receive royalties based on box office receipts; however, appreciable income from this source is only likely for productions in the larger theatres because usually the amount of the commission is deducted from the playwright's share of the royalties. The Arts Council has a rule that no writer may be offered awards totalling more than £6000 in the course of a year. Since bursaries are normally £3000 and rarely the maximum of £5000, it is highly unlikely that the Arts Council limit would be reached. Commissions and residencies are essential if one is to devote one's total energies to writing; and even then the living is marginal. A commission for a young writer is unlikely to be more £3800 (the minimum agreed to by the Theatre Writers Union). A six-months residency is £4000 to which the theatre must contribute an additional £1000. So if in a year a playwright were lucky enough to receive a bursary, a commission, and a residency which was renewed for a second six-months period the total income for the year would come to £16,800. However, one would have to be very optimistic indeed to count on all of these awards – especially since the success rate for bursary applicants is low and most often go to experienced writers (Hart).

It is always possible that a playwright will have a big success and gain breathing space. Max Stafford-Clark, says that 'playwrights are the one category of theatre workers who are still rewarded inordinately by success.' For actors a long run, of course, means their job lasts longer.

> For a freelance director it makes little difference financially if the production is a success or a failure. But for the playwright it can make a big difference. The revival of *Top Girls* will have made Caryl Churchill about $28–30,000. So at one end of the scale playwrights can survive very happily – and not just from a West End transfer. A good run at the Royal Court can net you £12–15,000. On the other hand, that kind of bonanza occurs only rarely.

James Stock is a good example of how a promising young play-wright gets started in the profession and manages to survive. As a student Stock had no interest in writing professionally for the theatre. He studied English and Drama and did an MA degree at Exeter followed by a teacher's course at Sheffield. He then taught English and Drama while working toward a Ph.D. intending to write a dissertation on the history play as exemplified in the work of Churchill, Barker, Brenton and Bond. Stock says, 'I am fascinated with how they use history in their work.'

That must have had a profound influence on me because I was then writing plays more in earnest. All of my plays deal with a dialogue between past and present. I discovered what I was researching was the means by which I could take myself seriously as a writer. As my interest in writing about others decreased, my interest in doing my own work increased. I made the effort to write a couple of plays I thought were good enough to go somewhere. I sent them off.

His first encouragement as a playwright came from the Northwest Playwrights Workshop which was set up by the Manchester Branch of the Theatre Writer Union. Writers are invited to submit a play and are guaranteed two written reports. About a hundred people enter and six or seven are chosen for a workshop with professional actors and a director who present a public rehearsed reading at the Contact Theatre in Manchester. Stock was encouraged.

I entered twice and was successful twice. I began taking myself more seriously. Then I wrote a play [*Kissing the Gargoyle*] that was rejected. It was definitely much better than the two that had been accepted. So, I decided I was right and the other people were wrong. I re-wrote it and sent it off to Paines Plough theatre. They did a rehearsed reading of it in 1989. That went down quite well, and then the play sank without a trace. The director of the Contact Theatre said it was quite good. She didn't want to produce it, but she did want me to become a writer in residence for a year.

While in residence at Contact he wrote *The Shaming of Bright Millar* which was produced there. In the meantime he had written *A Prick Song for the New Leviathan* which was produced at a pub, the Old Red Lion in London, by a group of Stock's friends calling themselves the Plain Clothes Theatre Company. They worked for nothing and Stock was paid nothing. Then they commissioned him to write another play for them and succeeded in getting three bits of funding: a grant for the company from the Arts Council, a Barclays' New Stages Award, and commissioning money from the Arts Council. Stock wrote *Blue Night in the Heart of the West* which was presented at the Bush Theatre in the summer of 1991.

About this time there were other encouraging developments. The people at the Royal Court liked *Prick Song* and commissioned him to write a play for Upstairs. And the RSC applied successfully for a Thames Television Theatre Writers award on his behalf. He received £5000 for a year to serve as a writer in residence for the year beginning January 1992. Stock was ecstatic.

> I have to write a play for them by the end of the year. That's quite daunting. It's a way for the RSC to work with me without commissioning me. They want to work with me on developing my writing, giving me a place to do that and actors and directors to help me develop. I think it's a brilliant idea.

If Stock is to be able to work full-time as a writer, the commissions and residencies must continue. But can he write good plays fast enough to fulfil the commitments and thereby continue to earn the money necessary to survive as a playwright?

Most playwrights must consider Howard Barker very fortunate. It is rare that a playwright other than Shakespeare has a relationship with a theatre company that produces his plays exclusively. While Alan Ayckbourn's theatre in Scarborough presents the premiere productions of almost all of his plays, the theatre also produces the work of other playwrights. Field Day Theatre Company was founded in 1980 by Brian Friel and actor Stephen Rea in Northern Ireland and since then has produced most of Friel's plays. The touring theatre Hull Truck, directed by the young playwright John Godber, produces his plays among others. And Plain Clothes Theatre was formed by James Stock and his friends to produce two of his plays; but now that Stock has commitments to larger theatres, it is unlikely the relationship will continue. On the other hand, the touring company called the Wrestling School, formed in 1988 to produce the plays of Howard Barker exclusively, may well continue for some time. Not only is Barker prolific enough to provide a steady stream of plays, but the intellectual complexity of his work tends to make the major theatres apprehensive and competition for his plays is limited. The Wrestling School, named to suggest the concept of wrestling with ideas, is directed by actor/director Kenny Ireland who assembles a group of artists for each project. Originally the company was formed by a group of actors who asked Barker if he would write a play for them. He wrote *The Last Supper* and has continued to provide them with plays.

Barker dates his beginnings as a writer to 1970 when he sent a script through the post to the Royal Court and William Gaskill produced it in the Theatre Upstairs. Before that he had written two radio plays, but had not studied drama or English and his working class family did not attend the theatre. 'The only sense in which I was fostered', he says, 'relates to the BBC Radio Drama Department.'

> What help I've received was simply people taking me seriously. I've never been advised or told or been able to rewrite. My whole practice is at the typewriter. I do a first draft, then I produce a second clean copy which varies very little from the first draft. That's the draft that is offered to the theatres. Thereafter the only changes are cutting to reduce the length of scenes or speeches. I've never rewritten in rehearsal.

He considers a play to be 'a work of spontaneous inspiration' which could not be accomplished through rewriting and which would be compromised if he wrote a scenario before hand. And he says he has a superstition about analyzing his process.

> A writer must beware of inflicting too much self consciousness on himself. Once you've traced the founts and the sources of your method and become too familiar with them, it seems to menace in some way. I prefer to be less knowing about what I'm doing.

Barker writes almost exclusively for the live theatre. It is not that he objects to television, but the governing aesthetic – non-verbal naturalism – is opposed to his and makes the medium a hostile environment. His recent plays have been produced at the Royal Court and the Almeida, but by his own prescription for play-wright promotion, his plays should be produced regularly at the National Theatre or the RSC. Barker has an explanation for why they are not.

> It's morality. I'm deeply opposed to national theatres. I think they are bearers of contemporary culture and ideologies, and if you infringe that you're not welcome. I've infringed it because I don't appear to go along with their sort of Marxist, humanist, analysis of contemporary society. They express their objections to my work by finding it 'bewildering' or they are 'not sympathetic' to it or 'this just isn't the one for us'. But I've made a point of sending every text I've written to the National Theatre in order to say that they have rejected the lot. There's much I would criticize

about the idea of a national theatre, but for someone who writes plays as big as I do, their resources are important.

He thinks it may be for similar reasons that the RSC has rarely produced his plays although they have offered him commissions. But there may be another reason as well: 'There is a commercial instinct at the RSC which makes them think that my work can't sell.' Even at the Royal Court Barker feels there is a tendency that works against the production of avant-garde plays.

Theatres like the Royal Court have become oppressive in their taste. It's inevitable that a theatre that has produced a revolutionary environment in a few decades develops reactionary tendencies. There is a governing aesthetic in these places which I believe is hostile to the development of new styles in the theatre. It's the play of domesticity, the play of humanism, the play of social criticism. That's certainly true of the regime at the Royal Court. However, if I were a young writer that is probably the first place I'd go.

Since 1988 the principal British producer of Barker's work has been the Wrestling School which, he says, is the finest experience he's had. They use many of the same actors from production to production which results in the kind of ensemble that doesn't often exist in Britain. And the actors come to trust the writing and are not troubled, for example, by the lack of obvious connections between scenes and by long speeches and poetry. He attends all rehearsals which he finds refreshing after spending so much solitary time writing. And because he and the other members of the company have come to know each other well, there is an open atmosphere in rehearsals which gives him access to the actors. This is necessary, Barker believes, in a company that exists for one writer.

Barker is a diligent persistent writer who manages, because of a meagre income provided largely by the Arts Council, to devote himself entirely to writing. As a result, by writing three or four hours every day, he completes about two plays a year and usually another project – perhaps a libretto – as well.

Each play leads to the next. My practice is very much based on routine. I think the reason for my persistent output is that I don't develop except through writing. Attitudes to life and art are a result of practice, they're not the result of living or political considerations. Being an artist in the theatre is a heroic job. Not just because of the rampant philistinism in this culture, Paris is just as bad, but the actual remaking of yourself through writing is very much a self-generating, self-creating process.

REFERENCES

(Unless otherwise noted, all quotations and paraphrases are from the interviews listed below.)

Interviews

Attenborough, Michael. Executive Producer. Royal Shakespeare Company. Interview by the author, 4 September 1991.
Barker, Howard. Playwright. Interview by the author, 24 August 1991.
Brown, Ian. Artistic Director, Traverse Theatre (Edinburgh). Interview by the author, 29 August 1992.
Burgess, John. Associate Director of the Royal National Theatre Studio and Literary Manager for New Work at the National. Interview by the author, 4 September 1991.
Furse, Anna. Artistic Director, Paines Plough. Interview by the author, 4 September 1991.
Hart, Charles. Officer in charge of Writer Schemes, Arts Council of Great Britain. Interview by the author, 5 September 1991.
Keidan, Lois. Coordinator for New Collaborations, Arts Council of Great Britain. Interview by author, 4 September 1991.
McGrath, Tom. Playwright and Associate Literary Manager at the Lyceum, Edinburgh. Interviewed by the author, 30 August 1991.
Stafford-Clark, Max. Artistic Director, Royal Court Theatre. Interviewed by the author, 18 July 1991.
Stock, James. Playwright. Interview by the author, 4 September 1991.

Unpublished Material

Arts Council of Great Britain. *Report on the English Stage Company at the Royal Court Theatre*. 1 August 1989.

Published Material

Arts Council Schemes for Writers and Theatre Companies 1992/93. London: Arts Council of Great Britain, 1992.
McMillan, Michael. *Cultural Grounding; Live Art and Cultural Diversity: Action Research Project*. A Report for the Visual Arts Department of the Arts Council of Great Britain. London: Arts Council, October 1990.

14

Directors: The New Generation

Jane Edwardes

ᐸ

INTRODUCTION

Directors have been the pantomime villains of recent years. Are they, some have asked, a necessary evil or just an evil? The overwhelming dominance of the Oxbridge educated director means that actors and directors no longer share their training in common and actors have become alienated by directors whose heads are crammed with intellectual concepts but who have little understanding of the process of acting. Directors are also criticised for productions laced with concepts that are designed to draw attention to their own talents rather than those of the playwright. The director is the most powerful figure in contemporary British theatre and yet he or she (increasingly a she) is often the only person in the room who has never been specifically trained for the job. And yet their job is enormous; directors are expected to be artists, leaders, administrators and enablers. Given such overwhelming expectations, it is perhaps not surprising that some directors are defensive and anxious not to reveal their insecurities, thus closing themselves off from the talents, intuition and potential of the different people in the rehearsal room who should eventually create the pudding that is the production.

However loud the complaints, it is impossible to imagine that directors are going to go away. Nor would it be desirable. The mishmash of styles that must have prevailed in the past is no longer acceptable. Efforts to reinstate the actor-director have met with mixed success. The best directors provide a vision, and a harmony of style and tone which enhance their material; so much so that we talk about Deborah Warner's *Electra* (1988) and Richard Eyre's *Richard III* (1990). These directors work from a profound understanding of the text rather than a desire to impose their will upon it.

The directors interviewed below conform to the stereotype in that all but Deborah Warner were educated either at Oxford or Cambridge. But they are not academics, rather they concentrate their minds on the shared experience of theatre, the ways in which it differs from film and television. They have little in common except for the high quality of their work, born out of the fact that they thrive on creating a demanding situation in which different talents can feed, nurture and inspire each other to reach new creative heights. They are collaborators, but collaborators with distinctive minds of their own. British theatre has always been a compromise between art, showbiz and commerce. Somehow these directors have managed to negotiate a path through that maze. Their work is the most effective rebuttal to the accusation that directors are an unnecessary invention of the Twentieth Century.

DECLAN DONNELLAN

Cheek by Jowl was started in 1981 by director Declan Donnellan and designer Nick Ormerod at a time when small-scale touring was struggling to find an audience for the new work that had drawn people in the seventies. From the beginning Donnellan and Ormerod were attracted to the classics. 'We like plays,' says Donnellan, 'that have an epic, poetic dimension. Plays about great issues that are not tied to any particular period. The great literary texts are so emotional.' The pair have created such a following for their work that alongside revivals of Shakespeare, they have been able to win audiences for the British premieres of Racine's *Andromache* (1984), Lessing's *Sara* (1990), Corneille's *The Cid* (1986) and Ostrovsky's *A Family Affair* (1988) just on the strength of the company's name. Not that they have buried themselves in the past. Ostrovsky's *A Family Affair* was as telling a comment on Thatcher's Britain as Caryl Churchill's *Serious Money* (1987) and the company's otherwise disappointing production of *The Tempest* (1988), which focused on the theme of political oppression, had an astonishing effect on audiences in Romania prior to the downfall of Ceaucescu. They recognised Elena Ceaucescu in Anne White's performance as the 'Queen' of Naples (gender bending is a common feature of the company) and, in the actors' revolt against Prospero at the end of the Masque, a call for revolution.

While the big musicals of the eighties relied on more and more spectacular effects, Cheek by Jowl did it all with just actors enhanced by the simple, effective statements of Nick Ormerod's designs. Donnellan dislikes intellectualising and will frequently attribute the most major of production decisions to simple pragmatism, but clearly he has the ability to guide actors into seeing the emotional decisions that lie behind the great texts without being intimidated by the formality and intricacy of the language. A Donnellan production of Racine manages to convince you that they are real people on stage not puppets dressed up in the costume of another age. 'Actors,' he says, 'should feel that they possess the play.' Touring throughout the world has convinced him that theatre can communicate whatever the language if the actors' imaginations are working.

> We've learnt that it is not really the surface of the words that communicates significantly. What really communicates is the imaginative spark that happens between people. If you go to a drama school production of *Romeo and Juliet* in this country, on the whole you won't know what people are saying even if you know the play terribly well. On the other hand, when I saw Lev Dodin's production of *Brothers and Sisters* in Russian, I felt that I understood the whole play.

Working on that 'imaginative spark' is Donnellan's obsession so that audiences imagine that the events are happening before their eyes and not in a playwright's mind four hundred years ago. 'There's a side of me that doesn't understand things very easily. On the whole, if I don't understand, it's because the actors' imaginations aren't working and they think the play can perform itself.' The excitement is in watching actors playing a scene. Especially those scenes in which the characters they are playing begin the scene as one person and by the close have emerged as another.

This concentration on the art of acting is harder to pin down than the excesses that have won the company devoted fans or disparaging critics. 'The road of excess leads to the palace of wisdom' is a quote from William Blake that appeared in the programme for *Twelfth Night* (1986) but it could equally have applied to many of their other productions. The Porter in *Macbeth* (1987) was played as a Glaswegian baglady mouthing a stream of obscenities at the audience and causing school parties to make a swift exit. Sir Toby Belch sported a Middlesex Cricket Club tie and burst into 'My Way'; Theseus in *A Midsummer Night's Dream* (1985) resembled Prince Charles and the mechanicals were all played by women; and in the most recent all-male production of *As You Like It* (1991), Rosalind was played by a six foot tall, black, male actor. Donnellan believes in following the spirit of the play and not the letter. Such risks can go badly wrong, but he is bravely determined to allow the energy of the rehearsal to take over.

> Sometimes you feel something has a gallop, an energy to it and you go for it. You may not like what you are doing but you think that it is inevitable because it has its own integrity. It's very good sometimes when I feel 'I don't like that but we've got to do it'. Then people can have a strong reaction to it.

It is a characteristic of the company that it doesn't let audiences off the hook. Although many of the company's critics have picked up on its name to condemn the work as cheeky; Cheek by Jowl refers to the relationship between actors and audience, and in a radio interview Donnellan explained why he thinks we need to go to the theatre.

> We can't live intensely in our own living rooms. We go to the theatre in order to do something that is dangerous. I don't think we go to see our lives exactly recreated. The extremities are uncomfortable and dangerous to live with all the time but we need to keep in touch with them.

In 1990, Donnellan and Ormerod were invited to produce *Fuente Ovejuna* at the National. The result was not only their best piece of work but also one of the most stirring productions ever seen in the Cottesloe. Lope de Vega's *Fuente Ovejuna*, in which the peasant community becomes the main protagonist claiming collective responsibility for the death of a ruthless overlord, cries out for the detailed ensemble work of a director like Donnellan. The solidarity of the community at the end was all the more powerful because the people had been introduced as individuals at the beginning. The production, set on a traverse stage with the King and Queen of Spain sitting at one end, also drew on Paddy Cuneen's music and the movement of Jane Gibson to create a stark contrast between hard-working physically fit peasants and the stiff-necked aristocrats. With black actors playing both aristocrats and peasants, including the Queen of Spain, it was a significant step forward in integrated casting for the National.

Donnellan's work at the National – he is now an Associate Director – has not meant an end to Cheek by Jowl. For a small company, it has had an enormous influence on British theatre, recognised in three Olivier awards. The exploration of a worldwide repertoire has encouraged other companies to follow suit. Its famous inventiveness and subversion has sometimes sent the company spiralling into chaos but its great achievement is to create real people on stage faced with real questions and having to come up with some awkward answers. When those 'real people' are some four hundred years old, that's quite an achievement.

SAM MENDES

Directors rarely hang around. If they are going to make their mark, their talent has usually been spotted somewhere before they reach the age of thirty. Even so, at 25, Sam Mendes has moved spectacularly swiftly. He has already directed three shows at Chichester, three in the West End, and two for the Royal Shakespeare Company as well as spending some time in Hamburg after winning the Hamburg Shakespeare Scholarship. Perhaps he was fortunate that his first job took him to the elderly and encrusted Chichester Theatre where a youthful, fresh eye was bound to be noticed. Put in charge of the new Minerva studio theatre at the age of 23, he attracted attention immediately with the opening production of Gorki's *Summerfolk* (1989). Dame Judi Dench, Michael Frayn and Michael Codron were sufficiently impressed to invite Mendes to direct Dench in Frayn's translation of *The Cherry Orchard* (1989) at the Aldwych. Since then he has managed to combine a career in the commercial sector with that in subsidised theatre culminating in his new position as artistic director of the re-opened Donmar Warehouse, a small two hundred seat theatre in the heart of the West End, once the home of the experimental wing of the RSC. There have been failures. In the event *The Cherry Orchard* merely grazed the surface of Chekhov's complexities and his production of *The Plough and the Stars* (1991) at the Young Vic, again with Judi Dench this time as the battling Bessie, was a sombre interpretation missing out on Sean O'Casey's Shakespearean mix of comedy and tragedy. *Kean* (1990) on the other hand at the Old Vic was a glorious celebration of the talent of Derek Jacobi, one actor paying tribute to another and was West End entertainment at its most audience friendly.

At the RSC, Mendes has turned in two productions – *Troilus and Cressida* (1990) and *The Alchemist* (1991) – that have been distinguished by the intelligence of the interpretation and the eclecticism of the settings. In *Troilus*, this combined anglepoise lamps with Trojan helmets and khaki tunics with a massive head of Apollo. Both of these productions originally opened in the Swan, the RSC's galleried theatre in Stratford where the emphasis is all on the actors and which Mendes compares working in to 'cooking on a hotplate'.

His production of *Troilus* drew one in to the density of the imagery focusing on the sour cynicism of the play. Inevitably in such a small space there were no splendid battle scenes. Simon Russell Beale as Thersites personified the cynicism of the play becoming almost orgasmic at the death of Hector. Only once did he show any humanity; when sniffing on a scarf that Cressida had dropped he briefly was lost in thought as though for once caught up in another person's pain.

Like many directors, Mendes was first attracted by the excitement and the conviviality of the rehearsal room.

> Then it shifted away from being about me and the cast and it became about a piece of work and an audience. I think you have to love that moment of performance. You have really to enjoy being in an auditorium watching people's responses and feeling the reactions. That horrible or wonderful moment when you first confront an audience with a piece of work that you have been beavering away on singlemindedly for weeks – that's the furnace and not really the rehearsal room.

It is maybe this showmanship that makes him enjoy working in the West End but experience has taught him that the play has to be right. Attempting to rehearse *The Cherry Orchard* in four weeks does not reveal any subtle insights. He is grateful that the RSC invited him to join the company at a crucial stage when he might have been deflected into endless West End revivals of Noel Coward for the rest of his career.

The major difference between the two worlds is working method. At the RSC you spend seven or eight weeks working on a play and after five weeks you move into a different area. You destroy what you've done and then reassemble it and it becomes something else. That's what happened with *The Alchemist*. After five weeks rehearsal, it had much more clutter and was full of Elizabethan knickknacks. That all went and it became much more about personalities. Going to the RSC at that stage in my career completely changed my perception of what it is that you do in rehearsal. It became about the collective consciousness of a lot of very intelligent, sensitive people and the imaginative exploration of an empty space. Also I was able to find a style that I thought was my own although influenced by Deborah Warner and Nick Hytner. In *The Alchemist* the characters are actually all from the same world because they are not from any period at all. It's fantasy but it's real. You have to believe that they all tread on the same street outside and that they are all splattered with the same mud. But beyond that the tiniest thing can set off mental ripples in your mind.

Working at the RSC, directors are obviously influenced by previous productions and none could have been more intimidating than Trevor Nunn's production of *The Alchemist*. Mendes has the advantage that he is too young to have seen many of the legendary productions, but for him the best way of counteracting the weight of such forebears is to have what he calls 'a secret'.

It's quite irrelevant sometimes. If you don't have a secret you are a victim of the play. That happened in *The Plough and the Stars*. I adored it but I had no secret. I just wanted to do it. In the end that means that you don't pick up a play by the scruff of the neck. You don't say that this is what the play's about. *The Alchemist* is a play about gullibility not about criminality, therefore it's about the need of the people who walk through the door to believe that gold can be made in the cellar. But the room is empty, there is nothing there. That's the trick of it. It's all done with words, with language. The alchemy of the play is linguistic. That was my secret. Its universal message is about imagination, needing to believe in something. The heart of the play lies with the people who walk through the door; the head is with the three con-artists.

None of this could be forced on the actors. They had to be persuaded that a specific setting as in Nunn's production was not essential. Mendes believes that directors have reacted to actors like Kenneth Branagh and Simon Callow who have criticised them for cracking the whip too much.

In the eighties, directors were getting too big for their boots. But now there is a new generation of directors who have tried to hark back to the Peter Brook experimental era and away from the empire building of Peter Hall, Trevor Nunn and John Dexter. They want something that is more studio based and unconventional and that also takes on board a great understanding of the actors' desires and their needs as human beings rather than as pawns in a master plan.

ANNABEL ARDEN AND SIMON MCBURNEY

British theatre is often accused of being insular, text-bound and dead from the neck down. None of these failings could be applied to the work of Theatre de Complicite, an artistic co-operative begun in 1983 by Annabel Arden, Simon McBurney, Marcello Magni and Fiona Gordon with a large floating membership. Arden and McBurney both act and direct and, like many others in the company, they have studied in Paris with the great theatre teachers Jacques LeCoq, Philippe Gaulier and Monika Pagnieux. McBurney has also worked with the mime artist Jérôme Deschamps. Arden describes their studies in France as not so much a reaction against British theatre but more a search for something that did not appear to exist here. 'When we started our basic desire was to do work that was physically based, highly visual and very funny. I was looking for a theatre that was as exciting as I remembered it when I was young.' LeCoq encourages actors to enjoy and exploit the moment of standing in front of an audience. Rather than imposing his style, he concentrates on developing the actors individual styles, providing them with the physical tools with which to do that and trying to re-awaken their childhood imaginations.

Theatre de Complicite (a French name was chosen as McBurney initially anticipated working in France) has fulfilled Arden's expectations. The focus is on the actors, many of them drawn from abroad and their appearance is often as striking as their talent. The theme of a new show may have been decided before rehearsals begin, but its development and shape depends on what happens in the rehearsal room. There the actors' own experiences and imaginations are drawn on to create shows that have usually been distinguished by a black humour that digs at the insecurities, isolation and failures of the human race. *A Minute Too Late* in 1984 drew on the company's feelings about death and bereavement; *More Bigger Snacks* (1985) was about having nothing and wanting everything; and *Please, Please, Please* (1986), according to McBurney, 'started being about love and sex and ended up with families who hated each other. Because of the subject matter we brought in a large bed for the first day of rehearsals.' The actors' commitment has to be total as they are involved in every stage of the process devising the show during long hours of argument, tears and great whoops of laughter. Sometimes objects can take on a life of their own.

> If you have a deck chair onstage, the audience can really see and enjoy that deck chair. You don't just sit down in it and start to act something out. There is this assumption that drama exists only between people and in the themes that concern those people. But drama is the whole act of the theatre. It's the building you're in. It's the props that you are using. It all communicates something. If you ignore it, then it will communicate ignorance.

'One of the things', continues Arden, 'that determined all those early shows was getting each actor really happy with a character; one that they can live with who they feel has got huge potential.'

> That can push events in all sorts of funny ways before you get to your final show. Because, as the characters start to emerge out of the mud, so the hierarchy starts to form, so you get a sense of where they could all co-exit together. In *Quiet Life* [1987] there were a few magical days when we just dressed up and Simon took photographs of us. Then, when we looked at the photographs, we said 'They [the characters] are arriving. What are they going to make us do?' It was a while before the plot was of any importance at all. What was important was to let those characters

roar around the rehearsal room. Attend funerals, weddings, fall in love, have sex, cry and go to church. We had to know much more about them before we could create the whole piece.

In 1989, the company, having already tackled street theatre, operettas and one man shows, decided to try its hand at a play. They chose Friedrich Dürrenmatt's *The Visit*, a playwright whose absurd vision of life matched their own. 'As well as wanting to be the author of your own work,' says McBurney, 'and to create an accurate reflection of the times, you are also working within a tradition, and part of that tradition is that there are these strange creatures who write plays, and as a theatre artist at some point you want to tackle that.'

For the first quarter of an hour of Arden and McBurney's production of Dürrenmatt's bleak fable of greed, collusion and revenge, the penniless townsfolk of Gullen, dressed in clothes that looked as though they had been dragged through birdshit, stand on a bleak, windswept railway platform beneath their grubby bunting, shaking to the vibrations of the passing trains. They are waiting for the return of billionairess Clara Zachanassian, once humiliated by the Gulleners when Albert Schill denied that he was the father of her child. Zachanassian returns to exact her revenge. Propped up on ermine covered crutches, swathed in furs and encrusted in make-up, Kathryn Hunter, in an Olivier award-winning performance, croaked her offer of unlimited wealth in return for the life of McBurney's Schill. As the evening progressed, McBurney's nervous cackle became more mirthless as he watched the Gulleners running up credit while protesting that they were not to be bought. The comic desperation, only alleviated by the tenderness of a meeting between Zachanassian and Schill beneath a magical forest created by the rest of the company, could not have been more pronounced. And Schill's silent, scrabbling death was a perfect illustration of the corruption that had corroded their souls.

'The character of Zachanassian fascinated me,' says Arden. 'And what a community does in that situation, and how does it do it? I've always liked revenge plays. And I've always thought it important to do something that directly refers to money which I believe is killing our society.' This specific reference to capitalism was disliked by some critics who felt that the play was more universal. Others relished the production's theatricality, including Richard Eyre who invited the company to perform *The Visit* in the National at the beginning of 1991. And Peter Brook who had directed the play himself with the Lunts in 1956, praised Theatre de Complicite for being true to Dürrenmatt's spirit. Sadly Dürrenmatt was too ill before he died to see it for himself.

The company is now planning a production of *The Winter's Tale*. 'You've got to do contradictory things', says McBurney. 'If there is anything good in what we do, it's that we do constantly try to look forward to something else. Not everything is equally successful. You need to be on a journey.' 'Yes' agrees Arden. 'But the journey is rocky. It's like a strange car that we are driving on a very odd bit of the road.'

DEBORAH WARNER

Fringe companies during the Edinburgh Festival will usually go to any lengths to lure audiences in to see productions. But in 1985, Deborah Warner, then the director of Kick Theatre, could be found marching up and down outside her company's venue warning audiences that the play – *King Lear* – was four hours long and the seats were hard. Those who defied her warnings were well rewarded and, in 1987, the RSC, scrambling to find somebody to direct Brian Cox in *Titus Andronicus* called upon 'that Kick woman' in desperation. It was an astonishing debut. The resulting production of Shakespeare's goriest number was a clear, unshirking eye on the face of evil undercut with a ferocious black humour. *King John* (1987) and *Electra* (1988) followed, the latter her first collaboration with Fiona Shaw in which two very different obsessives found inspiration in each other. The graphic simplicity of the images and the rawness of Electra's grief put audiences in touch with a play 2000 years after Sophocles sat down to write it. Later she directed *Good Person of Sichuan* (1989) and *King Lear* (1990) at the National and became an Associate Director.

In 1991, Warner directed Fiona Shaw in *Hedda Gabler* at the Abbey Theatre in Dublin. When it transferred to London's Playhouse it became the most talked-about production in the city. An old warhorse that is regularly trundled out of the stable suddenly learnt new steps and became almost unrecognisable. The controlled, hard-headed aristocrat of the past was transformed into a trapped, panic-struck woman witnessing the disintegration of her soul. Like Ingmar Bergman, Warner added a prelude in which Hedda was first glimpsed through a crack in the doors of Hildegard Bechtler's soaring set. (Bechtler who first worked with Warner on *Electra* has slowly influenced Warner to move away from a puritanical and stark emphasis on just the text.) Dressed in a nightdress and presumably escaping from the marital bed, she stumbled onstage, clutching her stomach and retching in disgust. In complete contrast to the breezy, plot-setting dialogue of Ibsen's opening scene, the prelude set the tone for Shaw's restless, courageous performance as a desperate woman who mocks her own aspirations and faults, both scornfully and ruthlessly.

Ironically, Warner had to be persuaded to overcome her aversion to plays with furniture in general and *Hedda Gabler* in particular, before she could be persuaded by Shaw and Bechtler to take on the production.

> Fiona had this idea that Hedda could make her first appearance in a face mask which historically was just about possible. And that this was how she would greet Aunt Juliane and deal with all those characters in the first scene as she had every reason to presume that nobody would call at such an early hour. This struck me as such a fantastic idea that I thought that if the play could allow that, then it was worth looking into. It woke the play up for me. I couldn't bear the idea of that awful monster's first appearance, but Fiona's idea suddenly made it incredibly messy, human and interesting. The idea maybe wasn't particularly good but that was irrelevant. We did try it and it didn't work but out of that came the idea of the prologue.

Once working on the play, Warner's other radical decision was her refusal to be constrained by Ibsen's stage directions, most notably in the case of the burning of the manuscript which Shaw hurriedly threw into the fire emphasising her despair rather than her calculation.

> The stage directions constantly pushed us towards the definition of Hedda that we were attempting to escape. It's such a tiny thing. The word 'sternly' may be in brackets but if you play it 'amusedly', it changes the whole play.
>
> We were completely stuck on the burning of the manuscript because we were burning it page by page as suggested in the text. And I couldn't make head nor tail of why she burnt it until long

past the press night in Dublin. Then one night I said in despair 'I could understand it if she just threw it in.' Then you realised that you could throw it in if you could find a way of getting through the next five lines. That was a massive revelation.

It was typical of Warner who sits in on performances, not to monitor but to develop, long after other directors have faded away, that such a crucial change could be acted on so late in the day. More than most, a Warner production is an everchanging affair.

In the past, Warner has been known for democratically exploring every actor's suggestion. *Hedda*, she confesses was more directed in her impatience to scrape off the years of varnish. She is hard on actors, frequently demanding a three session day and a commitment to match her own. She is eager for them to bring ideas into rehearsal. In this she is sometimes disappointed, and many actors she feels are not artists but rather searching in the theatre for some kind of therapy when they would be better off going to therapists.

Rehearsal is a place for exploration where ideally you play out various scenarios and see what emerges. You need a group that can play out infinite scenarios before you can start piecing it together. If somebody is behind or doesn't realise that a part isn't working yet, then you are in trouble. Some actors will say, 'I can't act it until I know what I am doing'; but as far as I am concerned acting is not to do with playing a character, it's to do with being yourself in a given situation and becoming defined by that situation. Fiona doesn't set out to play Hedda Gabler, she sets out to play the given situations that are on the page. And she can only play the situation that is given her by the other actors. If they don't do that then she is in trouble. And if she is not given the situation newly minted every night, then she is in trouble too. I think that is why Fiona is startling. You do get the feeling that it is being freshly created before your eyes, and you can't believe that the line has been previously written by somebody else. That is her bravery. Great acting is to do with being who you are. Not trying to be somebody else which is a very foolish and silly thing to be doing with your life.

Like Peter Brook, Warner is an uncompromising director and she struggles to find suitable working conditions within an economically threatened British theatre. One fears that, also like Peter Brook,

she may one day move abroad. Her commitment to a production is
so huge that it is a struggle to produce more than one a year. She
hankers after theatre that is an event, and in this she has succeeded
even in theatre-swamped London.

> Success changes a show. Suddenly everybody wants to go and
> you have an audience that absolutely wants to be there. Theatre
> should be an event and not just something that happens all the
> time. The genius of Peter Brook is that he persuades audiences
> that they want to see his shows so much that they are prepared
> to travel from London to Glasgow or get up at dawn and climb a
> mountain. I am delighted that *Hedda Gabler* is sold out alongside
> *Cats*, *Phantom of the Opera* and *Miss Saigon*. That makes sense of
> everything I've always wanted to do.

JENNY KILLICK

Max Stafford-Clark, Artistic Director of the Royal Court, wrote in
his book *Letters to George*, 'Putting on new writing for the theatre
remains at once the most risky and the most rewarding work.'
During the eighties directors were more aware of the risks than the
rewards as new plays became increasingly rare, confined to smaller
and smaller spaces, and seldom if ever attracting the attention and
audience following that pursued Antony Sher in *Richard III* or
Brian Cox in *Titus Andronicus*. Only Anthony Hopkins as Lambert
Leroux in David Hare and Howard Brenton's *Pravda* at the National
managed to rival the great classical performances.

   Directors of new plays rarely win awards. A production of *Hamlet*
can be compared, albeit often to the annoyance of the director, with
the great productions of the past and rated accordingly. But critics
of new plays tend to concentrate on the work of the playwright and,
providing a reasonably good job has been done by the director,
are uncertain whether the director has illuminated a bad play or
obscured a good one. Fortunately, in spite of the lack of glamour,
dwindling audiences and shortage of spaces, there are still a few
directors around committed to working with living writers, some
of them young enough not to have known a time when the concentration was all on the new plays rather than the old.

   At 31, this is certainly true of Jenny Killick who in 1985 became the
first woman artistic director of the Traverse Theatre in Edinburgh, a

theatre dedicated to the encouragement of new writing in general and new Scottish playwrights in particular. She had arrived two years previously as a trainee and quickly discovered that she had found her home. Anxious to avoid 'plays with sofas', the small-scale, naturalistic plays that were then familiar to the Traverse, she established a creative relationship with the playwright John Clifford who had until then been convinced that his plays would never be performed just because they didn't have any sofas. Her production of his play *Losing Venice* (1987), a historical fantasy set in Spain about a declining empire, opened her eyes to the excitement of new writing.

It's fabulous when you realise that the audience is having an active relationship with the things that are being said or enacted onstage. And it's a dialogue with somebody who lives in the same world. It's very heady and exciting. The first night of *Losing Venice* was completely extraordinary because of the play's allusions to the Falklands War and because of its mad theatricality – the idea that it was possible to have a new play with people running around in ruffs. And you felt that the play became the audience's property. When that happens you feel that there is nothing else that you would rather do in the world than direct new plays.

At the Traverse Theatre, she was in a position to commission new writing, to oversee early drafts and establish a close relationship with a writer – a rather different process from picking down from the shelf one of the great plays of the past. She says, 'You have to get off on the fact that you don't know how it's going to end up. That is quite crucial. You have these extraordinary visions of how it's going to be and then move through the dark. And if you are not happy doing that you'll hate doing new plays.'

Actors and designers as well as the director can talk to the playwright and through this creative process the play can develop. Killick believes that it is important for actors to feel part of the process and not be intimidated by the presence of the writer in the room.

Sometimes if the writer is in the room they feel there is a definitive way of playing the part that they have to discover. That can work negatively. Sometimes they feel there are two

people to please instead of one. I think once it is understood that
they are creating something new, then it becomes very exciting.
Watching an actor find a part that has never been performed
before has no precedent. They are not weighed down by the past
and nobody knows quite what the play is until it gets in front of
an audience. I think actors really enjoy that.

Three years ago Killick left the Traverse to go freelance. Away
from running a theatre where she had the opportunity to commission, she has encountered a different situation which is for her far
less satisfactory. More often than not a freelancer is delivered a
completed script metaphorically wrapped in pink ribbon perhaps
as little as six weeks before rehearsals are due to start. Under these
conditions, she directed *The Shape of the Table* (1991) by David Edgar
and *At Our Table* (1991) by Daniel Mornin at the National.

Danny's play was like a model National Theatre commission.
It was written. It went through the script department and was
delivered absolutely finished to the director who then had to
arrange a set design before rehearsals started. The director was
chosen after the play was written. It was very interesting but it
felt like doing only a fraction of the job. I can be accused of
wanting to meddle too early. Of being a frustrated writer. I have
no sense of wanting to be a writer but I feel that commissioning
provides a practical base. A play is written for a certain space for
a certain number of actors. Our theatre is really good when it is
rooted in practicality and understands the context in which it is
being performed.

This early relationship with the writer becomes more and more
difficult as few theatres dare to produce new plays. Killick is
convinced that the crisis in new writing is not a crisis of talent.

I think there is not enough money and not enough interest. People
at the very top of their profession should be encouraged to work
with new writers – the new play shouldn't always be given to
the trainee director. Everybody talks about the heady days of the
Royal Court when Gielgud and Olivier were acting there and I
think it is possible to attract the actors back. New writing has
possibly been underselling itself and there now needs to be a
new assertion. The Thatcher period engendered a whole desire

to appropriate and identify with cultural icons like *King Lear*. But I believe in what people have to say now. I think there is a great danger in the classical director's position of saying that what we have now is not as valuable as what was produced in the past. Then you are denying a sense of modern potential. I feel very strongly that we have in us enormous poetic, philosophical and spiritual potential. And I believe that each person has to believe in their own individual potential in order for things to move forward.

CONCLUSION

One of the distinguishing characteristics of the eighties is that directors who emerged during the decade were rigidly classified as directors of new plays or of classics. An unnatural schism has developed; classical directors are blamed, especially by new playwrights, for being reluctant to take the risk of directing a new play. Classical directors are widely seen as being too arrogant to want to play second fiddle to the playwright, and ambitiously aware that it is far easier to make one's name with a spectacular production of *Hamlet* than the more intimate work of today's playwrights. But, judging from these directors, it is more the case that the new generation of directors, far from being part of the heritage industry, seek to produce a uniquely theatrical experience and today's playwrights, nurtured on the limited fare of television, are not providing them with the raw material with which to do that. Peter Brook, whose work has been so influential for other directors, has himself found very few contemporary playwrights to work with. Killick declares herself not to be interested in plays with sofas and Warner had to be persuaded to do *Hedda Gabler* because she didn't like plays with rooms. Naturalism is out of vogue with directors, and audiences too, who, except for the occasional hit, are increasingly reluctant to see new work. The improvised work of the very popular Theatre de Complicite is far more expressionistic and alive than that of most playwrights. And yet for a theatre to be really vital it needs the unique vision of playwrights who share the same culture as their audience.

The whole basis of the RSC when it was first founded was to do the works of Shakespeare alongside those of contemporary playwrights so that a modern sensibility should inform the

Shakespearean work. If the rift widens it will become increasingly hard to live up to that ideal. Fortunately, there are some signs of change. Richard Eyre at the National Theatre is coaxing the classical directors into new work. Donnellan and Mendes are moving into new work and Stephen Daldry, who takes over in 1993 as artistic director of the Royal Court, the home of new writing, comes from the classically based Gate Theatre. He talks about drawing on a European repertoire that is less rooted in what he calls the Theatre of Dissent. Simon McBurney also looks to Europe and is inspired by the work of Arrabal and Ionesco as well as Dürrenmatt. Whether these directors will be able to persuade British playwrights to move out of the sitting room and to exploit the poetry of theatre remains to be seen but their efforts to do so should make for one of the more interesting developments in the nineties.

REFERENCES

All quotations and paraphrases are from interviews conducted by the author in September 1991.

15

Recent Tendencies in Design
Matt Wolf

As the 1990s take hold in the British theatre, the designer is once again news. Such was the case throughout the 1980s but often for the wrong reasons, as journalists focused on issues of aesthetic overkill and scenic bombardment that did the discipline of design no favours. Now, profiles of designers regularly appear on the pages of colour supplements and glossy magazines, often accompanied by elaborate reproductions of the individual's work. It's as if the general public has at last acknowledged what the industry itself always knew to be true: the important theatre of any epoch depends upon important designers, and Britain is lucky to have more than a few whose influence can be felt both on home ground and abroad.

That influence itself depends on outside sources, so it's fitting that one can talk about the apparent 'Europeanisation' of British design with 1992 now upon us. In part, such a sense is scarcely surprising given that many contemporary leading designers are not, in fact, English, or even British. Maria Bjornson, the most successful European female designer of her generation, was born in Paris of Norwegian and Romanian parents. Hayden Griffin and Johan Engels are both South African, whereas Richard Hudson, perhaps the most significant design 'discovery' – as it were – of the last decade, comes from Zimbabwe. All presently based in England, they join such Irish and Scottish talents as Bob Crowley, David Ultz and Philip Prowse in an extensive redefinition of what 'English' design these days even means.

Exposure to outside influences has made a difference, too. In 1987, Peter Stein electrified London with his Schaubühne staging of Eugene O'Neill's *The Hairy Ape*, designed by Lucio Fanti – notable both in terms of size (a floor-to-ceiling ship) and shape (in the last scene, the spherical monkey houses tilted away from their frames, a geometric effect David Fielding would later employ in the Royal Shakespeare Company *King Lear*). Predictably, it wasn't long before Fanti and Stein's German Expressionism had initiated an implicit dialogue with local teams like Antony McDonald and Tom Cairns, whose 1988 English National Opera *Billy Budd* was directly influenced by *The Hairy Ape*'s vertical partitioning of space, and individuals like Glasgow-based Philip Prowse, whose West End *The Vortex* (1988) [**Photo 13**] – with its angled mirrors and black suede walls – re-imagined for keeps that quintessential Englishman, Noel Coward.

British design suddenly seemed both responsive and innately ingenious. That fact must have come as a jolt to observers of the internationally successful British musicals of the eighties who associated English design first with scenery-laden, visually oppressive extravaganzas that reached their apotheosis with John Napier's futuristic set for the Dave Clark rock musical, *Time*. Napier, a Londoner who attended Hornsey Art College, spent years with the Royal Shakespeare Company working on *Nicholas Nickleby*, *The Greeks* and the Barbican's opening productions of both parts of *Henry IV*, but he hit paydirt with *Cats*, *Starlight Express* and *Les Misérables* [**Photo 7**], guaranteeing that the visuals of those shows were the primary attraction long after the original stars had decamped elsewhere.

By the time of *Time*, opinion was starting to turn: for many, state-of-the-art computerised technology and lasers did not a musical make, and Napier seemed to have been hoisted on the very petard of an aesthetic which he helped beget. His most recent West End show, the John Caird/Stephen Schwartz *Children of Eden*, expired early in 1991: self-important visuals were no longer enough without a quality experience to enfold them.

It's against this context, then, that a less-is-more aesthetic seems to have taken hold, certain designers notwithstanding. Preeminent, perhaps, on this front is Bob Crowley, an art college graduate from Cork in Ireland whose simplicity of visual effect is in fact deceptive. To be sure, his designs often utilise one key image: the formidable staircase in Christopher Hampton's *White Chameleon*, say, or the religious cross in David Hare's *Racing Demon*, not to mention the rich swatches of fabric defining the stage in *Les Liaisons Dangereuses*, for which he received two Tony nominations on Broadway (for sets and costumes).

Crowley's spareness comes from his own belief in the designer as literary critic. For him, as for his most provocative contemporaries, design works as metaphor; the designer's function is to be suggestive and allusive, not didactic and dogmatic. 'For me a stage design isn't just about providing the right environment for an actress to act in,' he told me in his office at the National surrounded by models of David Hare's new play, *Murmuring Judges*, and a revival of Edward Bond's *The Sea*. 'It's much more to do with the arc of a play: where you start on page one so that, 50 pages later, you've gone through a journey of some sort' (Crowley).

He acknowledges his minimalist tendencies but is quick to specify what underpins them: 'I suppose I do like the quality of an empty space above all, but it doesn't mean productions are minimalist just because there's a lack of scenery.' Influenced primarily by the cinema – Crowley storyboarded, film director-style, his 1991 Stratford designs for the *Henry* plays – his work imagines an environment that liberates the imagination of the viewer; rather than patronising his audience, Crowley frees them up just as he does the space of the stage. His *Murmuring Judges* design is his most filmic to date, cross-cutting freely between such settings as a prison cell, the Inns of Court, and the Royal Opera House as if David Hare's script had itself been written for the screen.

His 1989 design for *Hedda Gabler*, Howard Davies's Olivier Theatre production starring Juliet Stevenson, offers an apt case study in design-as-metaphor. Taking a play performed in London with some regularity, Crowley granted Ibsen's text a visual boldness, even effrontery, entirely in keeping with the production as a whole. Far from treating the play as some kind of reined-in domestic tragedy, Crowley's open and airy set – a staircase leading to the upstairs bedroom and the furnace centre-stage for the burning scene – transformed the Tesman residence into a key character in the play. The physical geography of the set corresponded to the emotional geography of the characters. Crowley explains: 'It had to do with privacy, and how you maintain privacy in a house that doesn't have it by virtue of its architecture; how do you keep secrets from people when there's the excitement of having them within earshot all the time?' (Crowley).

Crowley is a conceptualist who works with minimal amounts of *stuff*, and it's tempting to place him at one end of a spectrum occupied by Richard Hudson at the other. Like Crowley, Hudson is first and foremost an interpreter; unlike Crowley, Hudson tends to enclose or fill up his space, developing an Expressionist signature style of raked floors and ceilings and no shortage of visual effects and jokes. At the Old Vic Theatre under Jonathan Miller's artistic direction, Hudson won acclaim – and an Olivier award – for a season comprising, among others, Racine's *Andromache*, George Chapman's Jacobean *Bussy D'Ambois*, N.F. Simpson's *One-Way Pendulum*, and the Leonard Bernstein musical, *Candide*.

On the West End, his heavily Teutonic re-imagining of Stephen Sondheim's *Into the Woods* transformed the musical for those familiar with its lighter and more seductive Broadway look. Early in 1991, Hudson brought his rampant visual imagination to Broadway with his Tony-nominated work on David Hirson's *La Bête*, startling New Yorkers with a use of curtains, graffiti-scrawled walls, and rakes – *and* cheekiness – to which Londoners were long accustomed.

A graduate of the Wimbledon School of Art, where Yolanda Sonnabend was one of his tutors, Hudson began as an apprentice to Nicholas Georgiadis before he struck out on his own. Now well-established, he's forged crucial links to certain directors: Miller initially; then Richard Jones, who directed *Into the Woods* and *La Bête*; and Romanian Andrei Serban, for whom Hudson designed two of his starkest pieces – David Lan's *Desire* [Photo 1] and Euripides' *Hippolytos*, both at the Almeida Theatre. 'I'd hate to start doing the same thing again and again,' he says, eager to make clear that, however strong his own visual stamp may seem, the text itself comes first. He continues:

> I've always believed the most important thing for a director and a designer to do is to tell the story, to tell it really clearly. I don't believe in manipulating the text for your own devices or just because you've had a wonderful idea and want to set the show on the moon. (Hudson)

As a result, Hudson does extensive sketches and models, and believes in thorough consultation with the director. 'Hopefully, through discussion, you find something that will be truthful to the text' (Hudson).

Accordingly, he and Richard Jones sought a visually ingenious but also forbidding quality to the Sondheim in keeping with the musical's own subversive tone. *La Bête*, a play in rhymed couplets that proved unusual – to say the least – for Broadway, demanded a style as extravagant and intellectually alive as the mock-Molière pastiche of the writing. His *Andromache* design was simultaneously grand as well as 'precarious and dangerous' in keeping with the grand yet dangerous passions of Racine's lovesick characters: the result was a tilted floor in front of a commanding staircase impossible to climb because it in fact contained no stairs. Ostrovsky's *Too Clever by Half* [Photo 14], his Old Vic *coup de théâtre*, posited a world giddy with intrigue and gossip. Hudson and Richard Jones, in response, gave it a disorienting production to match, in which Alex Jennings's hair was only one of many components that were seriously out of place.

In Adrian Noble's 1989 Barbican mainstage production of *The Master Builder*, Hudson came up with a devastating final tableau to cap Ibsen's tragedy: as Solness fell to his doom, so, too, did the set collapse, revealing the Lilliputian scale of the structures which the architect himself had elevated to mythic proportions. 'We talked about the vertical nature of the play; I said I don't believe Ibsen writes about rooms with walls,' says Adrian Noble, recalling the collaboration. With Hudson, as with Bob Crowley, Noble points to an ability 'to make visible the inner architecture of the play. They help reveal the skeleton and thereby the meaning of a piece of work to an audience' (Noble).

Jonathan Miller says he admires Hudson's 'European sense of architectural space,' which might be another way of praising a tendency towards heightened abstraction characteristic of the best contemporary British design. As the curtain rose on Anthony Ward's Lyttelton Theatre set for *Napoli Milionaria*, the Eduardo de Filippo play revived in June 1991 by Richard Eyre, audiences gasped at a quality of light and space that seemed distinctively Neopolitan. This impression started with the long stone-walled passage at the rear and continued with the sheer height of the Jovines' front room crammed with a curtained-off sleeping area for Gennaro in one corner and a prevailing wartime seediness waiting for improvement. (Those 'improvements', in the form of the wife Amalia's fierce wish to transform her surroundings and, by extension, herself arrived on schedule at the start of act two.) Another emerging designer who has made his name over the past few years, Ward, too, prizes simplicity, opting where possible for the telling detail rather than a Massive Statement.

'Simplicity really hones the meaning of a play,' says Ward, aware that 'naturalism doesn't mean you have to have half a ton of dressing [on stage]' (Ward). Designing Martin Sherman's *When She Danced* in 1988 at the King's Head in Islington (Bob Crowley, incidentally, did its 1991 West End staging), Ward saw his task as one of 'going into a horrible little space and trying to make it look clean and simple.' His 1991 Paris Opera *Manon Lescaut*, by extension, was 'just four walls and a chair,' whereas his fresco-filled chateau for the Almeida revival of Jean Anouilh's *The Rehearsal* fell somewhere in between the two, being simultaneously pared-down and bold: not many objects but a sizable and elegant use of what ones there were. For Phyllida Lloyd's Stratford staging of *The Virtuoso*, Ward filled the Swan with nothing at first beyond a huge bed. Only gradually did he push the stage space back to reveal Sir Nicholas Gimcrack's cluttered shelves of vials and inventions which fall entertainingly apart as the play comes to a close.

The modus operandi? Ward says there is no formula. 'If I could tell you, I'd love to know,' he says. 'It's through slogging away looking at shapes and forms, talking (with the director) about the piece you're working on. I do find something goes click. There's an equation, and the equation solves itself. 'The creative partnership, again, is key, and Ward has worked often with Phyllida Lloyd, as well as Annie Castledine, Sue Todd, and Robert Carsen. 'I'm desperately collaborative,' Ward says with a laugh. 'I'm terribly open and sensitive [to others] in the work I produce' (Ward).

Most leading designers work best in tandem with a director. Alison Chitty, a Londoner who trained at St. Martin's and the Central School of Art and Design, has a rewarding, though hardly exclusive, partnership with Sir Peter Hall which embraces both the lush cornfields of the Lyttelton Theatre's *Martine* and the stylised, two-tiered Southern interior of Tennessee Williams's *Orpheus Descending* on the West End and on Broadway. Interestingly, it took a project like Williams's *The Rose Tattoo*, revived by Hall in 1991, for Chitty to appear to be repeating herself, imposing a cramped, bizarrely sky-streaked visual on a play that didn't warrant such fussiness.

Chitty works from models using all available references; so, too, does Maria Bjornson, whose evolving sense of scale has kept intriguing pace with the times. In 1981, she told the *Sunday Telegraph Magazine*, 'The theatre is a celebration; you don't want to see something pared down' (Bjornson, 1981). You certainly don't, especially when you're responsible for such visual events as *The Phantom of the Opera*, a show much more talked-about for Bjornson's lush, romantic designs than for Lloyd Webber's score; and, to a certain extent, the 1987 London premiere of Sondheim's *Follies*, with its decaying theatre of act one giving way to what the composer himself would call a visual 'cornucopia' in the act two *Follies* pastiche.

By the beginning of the nineties, though, Bjornson was telling *The Times*: 'I like working on smaller things' (Bjornson, 1991), which she was indeed doing in the Stratford studio productions of *The Blue Angel* and *Measure For Measure*, directed for touring by Trevor Nunn, her colleague on *Aspects of Love* and the Glyndebourne *Cosi Fan Tutte*. The cinema as an influence couldn't be ignored, and Bjornson, like Crowley, found herself applauded for a filmic fluidity that allowed for the different interiors – an artist's studio, a cafe, a train station – of *Aspects* as well as for the tiered sets for the two Other Place offerings. Her aesthetic has been consistently European throughout, building on what she calls 'a disturbed and heightened reality' that gets under the spectator's skin. This was Bjornson's decade for The Other Place and the Almeida (where she designed *The Lulu Plays*) – venues that allow for such visual and psychological burrowing – just as the eighties seemed ripe for her homage to an opulence and grandeur which society as a whole had decided, for the moment, to discard.

The best contemporary designs thrive on implication rather than illustration, which is why a stylised, abstracted view of reality is nowadays preferred theatrically to the real thing. Working in opera (the English National Opera *Peter Grimes*) and theatre (*Electra* and *Hedda Gabler* for Deborah Warner), German designer Hildegard Bechtler is known for sets as acclaimed for what they don't show as for what they do; indeed, the earth tones and trickling stream of *Electra* make clear immediately that the evening will be elemental, on every level. For Warner, Bechtler has transformed her innate suspicion of designers and design: 'I'm a great convert to design inasmuch as my work began without designers,' says the director, who points to fruitful partnerships with both Bechtler and also Sue Blane. What she admires in Bechtler is an ability 'to paint the thought.' The greenish tint, for example, of *Hedda Gabler* she describes as 'a colour of the human soul. Somewhere that green resonates. It's so much bigger than just a colour' (Warner).

While Bob Crowley and Anthony Ward tend towards designs grounded in reality that transcend that same reality, other designers start with pure metaphor. Hayden Griffin's set for the National Theatre premiere of Arthur Miller's *After the Fall* was an enormous spiral founded on principles of the golden mean that evoked the anguished recesses of the lawyer Quentin's mind; the design was astonishing coming from the same man behind the hyperrealism of David Mamet's *Glengarry Glen Ross* – the deep red banquettes of a Chinese restaurant followed in act two by a real estate office in disarray – which received its 1983 world premiere at the Cottesloe.

David Fielding's much-vaunted cube for the Nicholas Hytner *King Lear* resembled a sculpture brought to the stage that one could imagine seeing in a gallery, but it functioned as a piece of geometry literally enclosing the chaos of Shakespeare's text. (In the storm scene, appropriately, it kept revolving in accordance with the raging elements in the play.)

In contrast to this approach, one could point to someone like William Dudley, whose bigger-is-better aesthetic served not only the otherwise uninteresting David Essex musical *Mutiny!* but also the elaborate Victorian funfair of Ben Jonson's *Bartholomew Fair*, directed by Richard Eyre. Dudley, rather like John Napier, also enjoys the sheer machinery involved in making theatre happen. Small wonder that he was the first designer to exploit fully the revolving subterranean depths of the Olivier with his set for Boucicault's *The Shaughraun* (1988), which showed levels of Irish pastoral few admirers of the play can have envisioned. In a sense, Dudley has passed the scenic baton to a younger colleague, Mark Thompson, whose Olivier Theatre river bank in *The Wind In the Willows* went beyond loving detail to a sort of smothering verisimilitude that put off as many critics as it impressed.

Not that Thompson is incapable of wit and allusiveness; more to the point is the feeling that he embodies the bridge between the self-conscious virtuosity-turned-to-excess of the 1980s and the more oblique designer/interpreter of the nineties. For the Royal Shakespeare Company, Thompson has indulged a taste for the fanciful, whether it's the poppy-filled landscape of *The Wizard of Oz* or the gaudy technicolour world of Ian Judge's *Comedy of Errors* which bursts to life on the stage after a deliberately grey – and offputting – beginning.

The issue now, as the decade continues, is to specify exactly what design serves and who it's for. *The Hairy Ape* notwithstanding, both Deborah Warner and Adrian Noble express relief that, as Warner says, 'we're through that stage of aping German design and starting to be led by ourselves again, which is fantastic.' What she objects to is 'overdesign bearing no connection to what anybody else on stage was willing to or desired to do – actors wearing costumes they couldn't act in atop ledges they couldn't play the scene on'

(Warner). For Noble, the concern is design that looks outward rather than inward, towards the world of the text rather than that of 'dressing the designer's ego. I think most designers are as confused as most directors, actors, and writers as to what defines good theatre' (Noble). But as British theatre enters the nineties, there is no doubt that at its best, design can play an essential role. Gone are the days of Shaftesbury Avenue stage representations of three-piece suites eliciting applause because they confirm the world the audience already knows. Design, like the theatre it services, needs to chart new realms, not flatter a complacent public, and there's every evidence in these difficult times that the men and women to do so are out there and ready. When it comes to contemporary British design, the journey has only just begun.

REFERENCES

Bjornson, Maria. Quoted in Timothy Clarke, 'Measure of Mystery'. *The Times*, 14 September 1991.

Bjornson, Maria. Quoted in Jennifer McKay, 'Scenes of Spectacular Success'. *Sunday Telegraph Magazine*, 22 November 1981.

Crowley, Bob. Unpublished interview by the author. 9 September 1991.

Goodwin, John (ed.). *British Theatre Design; the Modern Age*. London: Weidenfeld and Nicolson; Zürich: The Weltkunst Foundation, 1989.

Hudson, Richard. Interview by Matt Wolf. *Harpers & Queen*, May 1988 and August 1990.

Miller, Jonathan. Quoted in Richard Hudson interview. *Harpers & Queen*, May 1988.

Noble, Adrian. Unpublished interview by the author, 10 October 1991.

Ward, Anthony. Interview by Matt Wolf. *Harpers & Queen*, August 1991.

Warner, Deborah. Unpublished interview by the author, 3 October 1991.

Index